Academic
R E C O V E R Y
Supporting Students on Academic Probation

Michael T. Dial, Editor

Cite as:
Dial, M. T. (2022). *Academic Recovery: Supporting Students on Academic Probation*. University of South Carolina, National Resource Center for The First-Year Experience & Students in Transition.

ISBN: 978-1-942072-59-1
ISBN (ePub): 978-1-942072-60-7
ISBN (eBrary): 978-1-942072-61-4

Published by:
National Resource Center for The First-Year Experience® and Students in Transition
University of South Carolina
1728 College Street, Columbia, SC 29208
www.sc.edu/fye

The First-Year Experience® is a service mark of the University of South Carolina. A license may be granted upon written request to use the term "The First-Year Experience." This license is not transferable without written approval of the University of South Carolina.

Production Staff for the National Resource Center:
Project Manager: Jennifer Keup, Executive Director
Design and Production: Stephanie L. McFerrin, Graphic Artist

Library of Congress Cataloging-in-Publication Data

Names: Dial, Michael T., 1986- editor.
Title: Academic recovery : supporting students on academic probation /
   Michael T. Dial, editor.
Description: Columbia, SC : National Resource Center for The First-Year
   Experience® and Students in Transition, University of South Carolina,
   [2022] | Includes bibliographical references and index. | Summary: "An
   academic resource for higher education professionals that provides
   guidance on how to better support students who are in endanger of or are
   on academic probation"-- Provided by publisher.
Identifiers: LCCN 2022035565 (print) | LCCN 2022035566 (ebook) | ISBN
   9781942072591 (paperback) | ISBN 9781942072607 (epub) | ISBN
   9781942072614 (eBrary)
Subjects: LCSH: Counseling in higher education. | College attendance. |
   Academic achievement. | College students--Rating of.
Classification: LCC LB2343 .A299 2022 (print) | LCC LB2343 (ebook) | DDC
   378.1/9422--dc23/eng/20220825
LC record available at https://lccn.loc.gov/2022035565
LC ebook record available at https://lccn.loc.gov/2022035566

About the Publisher

The National Resource Center for The First-Year Experience and Students in Transition was born out of the success of University of South Carolina's first-year seminar ("University 101") and a series of annual conferences focused on the first-year experience. The momentum created by the educators and advocates attending these early conferences paved the way for the development of the National Resource Center, which was established at the University of South Carolina in 1986. As the Center broadened its focus to include other significant student transitions in higher education, it underwent several name changes, adopting the National Resource Center for The First-Year Experience and Students in Transition in 1998.

Today, the National Resource Center collaborates with institutional partners in student success, student affairs, and academic units as well as with institutions, organizations, and affiliates across the country and around the world in pursuit of its mission to advance and support efforts to improve student learning and transitions into and through higher education. The Center achieves this mission by creating opportunities for the exchange of practical and scholarly information, facilitating the discussion of trends and issues in our field, and providing thought leadership. Its primary areas of activity include:

- convening conferences and other professional development events such as webinars, workshops, and online learning opportunities

- publishing scholarly practice books, research reports, guides, a peer-reviewed journal, and an electronic newsletter

- generating, supporting, and disseminating research and scholarship

- maintaining several online channels for resource sharing and communication, including a website, listservs, and social media outlets

The National Resource Center is the trusted expert, internationally recognized leader, and clearinghouse for scholarship, policy, and best practice for all postsecondary student transitions.

Institutional Home

The National Resource Center is located at the University of South Carolina's (UofSC) flagship campus in Columbia. Chartered in 1801, UofSC Columbia's mission is twofold: to establish and maintain excellence in its student population, faculty, academic programs, living and learning environment, technological infrastructure, library resources, research and scholarship, public and private support and endowment; and to enhance the industrial, economic, and cultural potential of the state. The Columbia campus offers 324 degree programs through its 15 degree-granting colleges and schools. In fiscal year 2021, faculty generated $225 million in funding for research, outreach and training programs. UofSC is among the top tier of universities receiving Research and Community Engagement designations from the Carnegie Foundation.

CONTENTS

TABLES & FIGURES

Tables

Figures

FOREWORD

Jennifer R. Keup

As noted by Nutter in chapter 2 of this book, "College students do not start their academic career with plans to fail" (p. 37). Yet, many students struggle with their transition—or, often, transitions given the non-linear path of many students through higher education—into the first year and during their college career. Students' difficulties may be the result of poor academic preparation, financial concerns, emotional health and well-being, demands of work and family on top of being a student, feelings of poor institutional fit or lack of belonging, or myriad other influences. Most recently, the COVID-19 pandemic exacerbated common challenges to student transition and success as well as introduced new obstacles to academic performance. Regardless of the reason, many students find themselves in a precarious position with respect to their academic performance that can trigger institutional processes such as academic warnings, probation, and/or dismissal as well as elicit personal feelings of isolation and self-doubt.

And yet, for a system dedicated to learning and development, those of us in higher education often forget that academic challenge, struggle, and even what we might deem "failure" represent profound teachable moments and critical junctures in the educational process. In other words, they are not necessarily always an interruption of students' academic trajectories as much as they may be considered an integrated part of their development in college. As the legendary college basketball coach, John Wooden, said "success is never final, failure is never fatal, and it's courage that counts." This edited volume seeks to reframe academic probation less as "failure" and more as a process of a courageous collaboration between the institution and the student on the path to learning, development, and success.

Such reframing requires that we interrogate and improve our institutional practices as well as provide guidelines for students to examine their own choices and commitment to their academic pursuits. Working with students who are struggling academically and on academic probation is a multipronged effort that requires thoughtfulness, empathy, and intentionality. It must address student mindset and resilience. It should enhance advocacy on behalf of students on academic probation by institutional agents such as advisors, coaches, faculty, academic support staff, first-year seminar instructors, and peer leaders. It requires strategic use of technologies, systems, and resources as tools for student support. It demands that we reframe policies and organizational perspective to be equity minded and incorporate a non-deficit perspective. Thus, there is a critical issue of mutuality and collaboration to the process of coaching students through academic challenge and onto a path toward a successful college performance.

Further, we must acknowledge that students are complex individuals with multifaceted identities, backgrounds, talents, capacities, challenges, and goals. There is no one successful route through higher education. Similarly, there is no one solution for students when they experience difficulties in their courses and, perhaps, encounter academic probation and dismissal. However, we cannot ignore that higher education as a system is still evolving to serve the rich diversity of students that come to its doors. As noted in this book, academic struggle is experienced by all students but is especially prevalent for certain populations such as students who are historically under-represented minorities, low-income, first-generation, and neurodiverse as well as those who have dependents, attend part-time, swirl between institutions, and commute. Consequently, supporting students in academic distress and on probation is not only an issue of student success, it is a critical tool to advance an equity imperative and a lever for social justice.

Therefore, as we approach student support and success for undergraduates who are facing the possibility or reality of academic probation, we must grapple with many questions both with and on behalf of our students:

- How do we normalize the discussion of academic struggle and keep the fear of failure from impairing student performance?

- How do we create safe spaces for students to reveal their concerns about academic performance or share their status as probationary students?

- How do we communicate and intervene with students in academic distress before they are placed on academic probation?

- How do we use inclusive and non-deficit language to communicate pending or current academic probationary status?

- How do we remove barriers to the pathway of reinstatement after dismissal as we help students return to their academic journeys at our institutions?

- How do we work in partnership across campus units to create collaborative advisement and advocacy on behalf of students headed toward or on academic probation?

Thankfully, this book offers answers to these questions and provides meaningful insight, examples, and guidance for our work with students. The National Resource Center for the First-Year Experience and Students in Transition is pleased to publish this book as a critical resource in the scholarly-practice literature on student transition, development, learning, and success. We hope you find it valuable to supporting your students.

Jennifer R. Keup
Executive Director
National Resource Center for The First-Year Experience and Students in Transition
University of South Carolina

INTRODUCTION

What We Know About Students on Probation and Supporting Them

Michael T. Dial

In recent decades, the bulk of the literature generated on student retention and attrition has focused on students who persist and those who opt to leave the university. Significantly less time and effort has been dedicated to exploring the experiences and needs of students on the brink of being dismissed by their institutions. Bledsoe (2018) contended that a surplus of literature on first-year and transition programs and assessment initiatives relate to retention and graduation rates at the conclusion of the student experience, but there is room for further investigation detailing "what goes on in between" (p. 561). This book focuses on one particular "in between" stage, that of academic probation. While students who are dismissed from their institutions account for only a small percentage of the attrition pie, institutions have both a moral duty and, as we shall see, a fiscal obligation to provide resources and support to struggling students prior to academic dismissal. Throughout the chapters that follow, you may see the terms "academic probation," "academic recovery," and "academic warning" used to identify the same general idea.

Every effort should be made to identify at-risk students early and connect them with academic and social resources to intervene prior to the student facing major academic consequences. From time to time, though, warning signs are missed and/or interventions may not be effective or received willingly. In these circumstances, students may find themselves on academic probation. This institutional label often triggers a variety of programmatic responses, including a host of interventions.

Surprisingly though, a common definition of academic probation is not as easy to capture as one would imagine because no national standards or guidelines dictate when students would or should be placed on probation. Often, a student earning below a 2.00 GPA on a 4.00 scale is placed on academic probation. This likely originates from the need to have at least a 2.00 to graduate from most academic programs and to receive various forms of federal financial aid. Arcand and Leblanc (2011, 2012) proposed a conceptualization for academic probation as a state in which students' grades have not met a satisfactory threshold, but they may remain enrolled and in their program of study while attempting to improve their grades. They stipulated that if the student's grades do not improve, they will be dismissed. They summarized that "academic probation can be seen as a transition between unsatisfactory performance to either acceptable academic standing or to dismissal" (Arcand & Leblanc, 2011, p. 3).

Although the literature does not explicitly state that students are on the proverbial clock in terms of achieving good academic standing, most if not all institutions give students a limited number of terms to improve grades. Providing students additional time to right their course is a compassionate policy that recognizes that students stumble and may need time to get back on track. It should be noted, however, that without deliberate, well-designed academic recovery initiatives, this approach may unintentionally provide students more time to struggle with recognizing their own academic challenges and prolong the student financial burden for a student who is already failing.

Academic probation is a university policy and label that results from students' poor academic performance. Consistent with Bénabou and Tirole's (2000) model of performance standards, being placed on academic probation has both discouraging and encouraging effects. Lindo, Sanders, and Orepoulos (2010) found that being placed on academic probation discourages some students from returning to the institution and encourages those who return to strive for improved performance. Institutions can take significant strides to support those who return after being placed on probation and improve the odds that they are able to recover academically.

Academic Probation as Transition

According to Goodman et al. (2006), a transition is any event or nonevent that results in changed relationships, routines, assumptions, and/or roles. Like other transitions, being placed on probation can be either a positive opportunity for growth or a negative experience. This will largely be determined by individual students' perceptions of their experience. A negative perception may lead students to experience feelings of shame, reduce their confidence, and cause them to disengage from campus life and academics (Goodman et al., 2006). Being placed on academic probation is likely an unexpected, negative event for many students. However, prior to being placed on probation, they were likely aware of their failing academic performance. What they may not have known are the institution's probation policies and how their poor academic performance in the present term could potentially change their status at the institution in future terms.

Students on probation, like those in other states of transition, may be confused and need support through the unfamiliar process (Goodman et al., 2006; Schlossberg, 2008). This book explores various theoretical approaches and practical applications to assisting students on probation. The chapters to follow present skills and knowledge that practitioners may rely on to help students on probation recognize, make meaning of, and manage this transitional state. Understanding that probation is a state of transition is only the first step, though. Awareness of the transition framework and its component parts (see Figure I.1) helps campus professionals – whether they are institutional leaders, program administrators, advisors, academic coaches, or caring instructors – support students on probation.

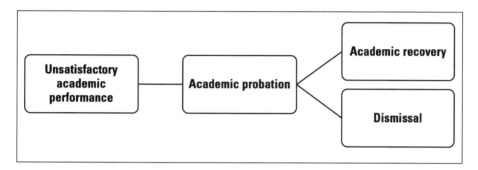

Figure I.1. Academic Probation as a State of Transition

Goodman et al. (2006) identified three component parts to the transition model: (a) transition identification and transition process, (b) taking stock of resources, and (c) taking charge. The first step in the process requires students to identify the type of transition that they are experiencing or have experienced. The student's evaluation of their own transition is paramount. Students in various states of transition may view their experiences as positive, negative, or somewhere in between. Upon being notified that they have been placed on probation, most students likely view their status change in a negative light.

In Chapter 2, Morris and Harris explore the use of psychologically attuned probation notifications (Waltenbury et al., 2018) to assuage some of this negative thinking from the onset. These psychologically attuned letters describe academic probation as an opportunity for growth, acknowledge common challenges students face, normalize academic struggles, and offer hope and support. An academic advisor supporting a student on probation in this first phase of the transition process could help them make meaning of their situation by ensuring they are fully aware of what the label of academic probation means for their status at and with the institution. They could go further and inquire how being placed on probation has affected the student's relationship with parents, other family members, friends, and perhaps even romantic partners. The nature of the transition will be experienced differently by each student. For example, an honors student who has rarely, if ever, struggled academically may find their perceived identity at odds with their current reality. Additionally, a first-generation student may doubt their place in higher education and experience increased feelings of impostor syndrome. Assisting students in normalizing and making meaning of this experience is vital in their eventual success at navigating academic recovery.

As students will experience the label of academic probation differently, so too will they approach the status with a host of different individual and community resources and challenges, which is the second step in the transition process (i.e., taking stock of resources). Student-support professionals including academic advisors, academic coaches, tutors, and course instructors may use the 4S system (see Figure I.2) to help students navigate their probation experience (Goodman et al., 2006). In this model, the 4 S's are

1. Situation – What is happening? What are the parameters for academic probation at the institution? What triggered this status change? What GPA must be attained to recover to good academic standing? How has this change affected a student's relationship with the institution?

2. Self – What personal characteristics does the student on probation bring into their new situation?

3. Support – What resources are available? Institutional supports may be available across the board, but family, social networks, and romantic partners will be unique to each student on probation.

4. Strategies – How does the student manage challenge?

By helping students take stock of their situation, staff members aid students in making meaning of the actions that resulted in their status, the timing of being placed on probation, and the control they have over their circumstances. Upon being placed on probation, students may perceive their role changing within the academic community. Finally, staff can help students consider prior experiences and other stressors active in their lives that may affect their ability to thrive and persist.

Students who return the semester after being placed on probation may need to be encouraged to consider the support available to them as they endeavor to recover academically and embrace the third component of the transition model: taking charge. Students likely have several supports available to them on campus, and some may be required as part of a mandatory academic recovery program. They may also lean on peers, intimate partners, and family as they navigate their experience on probation. Students on probation should also spend time scrutinizing their own personal characteristics and psychological resources. In fact, many academic recovery programs, specifically academic coaching (see Chapter 4), rely heavily on personality inventories and other assessments to help students do just that. Finally, students must consider various strategies and coping mechanisms necessary to recover academically. It should be noted that inaction is certainly an option but may lead to more serious consequences for students on probation, including dismissal.

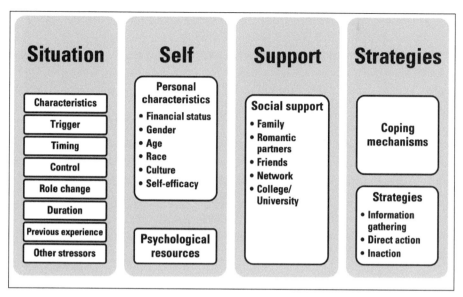

Figure I.2. Schlossberg's 4S Model (Schlossberg, 2008)

Who Are the Students on Probation?

Students may not meet required GPA thresholds for a variety of reasons, including inadequate academic strategies, poor time management skills, lack of motivation, and underpreparedness for collegiate academic requirements. They may also find themselves in majors and courses in which they have little interest or lack the necessary skills and/or knowledge to persist. Furthermore, student misunderstanding or lack of awareness of academic requirements and probation policies may also lead to inadequate performance (Barouch-Gilbert, 2015). In their review of the literature, Arcand and Leblanc (2012) pointed to yet more reasons that students struggle academically and find themselves placed on probation, including employment demands, physical and mental health issues, the requirements associated with serving as primary caregivers to minors and/or elderly parents, problems at home, and lacking connection or a sense of belonging to their campus. They posited, however, that overemphasis of these or any other factors deprives the student of recognition as a unique individual. As is the case with other student subpopulations, students on probation "do not form a homogenous group" (p. 218).

Up to a quarter of college undergraduates may find themselves on academic probation during their collegiate experiences (Greenfield et al., 2013). It is difficult, however, to specifically identify the characteristics of students on probation. One could reasonably assume though that the same demographic factors that affect students' retention and persistence rates (e.g., gender, race and ethnicity, age) also affect the rate at which students face academic challenges and find themselves on academic probation.

In Tovar and Simons (2006) study of 325 community college students on probation, the sample was relatively evenly split along gender lines (53% female; 47% male). Other studies (e.g., Mattson, 2007) have suggested that women are more likely to persist in university settings, for example earning higher first-semester and first-year grades than men do. Kamphoff, Hutson, Amundsen, and Atwood (2006–2007) found that while female students made up almost two thirds of the first-year class, they accounted for less than half of the students placed on probation in a given semester. In a large study of all first-year students enrolled at five Pennsylvania state universities over a 3-year period, Hamman (2018) found that 57.3% of students on probation were male and 42.7% were female. Interestingly, she found that female students were less likely than male students to return the semester after being placed on probation. They were, however, more likely than their male counterparts to recover academically if they returned the following semester.

Several studies (Mathies et al., 2006; Nance, 2007) suggest that minority students are disproportionally placed on academic probation. Tovar and Simon (2006) found that a majority (82%) of participants on probation identified as Latino, African American, Asian/Asian American, or other. Caucasians made up only 17% of the study population. While minority students may disproportionately find themselves on probation, Hamman's (2018) study indicated that African American students were more likely than other racial groups to return the semester following being placed on probation.

Further results of interest from Hamman's (2006) study were that traditional-age students (18 to 22 years old) are more likely to return to their institutions after being placed on probation, whereas adult students (over 22) are less likely to return. No significant age difference was found in the likelihood to recover academically upon return. Finally, regularly admitted students were more likely to recover academically after being placed on probation, while conditionally admitted students were less likely to recover.

It is important to note that academically at-risk and probationary students may share several similarities, but the two identifiers are not interchangeable. Many underprepared students lead productive academic lives and complete the requirements of their degree programs. On the other hand, some students admitted as high achievers face struggles and find themselves on academic probation. Interestingly, high-achieving first-year students, including those in honors programs, may be at greater risk than other students because they are not well equipped to handle failure and have not previously experienced academic disappointment. Facing academic challenges, honors students may hide warning indicators particularly well by remaining calm and positive to external audiences. Their portrayed self-assurance may make their struggles harder to identify for faculty, staff, and peers. They may also be less likely to seek help as they have not needed to in the past (Robinson, 2015).

Students of all backgrounds can and do face academic challenges and find themselves on academic probation. These results, however, exemplify opportunities to reduce institutional graduation gaps among various populations including men, minority students, and nontraditional-age students through high-quality academic recovery initiative design. The characteristics of students who find themselves on academic probation often correlate with a host of precollege inequities, including race, socioeconomic status, and access to academic opportunities. In addition, institutional helping professionals, from coaches and advisors to teaching faculty, should work to develop cultural awareness to support students on probation.

The Lived Experience of Students on Academic Probation

Most literature surrounding students on probation tends to flow from one of three topical themes. First, scholars are often concerned with the student characteristics and behaviors that may be predictive of failure to meet academic thresholds. Others detail programs and initiatives on local campuses that lead to academic recovery for students on academic probation. A third and more recent development in the literature has focused on the lived experiences of students placed on academic probation.

Barouch-Gilbert (2015) studied the experiences of students placed on academic probation in a qualitative study. In a review of the relevant literature, he found that students placed on academic probation ("labeled as academically deficient," in his words) expressed "feeling discouraged, emotionally damaged, fearful, and upset" (p. 102). Therefore, being placed on academic probation may lead students to doubt their ability to succeed academically and lower students' sense of self-efficacy (Arcand & Leblanc, 2011). When compounded with the fact that students placed on academic probation may already be more likely to be affected by various mental health issues such as anxiety and depression (Barouch-Gilbert, 2015), these negative reactions become even more important to recognize early in intervention strategies.

Barouch-Gilbert's (2015) research uncovered three themes expressed by students on probation. First, students expressed surprise or shock at finding themselves on academic probation. Students also reported being unclear on the academic expectations the institution had for them. These sentiments resulted from lack of awareness of their own academic standing and university policies. Consistent with prior research, students also expressed feelings of shame and embarrassment. Those delivering interventions should be purposefully mindful of the potentially fragile emotional state of students on probation (Arcand & Leblanc, 2011).

It's highly likely that students on probation experience intense feelings of shame. Brown (2012) defined shame as an "intensely powerful feeling or experience of believing that we are flawed and therefore unworthy of love and belonging" (p. 69). Shame is a complex emotion, and, unlike many emotions, it is learned throughout childhood. It's based in the family unit and eventually expands to include societal expectations. It is often confused with embarrassment; however, the emotions are drastically different. According to Brown, embarrassment results from a feeling of having done something bad, whereas shame results from feelings of being bad. As such, shame often causes feelings of disconnection and isolation.

Students on probation often feel as if their experience is abnormal. Upon being labeled as academically deficient, students on probation may feel distant from friends and peers who were more successful in their academic endeavors. They likely also feel disconnected from family and loved ones at home who had high expectations of them. Indeed, many students receive the letter notifying them that they are on probation at their home address while home for holidays or summer vacation. Finally, they may feel disengaged from the university community that welcomed them at the point of admission but are now warning they might not be cut out for success in college. Acknowledging the important role that sense of belonging plays in student persistence, it's evident that feelings of disconnection associated with shame could have a significant negative influence on a student's decision to remain in college.

Impacts of Academically Losing Students

Scholars have written whole bodies of work on the implications of student withdrawal, ranging from moral factors to financial impacts. Addressed in this section of the chapter is only a sampling of the implications for students, and institutions with respect to students' academic struggles and failure to persist.

Failure to Deliver on the Promise

The transition to college for new students likely starts at the point of admission – the moment when institutions inform them that they have met admissions standards, have what it takes to be successful on campus, and are welcomed into the academic community. At orientation, this line of communication continues when students and their families are introduced to countless resources available at the institution. Throughout the admission and orientation processes, students and their families are made both explicit and implicit promises about their ability to be successful and the institution's commitment to that success. Institutional faculty and staff have a moral obligation to meet these promises, to the best of their ability, for each student. When students slip through the cracks and are unable to perform and/or recover academically, institutions fail to deliver on promises made to support students on their pathway to becoming learners. Students, in these cases, lose the opportunity to enhance creativity, develop critical thinking skills, improve communication skills, and mature in character through the collegiate environment (Sanders, 2018).

Fiscal Implications for Institutions

Loss of Revenue

The college completion picture has significant financial implications for both students and the institutions in which they enroll. Given the plethora of options in the academic market, it is a costly endeavor to recruit students to colleges and universities. In fact, Cuseo (n.d., p. 1) noted that "retention initiatives designed to manage student enrollment are estimated to be three to five times more cost-effective than recruitment efforts." Swail (n.d.) suggested several ways to determine the cost of student attrition:

> The common logic regarding the cost of losing students is simply stated that an institution reduces its income when a student leaves. This can be considered on a given year or a degree-basis. For instance, if a student leaves after the freshman year, the institution can calculate the loss of that student by multiplying the lost tuition charges for subsequent years to degree. If tuition is $5,000 per year, a freshman dropout would relate to a net loss of $15,000 for a four-year degree program. (pp. 10–12)

Seidman (2012) further stipulated that, given this figure, the loss of 10 students would result in a revenue loss of $50,000 or more in a given term. Over the course of six terms, or the remaining semesters to degree following the first year, losses could amount to more than $300,000 for just these 10 hypothetical students. Seidman further cautioned that this figure does not include the lost revenue incurred in residence halls, campus dining establishments, bookstores, and attendance at college events. Additional future losses would most definitely be incurred because nondegree-earning students would lack the ability or the desire to give back to the institution as alumni.

Performance-Based Funding and Institutional Rankings

More than 30 U.S. states tie at least a portion of institutional funding to meeting certain metrics, including credit hours completed, overall persistence rates, and persistence rates for historically underserved groups (Ortagus et al., 2020). Losing students to academic dismissal following probation certainly has a negative impact on each of these outcomes and could result in institutional funding losses. Additionally, institutional retention and graduation rates factor into a host of college rankings criteria, which influence student enrollment decisions in the academic marketplace.

Fiscal Implications for Students

For students, the negative consequences of failing to complete a college degree are also noteworthy. Consistent with Bourdieu's (1984) concept of academic capital, higher levels of educational attainment result, in turn, in higher rates of employment. According to the National Center for Education Statistics, young adults (defined as 18- to 24-year-olds) with a bachelor's or higher degree achieved higher employment rates in 2017 than did young adults with some college credits, who had higher employment rates than young adults with only a high school diploma (86% vs. 80% vs. 72%; McFarland et al., 2018). It is also true that young adults with a bachelor's degree or higher have a significantly higher median annual income than do their peers with some college credits and those with only a high school diploma. In 2016, young adults with only a high school education earned just less than two thirds of what their peers with bachelor's degrees earned ($31,800 vs. $50,000; McFarland et al., 2018). In the same year, young adults with associate degrees on average had annual earnings totaling $38,000. Seidman (2012) also suggested that upon leaving college, students may have loans to repay. Given the lower employment and earnings potential for those without a degree, difficulty repaying loans could result in lowered credit ratings, impaired future borrowing potential affecting an individual's ability to purchase cars and homes, and potentially delayed traditional milestones, including marriage and the decision to have children.

What's in This Book?

This book is intended to serve as a resource and encourage discussion regarding supporting students who, for a variety of reasons, find themselves on academic probation. By supporting the developmental and emotional needs of first-year students on probation (including time management and academic skills, among others), colleges and universities can deliver on the promise of care made to students and their families in the admissions and orientation processes. Furthermore, the book presents a variety of interventions and institutional strategies for supporting first-year and other students on academic probation.

In Chapter 1, we begin with an exploration of institutional policies and procedures relating to probation, dismissal, and reinstatement. This chapter serves as the foundation for the approaches and strategies for supporting students presented throughout the remainder of the book. Chapter 2 covers a variety of issues relating to advising students on probation. Specifically, this chapter describes best-practice advising strategies for working with this population of students. It includes discussion of the unique developmental needs of students on probation, including noncognitive factors such as grit (Duckworth, 2016) and growth mindset (Dweck, 2008), and presents the concept of academic advising motivation, based on Maslow's motivational framework (Maslow, 1943). Chapter 3 introduces academic coaching, a popular and recent phenomenon in higher education, as an idealized approach to supporting student success and retention. This chapter defines academic coaching, differentiates coaching from advising, offers specific strategies for coaching students on academic probation, and explores how individualized coaching support can lead to a host of positive educational outcomes. Chapter 4 includes discussion of early-alert programs as a means of preventing students from facing the consequences of academic probation and monitoring and intervening with students in academic recovery. This chapter provides tools and context to facilitate early-alert programs that communicate care, foster community, and develop a sense of belonging among the students they serve. Chapter 5 reimagines the first-year seminar as an intervention for students on probation. The chapter begins with discussion of what makes the seminar an effective practice for all students and presents strategies to tailor seminar content to students on probation. Following these chapters covering effective interventions, Chapter 6 includes a description of a model of general assessment in higher education and potential outcomes for assessment of the aforementioned programs.

Following these content-based chapters are two case studies that allow readers to explore the principles and strategies for supporting students on probation. The campuses featured in these case studies are very different in terms of mission, size, control, and Carnegie classification, thereby illustrating the role and impact of institutional environment on approaches to supporting this student population. The first is a case study detailing Cabrini University's updated effort to support students in academic recovery through individualized advising and coaching. A second case study features the academic recovery section of UNIV 101, a first-year seminar, at the University of South Carolina.

Bledsoe (2018) posited that adequately supporting students on probation requires institutions to respond appropriately to changing student needs, nurture cooperative partnerships across campus, understand student populations, and make data-informed decisions while maintaining structure. Given these parameters, in Chapter 7 we argue for integration of programs designed to support students on probation – in effect, creating intentionally collaborative networks.

Call to Action

The chapters in this book are the result of years of dedication and passion for supporting students on probation by the individual chapter authors. Although the chapters reflect a culmination of combined decades of personal experiences and education, collectively they amount to the beginning of a conversation long past due. Significant promises are made to students and families upon their entrance into academia. Vast resources, including money, time, and personnel, are dedicated to first year and other transition experiences and rightly so because their impacts have been measurable. Far less time and far fewer resources have been spent on institutional efforts to support students on probation. This is often not the fault of the people doing the work, nor is it a suggestion that they lack passion or conceptual knowledge. They are often too busy, pulled in too many directions, understaffed, and under-resourced.

The goal of this book is to change that. As intended, this volume should be of interest to academics and practitioners focused on creating or refining institutional policies and interventions for students on academic probation. The aim is to provide readers with the language, tools, and theoretical points of view to advocate for and to design, reform, and/or execute high-quality, integrated academic recovery programs on campus.

Historically, students on probation have been an understudied and underserved population, and this volume should serve as a call to action for campuses to dedicate the personnel and intellectual and financial resources to supporting their success. Equipped with understanding of best practices, academic recovery program administrators must be willing to engage in critical self-reflection and remain capable of promoting and leading change efforts to improve the institutional supports available to students on probation.

References

Adelman, C. (1999). *Answers in the toolbox. Academic intensity, attendance patterns, and bachelor's degree attainment.* U.S. Department of Education, Office of Educational Research and Improvement. Retrieved September 1, 2018 from https://www2.ed.gov/pubs/Toolbox/toolbox.html

Arcand, I., & Leblanc, R. (2011). Academic probation and companioning: Three perspectives on experience and support. *Mevlana International Journal of Education (MIJE), 1*(2), 1-14.

Arcand, I., & Leblanc, R. N. (2012). "When you fail, you feel like a failure": One student's experience of academic probation and an academic support program. *Alberta Journal of Educational Research, 58*(2), 216–231.

Astin, A. W. (1975). *Preventing students from dropping out.* Jossey-Bass.

Bandura, A. (1976). Self-reinforcement: Theoretical and methodological considerations. *Behaviorism, 4*(2), 135–155.

Barouch-Gilbert, A. (2015). Academic deficiency: Student experiences of institutional labeling. *Journal of the First-Year Experience & Students in Transition, 27*(2), 101–111.

Bénabou, R., & Tirole, J. (2000). *Self-confidence and social interactions* (No. w7585). National Bureau of Economic Research.

Bledsoe, R. K. (2018). Facing academic dismissal: An adaptive organizational approach preparing all students for success. *Community College Journal of Research and Practice, 42*(7–8), 550–563.

Bourdieu, P. (1984). *Distinction: A social critique of the judgement of taste.* Harvard University Press.

Brown, B. (2012). *Daring greatly: How the courage to be vulnerable transforms the way we live, love, parent, and lead.* Penguin.

Cuseo, J. (n.d). *Fiscal benefits of student retention and first-year retention initiatives.* Retrieved September 10, 2018 from http://citeseerx.ist.psu.edu/viewdoc/download;jsessionid=F33863618246B6F78290EC2EA03524C1?doi=10.1.1.577.3510&rep=rep1&type=pdf

Duckworth, A. (2016). *Grit: The power of passion and perseverance* (Vol. 124). Scribner.

Dweck, C. S. (2008). *Mindset: The new psychology of success.* Random House Digital, Inc.

Earl, W. R. (1988). Intrusive advising of freshmen in academic difficulty. *NACADA Journal, 8*(2), 27–33.

Goodman, J., Schlossberg, N. K., & Anderson, M., (2006). *Counseling adults in transition: Linking Schlossberg's theory with practice in a diverse world.* Springer.

Hamman, K. J. (2018). Factors that contribute to the likeliness of academic recovery. *Journal of College Student Retention: Research, Theory & Practice, 20*(2), 162–175.

Kamphoff, C. S., Hutson, B. L., Amundsen, S. A., & Atwood, J. A. (2007). A motivational/ empowerment model applied to students on academic probation. *Journal of College Student Retention: Research, Theory & Practice, 8*(4), 397–412.

Lindo, J. M., Sanders, N. J., & Oreopoulos, P. (2010). Ability, gender, and performance standards: Evidence from academic probation. *American Economic Journal: Applied Economics, 2*(2), 95–117.

Lipsky, S., & Ender, S. (1990). Impact of a study-skills course on probationary students' academic performance. *Journal of the First-Year Experience & Students in Transition, 2*(1), 7–16.

Maslow, A. H. (1943). A theory of human motivation. *Psychological Review, 50*(4), 370-96.

Mathies, C., Gardner, D., & Bauer, K. W. (2006). *Retention and graduation: An examination of students who earn academic probation.*

Mattson, C. E. (2007). Beyond admission: Understanding pre-college variables and the success of at-risk students. *Journal of College Admission, 196,* 8–13.

McFarland, J., Hussar, B., Wang, X., Zhang, J., Wang, K., Rathbun, A., Barmer, A., Forrest Cataldi, E., & Bullock Mann, F. (2018). *The condition of education 2018 (NCES 2018-144).* National Center for Education Statistics. https://nces.ed.gov/pubsearch/pubsinfo.asp?pubid=2018144

Nance, M. (2007). The psychological impact of academic probation. *Diverse Issues in Higher Education, 24*(19), 12. http://nces.ed.gov/programs/digest/d12/tables/dt12_378.asp

Ortagus, J. C., Kelchen, R., Rosinger, K., & Voorhees, N. (2020). Performance-based funding in American higher education: A systematic synthesis of the intended and unintended consequences. *Educational Evaluation and Policy Analysis, 42*(4), 520–550.

Robinson, M. (2015). *The lived experiences of first-year, first semester honors college students placed on academic probation.* Electronic Theses and Dissertations. http://stars.library.ucf.edu/etd/718

Sanders, M. L. (2018). *Becoming a learner: Realizing the opportunity of education.* Macmillan Learning Curriculum Solutions.

Seidman, A. (2012). *College student retention formula for student success* (2nd ed.). Rowman & Littlefield.

Schlossberg, N. K. (2008). *Overwhelmed: Coping with life's ups and downs* (2nd ed.). Evans & Company.

Swail, W. (n.d.). *The art of student retention: A handbook for practitioners and administrators.* Retrieved September 10, 2018 from http://www.educationalpolicy.org/pdf/ART.pdf

Tovar, E., & Simon, M. A. (2006). Academic probation as a dangerous opportunity: Factors influencing diverse college students' success. *Community College Journal of Research and Practice, 30*(7), 547–564.

Waltenbury, M., Brady, S., Gallo, M., Redmond, N., Draper, S. & Fricker, T. (2018). *Academic probation: Evaluating the impact of academic standing notification letters on students.* Higher Education Quality Council of Ontario.

CHAPTER ONE

Institutional Policies on Probation, Dismissal, and Reinstatement

Caleb Morris and Andrea Harris

This chapter is an exploration of institutional policies and practices related to academic probation, dismissal, and reinstatement. Whereas later chapters delve into the specific interventions leveraged by institutions to support students in various states of academic recovery, this chapter focuses on the policies that often frame these interventions. Trowler (2002) proposed that policy is much more than a documented vision simply to address an identified issue or problem; instead, policymaking and implementation are "organic and complex" processes involving many institutional stakeholders at various levels and tied to action or inaction (p. 2). With that spirit, this chapter presents and discusses documented policies at a variety of institutions representing the diverse approaches to academic recovery. It also includes a case study and discussion on change management to elevate the journey that leads to finished policy.

Hoover (2014) identified four lenses for viewing higher education policy: disciplinary, interventionist, relational, and instructional. Policies to govern academic recovery, operationalized into academic probation, dismissal, and reinstatement, may similarly be viewed through these lenses. Academic recovery policies are at once disciplinary (intended to correct negative behavior), interventionist (intended to modify previous action or mis-action), relational (intended to foster a relationship between the institution and the student), and instructional (intended to involve the student in their own educational process). Thaler and Sunstein (2008) put forth the concept that policymakers are choice architects who, when designing policies, also organize the contexts in which people make decisions and the series of options they have available to them. As there is no such thing as a neutral design, any design or redesign of a policy will have an influence, small or large, on the choices made by those the policy affects. This chapter includes several policy examples, each showing different approaches to managing students in academic recovery. As each policy is examined, we consider the choice(s) the policy offer(s) for students and whether such choice(s) should be included at all.

Despite commonality in context and viewpoint, no consistent definition governs the conditions and procedures for academic probation, dismissal, and reinstatement, leading to a diverse array of policies and practices (Ferguson, 2017; Robinson, 2015). Because there is no standard to approaching interventions for students in academic recovery, interventions among institutions vary significantly (Lindsay, 2000). Common approaches include intrusive advising, registration holds, required minimum and maximum term credit hours, permission requirements for course drops/adds, required repetition of failed classes, required participation in academic recovery programming, and completion of contracts.

Overall, recovery intervention efforts fall on a three-system continuum: voluntary, intermediate, and mandatory (Ferguson, 2017), as shown in Figure 1.1.

Voluntary	Intermediate	Mandatory
Passive intervention. Only action by institution is notification. Responsibility for recovery falls on student	Nature of intervention varies by student population or academic unit, creating inequities in support.	Active intervention. Highly structured, coordinated, and applied across campus to ensure all students receive comparable support.

Figure 1.1. Academic Recovery Program Continuum (Ferguson, 2017)

The dividing principles between the systems concern the responsibility of the institution to the student, as demonstrated by the level of support involved. Student support across the systems ranges from the minimal-to-nonexistent support offered by voluntary interventions to the high level of support offered by mandatory interventions. This continuum and the differing levels of support represented therein lead to equity issues. One of the foundational theories of student development is Sanford's (1962) theory of challenge and support, whereby student growth is fostered by high challenge associated with high support. Students going through academic recovery experience a high level of challenge and will not grow if the interventions do not provide high support to match. In voluntary intervention, the only action initiated by institutions is notification, with responsibility for follow-up placed squarely on the student, who may or may not follow up. Conversely, student follow-up is required by the institutions for mandatory interventions, and this requirement ensures that all students in academic recovery are receiving an equitable level of support and the opportunity to grow. In later work, Tinto (1993) recognized that different student populations, such as first-generation, racial minority, adult, high-achieving, and transfer students, had distinctly different circumstances requiring population-specific retention policies and programs, which could resemble intermediate interventions. In these cases, equity for all can be maintained by different student populations engaging in interventions appropriate to their unique needs.

In summary, good academic recovery policy should address actions the institution can take to meet the needs of students experiencing high challenge. In addition, policy should be tied to intermediate-to-mandatory interventions that ensure students are receiving a high level of support to maximize the opportunity for growth. The next section of this chapter reviews a diverse array of policies from various institutional types, beginning with policies governing academic probation.

Academic Probation, Dismissal, and Reinstatement

Academic Probation

Although academic probation has no singular definition, research literature has identified certain elemental factors that are common among probation policies, namely GPA falling below a specific threshold, a defined period of time to raise the GPA, and dismissal if there is no improvement in GPA (Arcand, 2013; James & Graham, 2010; Robinson, 2015). As referenced earlier, intervention measures articulated in academic probation policy can vary, from voluntary interventions in which the impetus is squarely on the student to improve their GPA to mandatory interventions in which the institution has formalized structures to better support the student (Ferguson, 2007).

Although institutional policy may be silent on the matter of intervention methods, that does not mean that the institution is without an intervention program. But if such interventions are voluntary, inequity can arise because not every student will receive the same level of support. The literature suggests that for probation practices to be successful, participation should be mandatory. Much of the research literature on successful probation practices addresses programs that are mandatory interventions and fall between two approaches: one-on-one and group support (Kamphoff et al., 2006–2007). A one-on-one support could be between the probation student and an academic advisor or academic coach, while group support could be several students on probation enrolling in a for-credit or noncredit seminar (Coleman & Freedman, 1996; Pruess & Switalski, 2008).

Mandatory Group Interventions

Group interventions for students on probation involve the students enrolling together in a program or seminar. This type of intervention could be operationalized in several ways: linked courses, study-skills workshops, and academic recovery seminars (Brocato, 2000; Mackay, 1996; Martino & DeClue, 2003). Kamphoff et al. (2006–2007) found group interventions to be effective, though not without fault. Group interventions foster interactions among peers, faculty/staff, and the campus, which are key factors in retention literature (Astin, 1984; Tinto, 1993). However, group interventions could fall short if they have no focus on building community or addressing the holistic needs of students. For example, an intervention focused solely on study skills is not helpful for a student struggling with mental health (Hutson, 2006; Isaak et al., 2006; Trombley, 2000).

To examine a group intervention that focuses on community and holistic development, consider the policy and practice formerly in place at the University of North Carolina at Greensboro, a large public research institution. The academic probation policies of the university met the factors defined in the literature: GPA threshold, defined period to improve GPA, and dismissal if no improvement is made in GPA. The policy also prescribed the method of intervention: a course. It should be noted this policy was a mandatory intervention only for first-year students and therefore also contained elements of an intermediate (population-specific) and voluntary (responsibility on student) intervention. Per the policy, first-year students were immediately suspended if they did not enroll and attend the course, giving credence to the mandatory nature of the intervention, and the SAS 110: Strategies for Academic Success course covered a variety of topics and included an individualized learning plan (Hutson, 2006). The policy was found to be successful, with improved retention rates and self-reported growth in academic success attributes (Hutson, 2006).

The policy at the University of North Carolina at Greensboro distinguished conditions for probation and resulting intervention for first-year and continuing students. The GPA threshold was lower for first-year students, and the method of mandatory intervention, the SAS course, was explicitly restricted only to first-year students. The literature suggests several reasons for these targeted policies for first-year students. The first year of college is a critical transition period in a student's academic journey, as success in the first year is predictive of persistence and ultimate degree attainment. Because of this criticality, a large body of research addresses first-year student success and leading practices to foster that success. Per Robinson (2015), one focus of the first-year success research is mitigating adjustment difficulties, including academic failure. By creating an academic probation policy that targets first-year students, institutions can develop interventions to better support this specific population.

Mandatory Individual Intervention

Individual interventions involve students meeting on-on-one with an institutional representative, whether it be an academic advisor, success coach, peer mentor/tutor, or counselor (Arcand, 2013; Damashek, 2003; Mann et al., 2003–2004; Robinson, 2015). The literature suggests that individual attention greatly affects student retention (Drake, 2011; Kuh et al., 2005; Tinto, 1987). One study showed that even a simple phone call from the dean of student affairs to students had an impact on student performance and retention (Braxton & Brier, 1989). For advising students on probation, an intrusive advising philosophy has been found to be most effective (Preuess & Switalski, 2008). Intrusive advising combines student retention and advising theory and involves an advisor personally reaching out to students; meeting with them; helping them identify challenges, set goals, and create a plan to accomplish such goals; and following up with them (Cruise, 2002; Higgins, 2003; Tovar & Simon, 2006).

To put this advising theory into practice, consider the academic probation and suspension policy at Lamar University, a large public university in Beaumont, Texas. The policy at Lamar University meets the elemental factors found in the literature and has an intervention component, including immediate suspension for failure to comply with policy, similar to the policy from the University of North Carolina at Greensboro. Unlike the other policies examined, Lamar University does not distinguish the conditions for first-year students and continuing students, instead suggesting individual advising as a universal support practice. Students on probation are required to meet with an academic advisor, and this requirement is enforced through registration holds. With their advisors, the students develop academic action plans that may include further interventions such as counseling or tutoring (Lamar University, 2007). The policy at Lamar University showed success, with students achieving higher GPAs and reporting higher levels of satisfaction (Mann et al., 2004).

The architects of both policies examined gave limited choices for students to operate with. Academic probation was automatic if a student fell below a specific threshold, and interventions written into the policy were mandatory – the student could not register or continue enrollment if they did not engage in the intervention. The success of the policies at Lamar and UNC at Greensboro suggests that these limited choices are preferred for students on probation, ensuring engagement in interventions and ultimate recovery.

Psychologically Attuned Academic Probation Communications

Recent scholarship has examined the ways in which the language used in academic probation letters affects students on academic probation (Moss & Yeaton, 2015; Waltenbury et al., 2018). The institutional labeling of academic probation is often received as punitive, and probation letters themselves may have disparaging impacts on students. Research has shown that students report strong negative emotions tied to their experience of learning when they are on probation (Barouch-Gilbert, 2016). Therefore, a first step to better supporting students on probation is to examine the language used in these notifications.

According to Waltenbury et al. (2018), simply reframing the language used in institutional communications with students on probation is a cost-effective way that colleges and universities can demonstrate that faculty, staff, and peers care about students' emotional well-being and academic success. Using intentionally written, psychologically attuned language can help students feel connected to their universities, even as they find themselves on academic probation. A psychologically attuned probation notice takes into account the student's mental state, the hardship they may have experienced that led to low GPA and probation status, and the negative emotions they may feel about being on probation or even being a student at the institution. Waltenbury et al. (2018) found that psychologically attuned probation letters "reduced students' anticipated feelings of shame, concerns about stigmatization, and intentions to disengage from college" (p. 13). Administrators may debate the merits of a "tough love" versus a "soft" approach to probation notices; however, psychologically attuned communications strike a nice balance between being clear about institutional probation policies and addressing students' concerns about belonging and devaluation (Brady, 2017).

To evaluate the impact that institutional communications may have on students, locate a copy of the letter and/or email sent to students on probation. Read the letter from a student's perspective with two critical questions in mind: "How am I viewed by the institution?" and "What does probation mean for me and my relationship with the institution going forward?" (Waltenbury et al., 2018, p. 12). If the letter does not answer these questions – or worse, leads you to believe that a student might be ashamed, disheartened, or disengaged – it may be time to redraft these communications. To further this evaluation, Brady et al. (2019) suggested giving copies of the letter to students and then interviewing them to better understand their experience reading the letter.

Informed by psychological theory and research on students' sense of belonging, Brady (2017) postulated several strategies for crafting a psychologically attuned probation notice:

1. Frame probation as a process of learning and growth, not a label.

2. Acknowledge specific nonpejorative factors that contribute to academic difficulty.

3. Communicate that it is not uncommon to experience academic difficulties.

4. Offer hope of – and support for – returning to good standing.

By framing probation as a process of learning and growth, not a label, practitioners can help students move away from a fixed mindset, which could lead to "decreased effort, reduced help seeking, and avoidance of challenge" (p. 34) and instead adopt a growth mindset, helping the student to break the stigma by seeing that "intelligence and potential can be developed over time with effort, strategies, and support" (p. 34). By *acknowledging specific nonpejorative factors that contribute to academic difficulty*, institutions can recognize the plethora of reasons students may find themselves in academic difficulty (e.g., mental health, physical health, financial difficulty, personal relationships, underpreparedness, lack of awareness of resources) in a way that does not suggest a deficiency in the student in some way. By *communicating that it is not uncommon to experience academic difficulties*, institutions can aid student motivation and belonging by connecting the student with others having similar experiences, thereby reversing feelings of isolation or inferiority. And by *offering hope of, and support for, returning to good standing*, the institution can empower the student to connect with campus resources that will help the student return to good academic standing. The various strategies are grounded in social psychology literature, borrowing from Yeager & Dweck's (2012) research on mindset, Heider's (1944) attribution theory, Snyder's (2002) research on hope theory, and various studies on belongingness and self-determination theory applied to educational contexts (Brady, 2017).

In her study on psychologically attuned letters, Brady (2017) revised the probation notice at Stanford University, keeping in mind the student-perspective questions, "How am I viewed by the institution?" and "What does probation mean for me and my relationship with the institution going forward?" and the psychologically attuned strategies:

1. Describe probation as a process of learning and growth, not a label;

2. Acknowledge specific nonpejorative factors that contribute to academic difficulty;

3. Communicate that it is not uncommon to experience academic difficulties;

4. Offer hope of – and support for – returning to good academic standing.

Figure 1.2 includes content from Brady's dissertation, illustrating the differences between standard probation letter in place at the time and the revised psychologically attuned letter.

Standard Letter	Psychologically Attuned Letter
...You will be placed on Academic Probation effective [Term]. Let me make very clear that Probation at [School] is a warning, nothing more, and will not appear on your official transcript. Its purpose is to alert you to academic difficulties in time to identify those areas where you may be experiencing problems and determine how best to address them.	...You will have an academic probation status beginning [Term]. This process is simply designed to alert you to academic difficulties in time to help you identify those areas where you may be experiencing problems and determine how best to address them. It will not appear on your official transcript. Additionally, if you meet the requirements for satisfactory academic progress, this probationary status will end.
If you do not meet these conditions, you may be at risk for Restricted Registration status or Suspension.	We are confident that you can meet these standards. However, it is important that you take steps to address the causes of your academic difficulties. If these conditions are not met, you may be at risk for restricted registration status or suspension.
Placement on Academic Probation is a part of the University's commitment to offer students support for—and guidance through—whatever difficulties they may have experienced."	There are many reasons students enter the academic probation process. These reasons can include personal, financial, health, family, or other issues. Our goal is to help you identify the factors that are relevant to you and to help you address them. You should also know that you are not alone in experiencing these difficulties. Many students enter and participate in the probation process each year, and by working with their advisors, many leave the process and continue a successful career at [School]. For descriptions of the experiences of some past students who have gone through this process, please see the attached document.

Figure 1.2. Brady (2017) Example Probation Notice Refinement.

Note. The words Probation, Restricted Registration, and Suspension were capitalized in the university's standard letter.

In addition to embodying the student-perspective questions and the psychologically attuned strategies, the revised letter had an attachment with student stories, further humanizing the academic probation process. Brady (2017) provided an excerpt of one of the student stories:

> When I failed an important math class, I was devastated. If anything, getting the probation notice made me feel worse. I thought I was the only one having a hard time. Eventually, I got up the courage to talk to my RA. ... He told me, "You'd be surprised how many times I've had this conversation."... I learned something important in the process, about how to face up to challenges, to reach out to others for help, and find a way forward.

Revising the probation notices in a psychologically attuned manner and including student narratives reframed the probation process for students and helped students in this status feel connected to the institution and feel as if they knew a path to returning to good standing. The studies conducted by Brady (2017, Brady et al., 2019) reinforced this notion, and a new area of probation research is emerging, focusing on the psychological and emotional impact of academic probation on students (Barouch-Gilbert, 2016).

While this is an emerging area of the literature, institutions are already using the research to improve their own practices. The University of South Carolina recently revised its communications in a psychologically attuned manner (see Figure 1.3). Note the reframing of academic probation as a journey and normalizing the process by including language like "you are not alone," and "many first-year students experience a temporary setback after their first semester" followed by common factors that lead to probation, which the student may identify with. Yosso (2005) elevated counter-storytelling and reframing as tools to reverse deficit-based narratives about people of color, and the same principle can be applied to students on academic probation who are coping with negative emotions and narratives around their academic capabilities and may need help seeing probation as an opportunity for growth.

The language also iterates the institution's commitment to the student's success multiple times, ending with "we look forward to working with you." One area the probation notification could improve upon would be to ensure that students are feeling connected to the institution. One way to accomplish this would be to have the probation notice sent by an institutional representative the student already knows, such as their academic advisor. James and Graham (2010) asserted that intervention strategies should incorporate personal contact and individualization.

Because your cumulative UofSC GPA is below a 2.00 at the end of the fall 2019 semester you are part of the academic probation process—a journey to help you get back on the track to academic success. You are not alone. Many first-year students experience a temporary setback after their first semester for a range of reasons, from adjusting to university coursework to being away from home for the first time to learning to balance academics with social life.

We are committed to the academic success of each of our students. The first step in your academic probation process is attending an Academic Coaching appointment in the University Advising Center. At this appointment, you will create an Academic Plan that outlines your goals, incorporates your unique strengths, and identifies the steps you need to take to regain good academic standing.

[...] The University of South Carolina is committed to supporting you in your path to degree completion and personal success. Please visit www.sc.edu/advising/probation for more information or contact the University Advising Center at 803-777-1222 with questions about the probation process. We look forward to working with you.

(University of South Carolina, n.d., Academic probation notice sent to first-year students. Reprinted with permission)

Figure 1.3. University of South Carolina, Example Psychologically Attuned Probation Notice.

Suspension and Dismissal

The final elemental factors amongst most probation policies are suspension and possibly dismissal if no improvement is made in GPA (Robinson, 2015). Houle (2013) highlighted numerous tensions in the research regarding students who have been suspended from their institutions. While there is robust literature on the experiences of students who voluntarily withdraw (i.e., students who drop out or transfer), there is relatively little literature on the experiences of students who are suspended (Berkovitz & O'Quin, 2006; Houle, 2013; Suchan, 2016). A hallmark of retention literature is the importance of integrating students into the university, yet students who are suspended are purposely excluded from engaging in these integration opportunities (Astin, 1984; Tinto, 1993; Houle, 2013; Suchan, 2016). As is the case with academic probation status, institutions have wide variety of approaches for governing dismissal and academic suspension.

A GPA of 2.00 on a 4-point scale is the universally accepted threshold for meeting academic standards, yet some institutions hold differing expectations (Kopp & Shaw, 2016; Versalle, 2018). Central Michigan University automatically suspends any new student with less than a 1.00 GPA at the end of their first term, skipping probation, while the University of Alaska – Fairbanks places students with less than a 2.00 GPA on academic warning as a step prior to academic probation (Versalle, 2018). Some institutions have an appeal process for dismissed students who had extenuating circumstances, which may not be guaranteed or automatic (Versalle, 2018).

Review Process

At the end of each primary term, student performance is reviewed by members of the Financial Aid and Registrar's offices. Students who are meeting the above minimum standards are judged to be making satisfactory academic progress toward a degree.

Students who have been doing satisfactorily and then fall below any of the above standards are given a warning to improve performance. If they fail to meet the benchmark for the next semester or perform below the minimums for the primary terms, they are suspended. They may appeal the suspension or apply for readmission after spending some time away from DePauw.

Students who successfully appeal suspension are placed on probation. In most cases, they will have one probationary semester to bring their performance into line with the satisfactory academic progress standards. If they fail to do so they are again suspended. However, some students who come close to reaching the target may be continued on probation.

SAP progress is evaluated at the end of the Fall and Spring primary terms in order to give students who are suspended a chance to submit an appeal before the beginning of the next semester. Status determinations are provisional until the extended term is completed.

Appeals of Suspensions

Students who are suspended for failing to meet SAP guidelines may appeal their suspension in writing to the Academic Standing Committee, which includes representatives from the faculty, Academic Affairs, Student Life and Financial Aid. Usually, appeals are heard approximately two weeks after grades for the primary terms have been posted (approximately January 15 and June 10). In the appeal the student presents his/her case for continuing. If the student is behind in credit earned, the appeal should include a plan for catching up, which may include taking courses elsewhere over the summer. If the student has fallen below the minimum GPA standards, the appeal should include a plan for improving performance.

Students who successfully appeal a suspension may continue on probation in the following semester. Those whose appeals are denied may apply for re-admission after being away for a minimum of one semester.

(DePauw University, 2020, Academic Standing. https://www.depauw.edu/academics/academic-resources/advising/registrar/academic-standing/)

Figure 1.4. Dismissal Policy from DePauw University.

Figure 1.4 shows an example dismissal policy from DePauw University. The DePauw policy highlights an additional academic warning standing, with the probation standing in that example open only to students who appeal a suspension. The DePauw policy also presents an example of terms of dismissal. The policy stipulates that students must wait at least one semester before attempting to re-enroll in the institution (DePauw, 2020).

A defined suspension period is a common feature of dismissal policies, although the time away can vary from institution to institution. Versalle (2018) collected a series of policies:

- The website of Indiana University Purdue University Indianapolis (IUPUI) notifies potentially returning students, "Students dismissed for the first time must sit out for a minimum of one regular (fall or spring) semester" (2018).

- Florida State University's website informs academically dismissed students they can only be readmitted if they "have been absent for two or more consecutive semesters, including summer" (2016).

- Wright State University students are not permitted to enroll for any courses at the university for a full calendar year, or three consecutive semesters, including summer (2015).

While most institutions stipulate a defined waiting period, this practice is inconsistent with retention theory, which holds that integration with the institution fosters student persistence to completion (McDermott, 2008; Tinto, 1975, 1987, 1993, 2012). Houle (2013) recommended that institutions continue to provide engagement opportunities to students following dismissal, including campus activities, access to university resources like counseling and the health center, and direct communication.

Suchan (2016) found that many students experienced a sense of "healing" as a result of talking through their experience with the researcher, whether it started the healing process, brought a sense of closure, or allowed the student to actively reflect upon and examine the experience of academic suspension, make sense, and articulate their personal learning and development. Communication keeps students connected to the university and more likely to return and allows the institution to make it clear what is expected of students while on suspension and what the reinstatement process is (Houle, 2013). Such outreach could be through an institutional representative the student already knows, such as their academic advisor. These recommendations could shift institutional dismissal practices from voluntary interventions to intermediate interventions, offering more support.

The policies highlighted here exemplify practices in the literature that show policy architects more often build choices for students at risk of dismissal than students at risk of probation. Dismissal policies are more likely to include an appeals process, a pathway to avoid dismissal through major change or grade forgiveness, or a mandated break. While the institution cannot control individual actions of students, the design of policy can institutionally frame the pathways surrounding individual student action.

The preceding paragraphs have laid out a framework for academic dismissal, to include a defined GPA threshold after a certain number of credit hours or semesters, the opportunity for students to appeal to a committee, and a defined period of time students must sit out. Following this period of time, students may be reinstated to the institution.

Reinstatement

Similar to the policies for academic probation and dismissal, the approaches to reinstatement vary widely amongst institutions and, like the literature on academic suspension, the body of work on reinstatement is limited (Suchan, 2016; Versalle, 2018). Generally, the onus for reinstatement is squarely on the student, thus resembling a voluntary intervention, though institutions certainly could incorporate elements of intermediate and mandatory interventions to the reinstatement process. According to Bellandese (1991), the primary responsibility for hearing and deciding academic reinstatements often rests with academic standards committees, academic deans, or chief academic officers, although for at least one university, the responsibility lies with the academic advisor (Houle, 2013).

Giesecke and Hancock (1950) observed that the reinstatement decision "is made more often than not on the basis of inspired guesswork" (p. 72). Several variables have been tested to determine predictability of academic success for reinstated students, including high school performance, credit hours, duration of academic suspension, constructive activities during the suspension period, GPA, quality points, major change, and course enrollment (Suchan, 2016). Despite the number of variables that institutions consider when making reinstatement decisions, some common elements occur across institutions, such as a waiting period, application for readmission, and level of support upon reinstatement (Houle, 2013; Suchan, 2016; Versalle, 2018).

As mentioned previously when discussing dismissal, many reinstatement policies include a provision specifying that the student must sit out a defined period of time before pursuing reinstatement. The purpose of the waiting period is to allow for reflection, growth, and maturation (Osborne, 2013; Versalle, 2018). After this period of time, students can complete a reinstatement application, which could involve an essay, recommendation letter, academic plan, and/or interview (Central Michigan University, 2018; DePauw University, 2016; Versalle, 2018). The intent of such supplementary materials is to provide evidence that the student has used the time away to identify the challenges that led to the dismissal and create a plan for resolving and rising above those challenges when readmitted. If reinstated, the student's GPA would be below the threshold for good standing, so they might be readmitted on probation and required to participate in various probation initiatives such as meeting with an advisor or taking a course. Alternatively, the student might be required to take specific courses, repeat earlier classes, or take classes at a community college (California State University at Northridge, 2016; Colorado State University, 2015; University of Alaska – Fairbanks, 2016; University of North Carolina at Greensboro, 2013; Versalle, 2018). In most cases, reinstatement is a student-initiated process, although there are some rare examples of institution-initiated reinstatement processes, mostly limited to summer bridge or study-skills classes with a focus on study skills, academic planning, campus resource navigation, and time management (Berkovitz & O'Quin, 2006; Versalle, 2018).

In making reinstatement decisions, institutions should incorporate a holistic perspective. Suchan's (2016) research indicated that being placed on academic probation served as a trigger event for the critical reflection phase, and this experience led to transformational learning. Suchan recommended that students be required to respond in writing or verbally to key reflection prompts and questions. Responses should be deep, rich, and full and give insight to students' experience, critical reflection, learning, and development. Additionally, Houle (2013) recommended that institutions should closely examine the factors that contributed to the students being suspended as well as their plans for managing or eliminating these distractions if they are to be reinstated. Asking students to reflect could be one way to accomplish this. Houle further recommended this reflection could lead the institution to impose additional conditions for the student's reinstatement. This additional support could benefit newly readmitted students.

Regardless of who holds responsibility, a framework for reviewing and deciding on readmission applications should be established to guide institutional officials who have the responsibility for reviewing applications and deciding which students will be granted readmission (Houle, 2013; Suchan, 2016). Institutions should provide clearly defined expectations to students regarding the process to reinstate and should publish a reinstatement policy that outlines institutional policies and procedures in the university handbook. Such policies and processes should also be easily accessible online. It is also a good idea for universities to designate a person or committee to whom students on academic suspension may reach out to seek guidance or assistance with questions regarding the reinstatement process. Such person or committee should make active, intentional efforts to contact academically suspended students (Houle, 2013; Suchan, 2016).

Figures 1.5a–c show various reinstatement policies. The reinstatement policies from these institutions represent the varied approaches to handling students who are returning from a dismissal. The policy at Central Michigan University makes it explicit that "permission to return is not automatic and is based upon individual circumstances" while remaining vague in criteria for reinstatement, representing Giesecke and Hancock's (1950) "inspired guesswork" observation. California State University at Northridge has a highly defined eligibility for reinstatement policy that includes the completion of certain courses and the demonstration of "acquired skills or achievements," representing the strategic use of the time away (California State University at Northridge, 2020; Central Michigan University, 2020). Similar to the institutions profiled in the Dismissal section, these institutional examples of reinstatement policies all have different length of time requirements. More specifically, California State University at Northridge doesn't articulate a defined period of time, Central Michigan University defines the time in months, and the University of Alaska – Fairbanks defines the time in semesters. Each institution approaches the process for reinstatement similarly, though with nuances: All involve a written application, but additional requirements include a personal interview with advisors, completion of courses at a separate institution, and

Rematriculation/Reinstatement

A student whose eligibility to enroll (matriculate) has been canceled for academic reasons may appeal to return through the Academic Advising and Assistance office. Students who have been dismissed may appeal for reinstatement consideration usually 12 months after dismissal. A student who has been dismissed twice will be rematriculated only under extraordinary circumstances.

Rematriculation/reinstatement requires a written application, payment of the rematriculation application fee and a personal interview with the Academic Advising and Assistance office. Supporting documents may also be required. Interviews for students seeking to return will be scheduled in advance of each enrollment period.

Permission to return is not automatic, and is based upon individual circumstances.

(Central Michigan University, 2020, Undergraduate Academic Probation, Suspension, Dismissal, and Rematriculation Policies and Procedures. http://cmich.smartcatalogiq.com/2021-2022/Undergraduate-Bulletin/Policies-and-General-Information/Academic-Policies-and-Information/Undergraduate-Academic-Probation-Suspension-Dismissal-and-Rematriculation-Policies-and-Procedures)

Figure 1.5a. Central Michigan University.

Returning Student Admission Requirements – Previously Disqualified Undergraduate Students

Undergraduate students wishing to return after previous disqualification in their last semester at CSUN must demonstrate acquired skills or achievements that support a successful return to the University. Such evidence may include successful completion of courses in their degree program at another institution or through The Tseng College (Extended Learning) with grades that demonstrate the ability to achieve good standing in a reasonable time frame if they are readmitted to CSUN. Students are strongly urged to meet with their CSUN academic advisor to discuss readmission requirements.

To be considered for readmission, previously disqualified freshmen, transfer and second bachelor's students will need to meet the following **eligibility requirements**. Students should:

1. Complete the four basic subjects for CSU general education: Writing, Mathematics, Critical Thinking, and Speech Communication courses with a "C–" or better. (Students reapplying as Engineering or Computer Science majors do not have to complete Critical Thinking prior to admission.)

2. Before applying, contact the CSUN College Advising Center for the major to determine major-specific readmission criteria. After the student applies, the College of the major and the Office of Undergraduate Studies will complete a review to determine the student's admissibility.

3. Determine whether or not a new application for admission via Cal State Apply is required.

4. Complete and submit the "Previously Disqualified Student Questionnaire" before the published deadline.

Admission procedures for previously disqualified students are published at Returning to CSUN.

(California State University at Northridge, 2020, Policies and Procedures. https://catalog.csun.edu/policies/returning-student-admission-requirements/)

Figure 1.5b. California State University at Northridge.

Readmission

An academically disqualified student who desires to continue admittance to the same program or another baccalaureate program may submit a request for readmission after not attending the University of Alaska – Fairbanks for one academic semester. The student should complete a form for readmission, which includes a plan for academic success. This form must be reviewed and approved by an academic advisor. Completed readmission forms must be submitted to the Office of the Registrar no later than the first day of instruction in the semester for which a student wishes to be reinstated. An academically disqualified student must successfully be readmitted within two years of disqualification or will need to reapply for admission.

If readmission is granted, the student will remain on probation and be required to meet with an advisor prior to registration for classes until their cumulative GPA is 2.0 or above. Students must achieve a term GPA of 2.0 or above for each term. Readmitted students who achieve a term GPA of below 2.0 will again be disqualified and will not be allowed to attend UAF for one academic year.

Baccalaureate students who wish to continue attending may apply to the UAF Community and Technical College (CTC) or College of Rural and Community Development (CRCD) for admission into an associate-level degree, certificate or occupational endorsement program with dean approval. This process can be completed with a full plan for academic success that has been developed with an academic advisor.

Readmitted students will have a maximum semester course load limit of 13 credits.

(University of Alaska – Fairbanks, 2020, Academic Standards. https://catalog.uaf.edu/academics-regulations/academic-standards/)

Figure 1.5c. University of Alaska – Fairbanks.

a plan for academic success. The policies also have different temperaments toward students who have been dismissed multiple times, with Central Michigan University explicit that reinstatement only occurs in extraordinary circumstances and the University of Alaska – Fairbanks conceding that students who have been dismissed multiples times can serve the dismissal period at the local community and technical college.

The policies showcased here reveal the many ways that choice architecture can affect how students navigate their reinstatement process. Suchan's (2016) advocacy of the reinstatement process as a trigger for critical reflection shows how designing reinstatement processes could elevate this practice from rote administrative action to transformational learning. For instance, California State University at Northridge's inclusion of highly defined eligibility requirements for reinstatement fosters a pathway for students to make strategic use of their time away from the institution. In another example, offering enrollment at a community or technical college allows for students at the University of Alaska – Fairbanks to have additional access points to continue their pursuit of degree attainment. Such choices not only offer additional pathways but also increase access, learning, and engagement.

While some institutions have reinstatement policies that include interventions similar to those for students on academic probation, this is not a universal practice. Reinstated students are still a vulnerable population in need of intervention support. Trombley (2001) noted that academic interventions that include strategies such as group intervention, individual advisor sessions, a study-skills course, goal-setting classes, and interpersonal problem-solving training have been shown to be successful initiatives. Other researchers have determined that intervention through advising and academic support services with unsuccessful students could be effective (Pascarella & Terenzini, 2005). Noel-Levitz (2009) found that students who did well following an academic suspension were enrolled in programs with strong administrative support services.

Change Management Case Study

Because of the various approaches to academic recovery policies, institutions will likely identify a need to change policy to align with leading practices. One such update occurred at Pepperdine University, a private, faith-based institution in California. In 2007, the University's Seaver College redesigned its probation policy after a survey revealed the majority of the students, faculty, and staff had no idea exactly what determined the probation status someone received, nor what the student had to do to comply with the vague stipulations.

The original probation policy, which went into effect in 1990, is shown in Figure 1.6. The policy was unclear, difficult to interpret, and cumbersome. It included no definitions for standards like "lack of progress" or "significantly high." The committee administering the policy used lengthy mathematical computations to determine who should stay and who should go, and the same computations determined add-ons to the standard probation statuses, which appeared as text in the letters the students received but were not written in the policy. The notification letters sent to students were severe, information-heavy, and in a small font to ensure one sheet of paper. The outdated policy raised several questions among stakeholders: Who determines lack of progress? What is a grade point deficiency? What if the institutional assessment is different from the student's?

Students falling below a grade point average of 2.0 in either their cumulative college work or work taken at Seaver College will be placed on academic probation. Any student who 1) is on probation and shows lack of progress, or 2) has a grade point deficiency which is significantly high, or 3) fails to clear probation within one calendar year is subject to dismissal.

(Pepperdine University, 2007, Academic Probation and Dismissal. https://seaver.pepperdine.edu/academics/content/2007seavercatalog.pdf)

Figure 1.6. Pepperdine University Policy, 1990–2008.

When redesigning the probation policy, staff researched NACADA the Global Community for Academic Advising journals and its clearinghouse, as well as all peer and aspirational school policies to formulate the updated policy. The policy that staff crafted is shown in Figure 1.7. While not dramatically different from the 1990 policy, the revised policy provides a clear structure for probation, dismissal, and reinstatement, making it easier to interpret and enforce.

When a student's cumulative GPA falls below 2.000, that student is placed on academic probation, which is considered a warning. Any student on academic probation must: (1) earn a minimum GPA of 2.000 in the next term of enrollment, and (2) be removed from academic probation. Failure to meet either stipulation will result in academic dismissal. Before requesting readmission, students who are academically dismissed must demonstrate successful completion of a full load of classes elsewhere for at least one term and fulfill all other requirements as specified by the Credits Committee.

(Pepperdine University, 2007, Academic Probation and Dismissal. https://seaver.pepperdine.edu/academics/content/2021-seaver-catalog.pdf)

Figure 1.7. Pepperdine University Policy, 1990–2008.

Pepperdine University's Seaver College engaged in a change management process to provide the necessary update to the probation policy. The literature suggests no singular proven change management framework; instead, there are many models, which sometimes come into conflict with each other (McCaffery, 2010; Tondnem, 2005). Change catalysts must be aware of the various models and understand which approach may apply in any given situation (Herbst, 1999). Pundyke (2020) identified various models of change management, though emerging constants were that change was continuous and iterative, involved many stakeholders yet was individualistic, and was guided by reflection and goal setting. Through benchmarking, peer review, and asking generative questions, Pepperdine staff engaged in a process-oriented and appreciative inquiry approach to change management when updating their probation policy (Cooperrider & Whitney, 2005; Herbst, 1999; Pundyke, 2020).

Some general leading practices for change management in higher education with respect to academic recovery policies include

- Gain buy-in from key constituents who are in the process and/or make the decisions, keeping in mind that they may be resistant to change. Such constituents could include the university registrar, chief academic officer, faculty, and vice president of student affairs or the directors of the various student-support units.

- Access probation, dismissal, and reinstatement data from institutional student information systems to inform current and future impact.

- Conduct peer review using the institution's list of peer and/or aspirational institutions, consult the literature maintained by professional organizations like NACADA, and benchmark by connecting with colleagues using email discussion lists to collect information that can be provided to leadership.

- Use information to construct a sample policy to share with campus decision makers and begin to build a coalition of support around the proposed plans. Sell the problem, not the solution – if the focus is a proposed new policy and a compelling need has not been demonstrated, it will be much harder to win over necessary buy-in.

Conclusion

This chapter provides an exploration of institutional policies and practices related to academic probation, dismissal, and reinstatement. Good academic recovery policy should address actions the institution can take to meet the needs of students experiencing high challenge, and policy should be tied to intermediate-to-mandatory interventions that ensure students are receiving a high level of support to maximize the opportunity for growth. There is a wide variety of institutional approaches to govern academic probation, dismissal, and reinstatement policies. When designing or redesigning policy, administrators must remember their role as choice architects and understand that the policy will ultimately frame the actions students are able to move forward with.

Although academic probation has no singular definition, elemental factors include GPA falling below a specific threshold, a defined period of time to raise the GPA, and dismissal if there is no improvement in GPA. Successful probation practices more often represent mandatory interventions and fall between two approaches: one-on-one and group support. An emerging practice in academic probation is to support student mental health using psychologically attuned probation letters.

While academic probation is more well documented in the literature, dismissal and reinstatement remain emergent. Common elements to both dismissal and reinstatement are a defined period of time away from the institution to allow a period for growth and maturation. As policymaking and implementation are organic and complex processes, change catalysts must be aware of the various models for managing change, and which approach may apply in any given situation, and must ensure that change is continuous and iterative, involving many stakeholders yet individualistic, and guided by reflection and goal setting.

One final factor to consider with policy approaches to probation, dismissal, and reinstatement is that there's no "one size fits all." A consistent theme is the wide variety of approaches to supporting this population of students. Kamphoff et al. (2006–2007) advocated that administrators create a program that works for the individual institution, but these policies also need to work for individual students. For example, an advisor would likely not use the same approaches when advising a first-year student as they would a junior. Advisors also need to consider the personal circumstances unique to each student to determine the best way to support them.

Professional experiences and related graduate and professional programs encourage educators in higher education to value the diversity of experience and to see each student as an individual. If each of us is prepared to treat each student as a unique person, how do we manage when our policies do not match up? Ideally, probation policies could be "one size fits most," with academic departments having latitude to use grace and make individual decisions (likely on appeal) that reflect an interest in treating students as individuals. If institutions are committed to that, it is incumbent that they take into account the issues unique to first-year students and others in transition and seek to create or amend probation policies that are consistent with our understanding of their unique circumstances.

As posited in the introduction to this book, institutions have a moral duty to provide resources and support to first-year students prior to academic dismissal. Implementing mandatory interventions that provide high individualized support can ensure student success.

References

Arcand, I. (2013). *A qualitative investigation of the conditions and experience undergone by students on academic probation who participated in academic companioning in a university context* [Unpublished doctoral dissertation]. University of Ottawa.

Astin, A. W. (1984). Student involvement: A developmental theory for higher education. *Journal of College Student Personnel, 25*(4), 297–308.

Barouch-Gilbert, A. (2016). Academic probation: Student experiences and self-efficacy enhancement. *Journal of Ethnographic and Qualitative Research, 10*, 153–164.

Bellandese, D. W. (1991). *A study of undergraduate academic dismissal policies and procedures at American colleges and universities* [Doctoral dissertation, University of Connecticut]. Dissertation Abstracts International: Section A.

Berkovitz, R., & O'Quin, K. (2006). Predictors of graduation of readmitted "at risk" college students. *Journal of College Student Retention: Research, Theory, & Practice, 8*(2), 199–214.

Braxton, J., & Brier, E. (1989). Melding organizational and interactional theories of student attrition: A path analytic study. *Review of Higher Education, 13*, 47–61.

Brady, S. (2017). *A scarlet letter? Institutional messages about academic probation can, but need not, elicit shame and stigma* [Doctoral dissertation, Stanford University]. ProQuest Dissertations and Theses Global.

Brady, S., Fricker, T., Redmond, N., & Gallo, M. (2019). *Academic probation: Evaluating the impact of standing notification letters on the experience and retention of students, followup report.* Higher Education Quality Council of Ontario.

Brocato, P. (2000). *Academic workshops: A plan to help students experiencing academic probation and disqualification* (ED 461349). ERIC.

California State University at Northridge. (2020). *Policies and procedures.* https://catalog.csun.edu/policies/returning-student-admission-requirements/

Central Michigan University. (2020). *Undergraduate academic probation, suspension, dismissal, and rematriculation policies and procedures.* http://cmich.smartcatalogiq.com/2021-2022/Undergraduate-Bulletin/Policies-and-General-Information/Academic-Policies-and-Information/Undergraduate-Academic-Probation-Suspension-Dismissal-and-Rematriculation-Policies-and-Procedures

Coleman, H. L. K., & Freedman, A. M. (1996). Effects of a structured group intervention on the achievement of academically at-risk undergraduates. *Journal of College Student Development, 37*(6), 631–636.

Cooperrider, D. L., & Whitney, D. K. (2005). *Appreciative inquiry: A positive revolution in change.* Berrett-Koehler.

Cruise, C. A. (2002). Advising students on academic probation. *The Mentor: An Academic Advising Journal, 4.* https://journals.psu.edu/mentor/article/view/61709/61354

DePauw University. (2020). *Academic standing.* https://www.depauw.edu/academics/academic-resources/advising/registrar/academic-standing/

Drake, J. K. (2011). The role of academic advising in student retention and persistence. *About Campus 16*(3), 8–12. https://doi.org/10.1002/abc.20062

Ferguson, N. S. (2017). Academic recovery in the first year. In J. R. Fox & H. E. Martin (Eds.), *Academic advising and the first college year.* Styles Publishing. 107-124

Giesecke, G. E., & Hancock, J. W. (1950). Rehabilitation of academic failures. *College and University, 26,* 72–78.

Herbst, M. (1999). Change management: A classification." *Tertiary Education and Management, 5*(2), 125–139. https://doi.org/10.1080/13583883.1999.9966986

Heider, F. (1944). Social perception and phenomenal causality. *Psychological Review, 51*(6), 358–374. https://doi.org/10.1037/h0055425

Higgins, W. M. (2003). *When expectations and reality collide: Working with students on probation.* NACADA Clearinghouse of Academic Advising Resources. http://www.nacada.ksu.edu/Clearinghouse/AdvisingIssues/Probation.htm

Hoover, C. (2014). *The purpose and practice of academic probation* [Doctoral dissertation, East Tennessee State University]. Digital Commons Electronic Theses and Dissertations. https://dc.etsu.edu/etd/2449

Houle, N. M. (2013). *Academic suspension and student adjustment: how students make meaning of their experiences* [Unpublished doctoral dissertation]. Northeastern University.

Hutson, B. L. (2006). *Monitoring for success: implementing a proactive probation program for diverse, at-risk college students* [Unpublished doctoral dissertation]. University of North Carolina at Greensboro.

Isaak, M. I., Graves, K. M., & Mayers, B. O. (2006). Academic, motivational, and emotional problems identified by college students in academic jeopardy. *Journal of College Student Retention: Research, Theory and Practice, 8*(2), 171–183.

James, C. L., & Graham, S. (2010). An empirical study of students on academic probation. *Journal of The First-Year Experience & Students in Transition, 22*(2), 71–92.

Kamphoff, C. S., Hutson, B. L., Amundsen, S. A., & Atwood, J. A. (2006–2007). A motivational/empowerment model applied to students on academic probation. *Journal of College Student Retention, 8*(4), 397–412.

Kopp, J. P., & Shaw, E. J. (2016). How final is leaving college while in academic jeopardy? Examining the utility of differentiating college leavers by academic standing. *Journal of College Student Retention: Research, Theory & Practice, 18*(1), 2–30. https://doi.org/doi:10.1177/1521025115579670

Kuh, G. D., Kinzie, J., Schuh, J. H., Whitt, E. J., & Associates. (2005). *Student success in college: Creating conditions that matter.* Jossey-Bass.

Lindsay, D. (2000). *A study to determine the characteristics of effective intervention programs for students on probation* [Doctoral dissertation, Pepperdine University]. ERIC Document Reproduction Service.

Mackay, J. (1996). *Establishing a learning community for community college students: STAR-students and teachers achieving results.* ERIC Document Reproduction Service No. ED393514.

Mann, M. M., Hosman, C. M., Schaalma, H. P., & De Vries, N. K. (2004). Self-esteem in a broad-spectrum approach for mental health promotion. *Health education research, 19*(4), 357-372.

Martino, T. L., & DeClue, J. (2003, October). *It's time to ACT!: Helping students get back to good standing* [Conference paper]. National Academic Advising Association Annual Meeting, Dallas, TX.

Mann, J. R., Hunt, M. D., & Alford, J. G. (2003–2004). Monitored probation: A program that works. *Journal of College Student Retention, 5*(3), 245–254.

Moss, B. G., & Yeaton, W. H. (2015). Failed warnings: Evaluating the impact of academic probation warning letters on student achievement. *Evaluation Review, 39*(5), 501–524. https://doi.org/10.1177/0193841X15610192

McCaffery, P. (2010). *The higher education manager's handbook: Effective leadership and management in universities and colleges* [EBook]. Routledge.

McDermott, M. L. (2008). *The relationship between suspension and subsequent student success* [Doctoral dissertation, University of Minnesota]. ProQuest Digital Dissertations.

Noel-Levitz, Inc. (2009). *2009 student retention practices and strategies at four-year and two-year institutions.* https://www.noellevitz.com/documents/shared/Papers_and_Research/2009/StudentRetentionPracticesandStrategies09.pdf

Osborne, J. A. (2013). *Gaining insight on the experiences of reinstated undergraduate students.* California State University, Long Beach.

Pascarella, E. T., & Terenzini, P. T. (2005). *How college affects students: Vol. 2. A third decade of research.* Jossey-Bass.

Pepperdine University. (2007). *Academic probation and dismissal.* https://seaver.pepperdine.edu/academics/content/2007seavercatalog.pdf

Pepperdine University. (2021). *Academic probation and dismissal.* https://seaver.pepperdine.edu/academics/content/2021-seaver-catalog.pdf

Preuss, M., & Switalski, R. (2008). *Academic probation intervention through academic assistance advising.* Rockingham Community College. (ERIC Document Reproduction Service No. ED 502891)

Pundyke, O. S. (2020). Change management in higher education: An introductory literature review. *Perspectives: Policy and Practice in Higher Education, 24*(4), 115–120. https://doi.org/10.1080/13603108.2020.1809545

Robinson, M. M. (2015). *The lived experiences of first-year, first semester honors college students placed on academic probation* [Doctoral dissertation, University of Central Florida]. Stars Electronic Theses and Dissertations, 2004–2019. https://stars.library.ucf.edu/etd/718

Sanford, N. (1962). *The American college.* Wiley.

Snyder, C. R. (2002). Hope theory: Rainbows in the mind. *Psychological Inquiry, 13*(4), 249–275. https://doi.org/10.1207/S15327965PLI1304_01

Suchan, J. J. (2016). *Exploring the experience of academic suspension and subsequent academic resilience for college students who were reinstated to the institution: A phenomenological analysis* [Doctoral dissertation, Iowa State University]. Graduate Theses and Dissertations. https://lib.dr.iastate.edu/etd/15816

Thaler, R. H., & Sunstein, C. R. (2008). *Nudge: Improving decisions about health, wealth, and happiness.* Penguin.

Tinto, V. (1975). Dropout from higher education: A theoretical synthesis of recent research. *Review of Educational Research, 45,* 89–125.

Tinto, V. (1987). *Leaving college: Rethinking and causes and cures of student attrition.* University of Chicago Press.

Tinto, V. (1993). *Leaving college: Rethinking the causes and cures of student attrition* (2nd ed.). University of Chicago Press.

Tinto, V. (2012). *Leaving college: Rethinking the causes and cures of student attrition* (3rd ed.). University of Chicago Press.

Tovar, E., & Simon, M. (2006). Academic probation as a dangerous opportunity: Factors influencing diverse college students' success. *Community College Journal of Research & Practice, 30*(7), 547–564.

Trombley, C. M. (2000). Evaluating students on academic probation and determining intervention strategies: A comparison of probation and good standing students. *Journal of College Student Retention, 2*(3), 239–251.

Trowler, P. (2002). Introduction: Higher education policy, institutional change. In P. Trowler (Ed.), *Higher education policy and institutional change: Intentions and outcomes in turbulent environments* (pp. 1–24). SRHE and Open University Press.

University of Alaska – Fairbanks. (2020). *Academic standards.* https://catalog.uaf.edu/academics-regulations/academic-standards/

University of South Carolina (n.d.). *Academic probation notice sent to first-year students.* Columbia, SC: University of South Carolina

Versalle, G. L. (2018). *Understanding the experiences of students re-admitted after academic suspension as part of a university-initiated process: a qualitative study* [Doctoral dissertation, Western Michigan University]. ScholarWorks. https://scholarworks.wmich.edu/dissertations/3357

Waltenbury, M., Brady, S., Gallo, M., Redmond, N., Draper, S. & Fricker, T. (2018). *Academic probation: Evaluating the impact of academic standing notification letters on students.* Higher Education Quality Council of Ontario.

Yeager, D. S., & Dweck, C. S. (2012). Mindsets that promote resilience: When students believe that personal characteristics can be developed. *Educational Psychologist, 47*(4), 302–314. https://doi.org/10.1080/00461520.2012.722805

Yosso, T. J. (2005). Whose culture has capital? A critical race theory discussion of community cultural wealth. *Race Ethnicity and Education, 8,* 69–91.

CHAPTER TWO

Theory and Practice for Academic Recovery Advising

Catherine Nutter

College students do not start their academic career with plans to fail. Even so, roughly 40% of those who start college will not finish (Boswell, 2012; National Student Clearinghouse, 2016). Some will stop their college career to work; others will believe they are "not college material"; and still others will not make the required grades to continue according to academic standing requirements. It is this last group, students we term academic recovery students, on whom we focus this chapter.

Academic recovery students bring with them unique situations that can challenge even the most seasoned academic advisor. Students may have failed courses because of financial concerns that led them to prioritize a job and its income, or students may have had emotional or personal situations arise that caused them to completely shut down, or students may have faced academic struggles without knowing where to turn for appropriate and available remediation or tutoring. Very often, students may have been in all three of these categories and a few more.

While research has made it very clear that the academic advisor is one of the most significant contacts a student has in college (Campbell & Nutt, 2008; Drake, 2011; Karp, 2011; Vander Shee, 2007), traditional advising approaches often prove ineffective with students in academic jeopardy simply because they are not on a traditional trajectory, moving toward graduation (Baloul & Williams, 2013; Laskey & Hetzel, 2011). Student outcomes, student needs, and even student motivation can differ vastly for academic recovery students. Academic advising holds reign as the primary intervention for student success, and the academic recovery student needs even more of that connection, more of that guidance, more of that relationship to succeed.

The causes for students landing on academic probation and academic dismissal are vast. Just as varied are the strategies that can make a difference for the student's academic success. No single theory or advising method addresses all possible issues facing students in academic jeopardy. The academic recovery advisor needs a set of strategies that can blend, combine, and bundle ideas from a host of theories, thoughts, and practices. Strategies based on student development theory, Dweck's mindset theory (1986, 2000; Dweck et al., 1995), and Duckworth's grit theory (2007, 2009) can combine with developmental and prescriptive advising components, academic advising motivation based on Maslow's motivational framework (Maslow, 1943), and student self-efficacy activities (Bandura, 1977) to create sound yet flexible strategies for advising this specific population of students.

If that sounds like a great amount of information, it is. The rest of this chapter will help unpack it and provide examples and questions to help develop a practice and process for working with the academic recovery student. While academic advising takes center stage in this chapter, advisors are encouraged to remember the importance of teamwork and interdependence for the student and for our practice as well. Very often, student needs are best addressed through a team approach.

Advising as a Retention Strategy

Academic advising and college student persistence and retention are inextricably linked (Campbell & Nutt, 2008; Drake, 2011; Karp, 2011). An ACT policy report cited academic advising as one of the least used but most beneficial nonacademic programs on campus in terms of affecting student persistence and retention (Lotkowski et al., 2004). The ACT report examining academic and nonacademic factors in college student retention promoted academic advising as one of the key programs on campus that allows students to create strong professional relationships within the institution. The authors of the report drew from Tinto (1987, 1998) when they mentioned the impact of advising interaction on retention: "One of the primary factors affecting college retention is the quality of interaction a student has with a concerned person on campus" (Lotkowski et al., 2004, p. 16). While this relationship is important and not to be dismissed, academic advising improves a student's chance at academic success beyond simply providing an interested person with whom to talk. Access to quality, instructive academic advising can mean the difference between a marketable degree or just a short yet expensive foray into higher education (Nutter, 2017).

Swecker, Fifolt, and Searby (2013) found the impact of academic advising on retention more significant than any other single variable they evaluated. Their study found that each meeting with an advisor increased the odds of the student being retained by 13%. Gender, race, and major showed no significant relationship to retention, but meeting with an academic advisor did. In another study related to student retention and success, Young-Jones, Burt, Dixon, and Hawthorne (2013) provided quantitative analysis to support six factors related to student academic success. Three of those factors are identified specifically as related to advising: academic advising meetings, advisor empowerment, and advisor accountability. In the author's department, advisors call this process guided autonomy. In simple terms, it is helping the student navigate the path toward independence and interdependence from an academic perspective. In the Young-Jones et al. (2013) study, interactions with a positive and responsible person who supported the student's ownership of the educational process and provided guidance were responsible for enhanced student self-efficacy, which was in turn related to higher GPA.

One of the chief suggestions in the ACT policy report was the creation on college campuses of formal, structured academic advising programs to promote retention of students (Lotkowski et al., 2004). How to implement these programs was left to insight and imagination. A variety of advising practices were created in the 10 years after the ACT policy report, including the rise of professional, trained academic advisors in departments, colleges, and career centers across the nation (Doubleday, 2013). What remains consistent within those varied practices is the fact that institutions have enhanced student-support programs such as academic advising to facilitate retention and persistence in the wake of increased student need and increased student turnover (Dickson, 2006). The advent of specific academic advising programs for students in academic distress has also increased.

Advising Approaches

Academic advising methods can be categorized into two major approaches: prescriptive and developmental (Barbuto et al., 2011). Prescriptive advising, positioning the advisor as in charge and the student as simply a follower, is losing its hold as a primary framework for advising as programs move toward understanding student needs, student development, and student goals (Crookston, 1972; Grites, 2013). However, prescriptive advising has its place when working with students, especially those in academic jeopardy.

Developmental Advising

Gordon (1994) referred to developmental advising as an "elusive ideal," one that can often seem unrealistic in the wake of practices and processes in many advising offices. Grites (2013) called developmental advising "one of the most fundamental and comprehensive approaches to academic advising" (p. 5). Developmental advising is not a theory; it is an approach to academic advising that considers all aspects of a student's development – educational, professional, and social (Gordon, 1994; Gordon & Grites, 2001; Grites, 2013):

> The developmental academic advisor gathers information to recognize where the student stands along the educational, career, and personal dimensions of her or his life, discusses where the student plans to be, and assists the student in getting to that point as readily as possible. (Grites, 2013, p. 13)

Frost (1993) was able to identify key elements of developmental academic advising by surveying faculty advisors whom students identified as using a developmental approach. Those elements included involving the student in the advising experience, exploring success factors with the student, and displaying interest in the student's progress – academically and otherwise. Because of the focus on including students as actors and participants in the advising process, multiple research studies suggest that students prefer developmental advising practices to those that are more prescriptive (Beasley-Fielstein, 1986; Frost, 1993; Grites, 2013; Mottarella et al., 2004; Paulsen, 1989).

Prescriptive Advising

Prescriptive advising also has a place in the academic advising relationship, especially for the student in academic jeopardy (Fielstein, 1994). Students who are on academic standings that limit activities or require specific course enrollment very often need direction on those requirements, policies, and rules. A more prescriptive approach is necessary when the student has rules, regulations, and policies to navigate. One of the chief complaints about prescriptive advising is that it leads to fewer advising interactions, thus limiting the effectiveness of academic advising. However, several recent studies suggest that prescriptive advising has its place in academic advising programs, especially if institutional policy is at play. Researchers from California State University found that including prescriptive elements into academic advising, especially where degree planning, graduation requirements, and course load were concerned, increased four-year graduation rates (Bolkan et al., 2021). Providing clear expectations through a prescriptive advising approach benefit students by providing "uncluttered pathways" to graduation (Bolkan et al., 2021).

Nutter (2017) conducted a study of students who had been placed on academic probation or had just returned from academic suspension. Students who were meeting with an academic recovery advisor instead of a traditional advisor regarded their academic advising interactions as more prescriptive than developmental. However, the students who identified their advisor as using a more prescriptive advising style also reported more advising interactions and more meetings. In other words, a more prescriptive advising style did not lead to fewer interactions, but more. According to Shelton (2003), the level of support students feel, which can be linked to the frequency of academic advising appointments, is directly linked to student retention and success. Those results suggest that prescriptive advising, including small steps and checks on progress more frequently, may be what students in academic jeopardy need.

Discussion

Developmental academic advising can be difficult to achieve in practice, as Gordon (1994) suggested. Academic recovery advising (ARA) is very often an additional responsibility for the traditionally assigned department or major advisor. Many academic advisors are already working with hundreds of students and are responsible for a range of responsibilities, including course advising, registration, and degree audits. The academic recovery student needs different guidance. This student still wants and needs to register for appropriate classes, but this student may also need additional support with resource use, academic skills development, time management strategies, and more.

The sheer number of students assigned per advisor makes a developmental, relational, transformative advising practice for all students elusive at best and impossible at most (Gordon, 1994). So how does an academic advisor with a 300+ student population support the student in academic jeopardy? The short answer is – creatively.

The traditional 30-minute in-person advising appointment can be and maybe should be reimagined. A brief video check-in with students keeps the relationship active and also respects busy schedules. We often discuss advising in terms of the advisor's schedule, but we should not discount the student's schedule of classes, study time, homework, family, and social time. A 10-minute virtual check-in at the beginning of the week to recap short-term goals or to celebrate a successful midterm grade keeps the student on track and helps the advisor assess and augment the academic recovery plan.

While ideally ARA is an entirely separate intervention, it can be done – and done well – by the department or major advisor. As we move forward into theories that help define the ARA practice, we discuss how each of those theories could look in an advising meeting.

Theories of Note

To develop theories, researchers start with questions. Then they seek answers to those questions, looking at practice, process, and variables. They study how variables influence practice and how process could affect variables. They look for commonalities to suggest explanations. They check results for data integrity, process integrity, and practical integrity. But most important, they start with questions. As we begin to layer prior knowledge with theories and philosophies, we should remember to question. When reading through theory, practice, or any professional literature, it is helpful to keep in mind key questions: What is here that addresses the situation or needs of the ARA student? How can I implement this idea in my practice?

Mindset

The first and likely most well-known theory to inform ARA practice is growth mindset. Carol Dweck (1986, 2000) maintained that the ideas people construct about themselves, which she calls self-theories, play into motivation, success, and locus of control: "People's implicit theory about human attributes structure the way they understand and react to human actions and outcomes" (Dweck et al., 1995, p. 267). She identified two primary theories of intelligence that affect how and why people behave the way they do in a crisis or when faced with adversity (Hong et al., 1999). Her model suggests that people who believe intelligence to be fixed (*entity theory*) tend to focus more on performance goals, as opposed to those with a fluid or malleable perception of intelligence (*incremental theory*), who instead focus on learning goals (Dweck, 2006; Dweck & Yeager, 2019). "Although [students] displaying different patterns do not differ in intellectual ability, these patterns can have profound effects on cognitive performance" (Dweck, 1986, p. 1041). Students challenged by learning, those with the malleable view of intelligence, will strive to find ways to foster their learning and to work harder, such as taking foundation classes as a way to build skills or seeking out tutoring opportunities. Those with more of a fixed mindset will avoid a challenge because they will evade a situation that shows their knowledge to be limited or less competent (Dweck, 1986).

The fixed, or entity, mindset emphasizes traits to explain behavior. For example, in the case of our academic recovery student, poor academic performance would be attributed to a lack of intelligence in a subject, not a lack of effort or a lack of strategy development. These traits can be tied to goals as well. Dweck (1986) suggested that "performance goals (as often attributed to fixed mindset) appear to promote defensive strategies that can interfere with challenge seeking" (p. 1042). Incremental, or malleable, theory tends to look more at mitigating factors, such as needs and intentions. The goals most often expressed are learning goals, an aim to increase knowledge or competency. In this mindset, poor academic performance could be attributed to effort or to ineffective study skills. In other words, entity theorists will focus more on ability whereas the incremental theorists will emphasize effort (Bouffard et al., 1995; Dweck, 2008). "In the face of failure, incremental theorists would then be more likely than entity theorists to exert effort to remedy the skills they lack" (Hong et al., 1999, p. 589).

A point that bears noting in Dweck's discussion of mindset is that of stereotypes. When people belong to marginalized groups that have negative stereotypes, the fixed mindset effects can be magnified intensely (Dweck, 2006, pp. 74–78). For example, a high-performing female student who believes she is simply smart in math has consistently scored in the top of the class until she is presented with the teacher-reinforced stereotype that girls are not good at math. Suddenly, that math genius is making lower grades, questioning her ability in a subject she has succeeded in for years prior. A person with a fixed mindset, who believes that intelligence is innate, given, constant, will have trouble standing up to a negative input (Dweck, 2006). Now imagine the stereotypes faced by first-generation students, students from low socioeconomic environments, or those from ethnic backgrounds that are so often marginalized.

The biggest difference between the two types of mindset is that the growth mindset allows for education and reform (Dweck et al., 1995). Even better, the growth mindset can also be taught (Dweck, 2006). Teaching the malleable mindset is as easy as paying attention to what behavior nets praise. Praising process over performance and effort over grades reinforces the importance of learning and growing. Setting goals that reward effort and strategy, for example, moves students from performance to learning goals (Dweck, 2006). "A strong wish to prove the adequacy of one's ability makes that ability seem like a deep-seated, fixed attribute of the self, whereas a strong desire to improve one's ability makes it seem like a more dynamic quality that can be developed" (Dweck & Yeager, 2019, p. 483).

Application in Academic Recovery Advising

Think about this scenario: A student is on academic probation. The advisor is talking with the student about the situation. The student says, "I'm on probation because I just don't get math (or history or English). I am just not good at it. I DO NOT want to take that class again, but I know I have to." The student has a rather fixed mindset, especially in terms of performance avoidance. The advisor knows that the surest way to help the student's GPA is grade replacement. Now what?

The first step is to introduce the student to the concept of growth mindset. Perhaps find a quick video that summarizes growth mindset or spend the first 10 minutes of the appointment watching Dweck's 2014 TedTalk (Dweck, 2014). Ideally, add the video to a seminar for ARA students but introduce the concept, regardless of the method. Very likely, students will recognize the benefits of a growth mindset but also admit to experiencing the fixed mindset in the face of academic struggles. Now it is possible for an honest discussion to begin.

For ARA, the key to using growth mindset may be in how advisors and students set goals. By guiding students toward improvement through learning goals, not performance goals, advisors can facilitate a growth mindset with students. Instead of focusing on a particular grade in a class, for example, setting a goal of understanding a particular subject better or learning a specific mathematical process teaches students that learning is the goal, not necessarily the grade. An improved GPA will almost always follow improved learning in class. Focusing on activities that improve learning will guide students toward the more malleable, growth mindset and help them understand setbacks (such as academic probation) as opportunities for improvement, not failure of performance. Since the ARA meetings are frequent, advisors can help students identify multiple strategies and resources to help define and reach the learning goal, such as tutoring or instructor office hours.

Grit

The next theory related to success with academic recovery students is grit, identified by Duckworth et al. (2007). As defined by Duckworth, grit is perseverance and passion for long-term goals. The concept of grit has seen its share of success and implementation as well as concerns and questions. It has been adopted as process in some public schools as a means to increase completion and improve grades. It has been studied as a predictor of academic success with mixed results (Bazelais et al., 2016; Kannangara et al., 2018). It has been redressed as a repacking of conscientiousness (Crede, 2018) and identified as a privilege based on socioeconomic factors (Schreiner, 2017). What we know is that grit (and the research concerning it) is much deeper and much more nuanced than what many initially believed. While grit may support growth mindset, or vice versa depending on the literature you read, the two theories complement one another and provide strategies for working with at-risk students.

In ARA, grit can be defined as the reason students come back to college after academic suspension or dismissal. Grit is why students continue to work toward a college degree after facing setbacks and obstacles.

After evaluating factors that lead to success in a variety of settings, including universities, military institutions, and academic competitions, Duckworth's research showed that self-discipline, perseverance, and interest were far and away better predictors of success than were background, education, or IQ (Duckworth, 2014; Duckworth & Gross, 2014; Duckworth et al., 2007; Duckworth & Quinn, 2009; Eskreis-Winkler et al., 20014; Maddi et al., 2012). According to studies, grit is more positively associated with success, completion of tasks, and attainment of goals than is IQ, GPA, standardized tests, and even prior success (Duckworth et al., 2007). In Duckworth et al.'s (2007) study of college students, grit was associated with higher GPAs for undergraduate students, even when factors such as SAT scores were held constant. In addition, studies have found that grit can be increased and developed over time, especially with specific interventions such as strengths-based goals (Duckworth, 2007) and academic rational beliefs (Warren & Hale, 2020).

Grit in our context – perseverance and passion for a college degree – may very well explain why some students return to school after academic suspension and why they succeed after facing such an extreme setback. Perseverance and passion outweigh failed attempts and low GPAs that accompany academic probation, suspension, and dismissal. Duckworth et al. (2007) found that *perseverance of effort* is a far better predictor of success through grit than is *continuity of interest*. For academic recovery advising, this means the quest for the degree is more a leading indicator of continued enrollment than is the quest for a degree in a specific major.

Duckworth and colleagues (2007) collected data in six separate studies to address the basic question of why some people achieve more and accomplish more than others of equal intelligence. These studies were conducted with different population samples in different environments using different success measures. Without getting into all of the data details, the research provided a key finding. The data generated from the Short Grit survey (Grit–S) showed a two-factor solution linking perseverance of effort and consistency of interest as key elements in persistence.

Nutter (2017) used the same grit measurement scale with students who had been in academic jeopardy (on academic probation or previously dismissed from the university because of insufficient GPA). Students who had faced the highest level of consequence – academic dismissal – and recovered showed the highest self-reported grit scores. That makes sense if we consider that students who have been academically suspended had to work harder just to be allowed to enroll in classes than did students who were on academic probation. In the campus study, Nutter noted that effort was more pronounced than interest. And the data showed an interesting correlation between effort and advising. The more student advising centered on nonacademic topics such as what students were doing outside of class, the lower the students reported the effort aspect of grit. In simple terms, the more a student's advising appointments focused on nonclass behavior, the less effort students reported on the grit survey. What we can suggest from this result is that effort must be coupled with academic focus for a student to improve academically. Fosnacht, Copridege, and Sarraf (2018) also reported that persistence of effort tends to be more predictive of grit than consistency of interest is.

Why was interest reported less than effort was in Nutter's (2017) study? A couple of possibilities exist to help explain that result. One is that students have changed their interest in a specific degree. Many of the majors at the institution where the study occurred have competitive GPA requirements or restrict the number of unsuccessful attempts in key courses. Students who are on academic probation or returning from academic dismissal very likely have changed their academic focus to a different major, which likely manifested as a lower interest score. Similarly, it is possible that the primary interest these students have is recovering their academic standing, not focusing on a particular major or set of classes.

Application in Academic Recovery Advising

Grit provides insight into why students persist, even in the face of academic probation or suspension. Sustained effort is more important than sustained interest. For advising, this statement translates into effort to graduate instead of interest in a particular major. This information is encouraging when considering the number of GPA-restricted majors and colleges at many institutions. Students who are working with low GPAs but have interest in a restrictive major may be willing to reconsider the major if the goal of a degree can be reinforced.

Grit can be affected by mental well-being and self-control as well as resilience and mindset (Kannangara et al., 2018). Advisors can use this knowledge in advising meetings to offer referrals as necessary to counseling services or other resources as well as to help set goals and plan around potential obstacles. When students can identify the obstacles that might appear and put strategies in place to address those issues, they are much better suited to work through the issues and achieve the goal.

Student Self-Efficacy

When it comes to theory on student success, one of the most seminal and still in use is Bandura's (1977) theory of self-efficacy. To summarize, people in general, and students in particular, who believe in their ability to perform a task are much more likely to be successful in that performance (Bandura, 2010). Without a belief in outcome, motivation to act is limited. Therefore, part of any academic recovery program should facilitate self-efficacy growth and development.

Testing self-efficacy in an educational setting, researchers have discerned that motivation reinforced by high self-efficacy could lead to better habits related to learning – including persistence when faced with a challenge. Hsieh et al. (2007) defined goal orientation (motivation) as one of three types: mastery (the desire to improve ability), performance approach (the desire to demonstrate ability), and performance avoidance (the desire to hide inability). Not surprisingly, students who scored their self-efficacy highest reported their goals in the mastery level more than did those who reported a lower self-efficacy score. However, an interesting development showed with students in academic jeopardy: Students who were in academic trouble tended to sabotage their success by adopting more performance avoidance goals, even if those students reported high self-efficacy. For advising, the takeaway here is that without direction and guidance, students will avoid those classes, those tasks, those situations that they believe point to an inability on their part. Even if grade replacement is an option (and, as such, could significantly improve the student's academic standing), students in academic jeopardy prefer to avoid the "hard" class or elect to completely change academic direction to keep from looking unintelligent.

High self-efficacy can be developed, and it can be developed in academic advising meetings. Bandura (1977) discussed four main sources of influence in creating high self-efficacy. The first is mastery experiences. Success breeds success and a success-oriented outlook. Just like in our discussion of grit, how people handle setbacks is more the definition of self-efficacy than how they approach success. For a student in academic trouble, repeating a failed class may pose some trepidation, but success in that class may very well lead to success in other classes and in other situations.

The second realm of influence with self-efficacy is vicarious experiences – watching others do the same thing with success. Knowing or knowing about someone in a similar situation who achieves success raises the viewer's sense of self-efficacy (Bandura, 1977, 2008). While we want to maintain confidentiality in academic advising, talking about a redacted situation with a student can help build self-efficacy by showing that others have had success following the same model as the one being suggested for the student. While students may not want to hear about research studies necessarily (although some students will find these studies evidential and supportive of the intervention), working with peer mentors or talking with an accountability partner or success team members will provide a path to that vicarious experience.

The third method of increasing self-efficacy is called verbal or social persuasion. Bandura (1977) explained verbal persuasion this way: "People are led, through suggestion, into believing they can cope successfully with what has overwhelmed them in the past"

(p. 198). We know that simply telling someone they can succeed does not often lead to success. Social support or social persuasion is more than just telling someone, "You can do this." Social support is providing a helpful environment and providing resources and tools to facilitate success (Bandura, 1977). Even though social persuasion is not as strong a creator of self-efficacy as a stand-alone strategy is, it often leads to a self-fulfilling prophecy effect. When students are told by a trusted advisor that they have the abilities and the intelligence to succeed and are provided the tools, resources, and practices known to work, students begin to believe it (Bandura, 2008).

Finally, Bandura (2008) discussed building self-efficacy through responses to stress and negative situations. Negative perceptions of stressful situations or of responses to stressful situations can influence a person's sense of self. Part of an academic recovery program could include healthy responses to stress and positive perceptions of emotions. That stress is natural and that responses can be managed as energy and not paralysis can be key topics during academic advising sessions and can be an integral part of an academic recovery program.

The fact that students return to the university after an academic suspension says something about their self-efficacy. Their belief in their ability to complete a degree program, even when faced with tangible evidence to suggest otherwise, points to high self-efficacy. However, self-efficacy without guidance may not lead to any better results a second or third time around.

Application in Academic Recovery Advising

Imagine a student in the second semester of school has earned a 1.8 GPA. The student is on academic probation and is questioning whether attending college was a good idea. The student tells you in the first meeting, "I don't know that I'm really cut out for college. I don't seem to know anything I'm supposed to know. I'm not as smart as everyone else, and I just stay confused and lost in all of my classes. Maybe I just need to put in more hours at work and come back to school when I'm older." As the advisor begins to unpack this statement, it becomes evident that the student is facing multiple obstacles and may be a first-generation student who is working at least part-time to help pay for college. Very likely, the student needs help with time management, study skills, notetaking strategies, and socialization. Where does our advisor begin?

Step one for the advisor is recognizing that all issues cannot and will not be resolved in a single meeting. Effective change, enhancing self-efficacy, and promoting growth take time, repetition, and reinforcement. ARA is not a once-a-semester advising practice. It is a functional, supportive, learning relationship between a student in need and a practiced and caring professional.

Remember, the main influences to promoting self-efficacy are mastery experiences, vicarious experiences, social or verbal persuasion, and response to stressors. Helping the student remember why they applied for college can get the conversation moving toward goals and aspirations. Reminding the student that they were admitted (mastery experience) lays the foundation for seeing past success as an indicator for future success. Putting the student in touch with successful peers who can identify with the feelings of confusion, loss, and isolation will also begin to enhance self-efficacy (vicarious experiences as well as social persuasion). Creating goals and plans for learning how to talk with instructors, how to create a study plan, how to manage time commitments for both work and school, and how to prepare for class will help move the student out of the stress response of "Maybe I should just quit" to a more positive "I need to find a better way to do this."

Academic Advising Motivational Factors

Students in academic recovery have motivations related to academic advising that may differ from the traditional student. Where the traditional student may be looking for advising to discuss internships, graduation requirements, or degree completion, the academic recovery student wants back on track.

Similar to how Maslow's (1943, 1954, 1962) hierarchy of human needs explains the growth and development of an individual, we can create a hierarchy of academic recovery advising, identifying which students are motivated by which levels of need. Taking Maslow's hierarchy and repurposing it specifically for the academic recovery student (see Figure 2.1), we can see better where students are, what they need, and where they are headed. This approach may also help us unpack some of the nonacademic issues that students face related to situations such as cultural capital, social and/or racial diversity, and low or lower socioeconomic status.

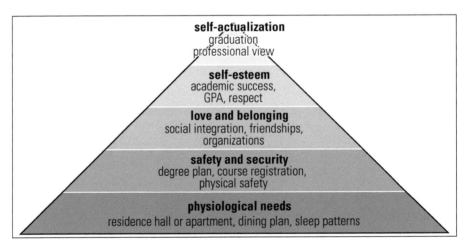

Figure 2.1. Academic Recovery Student Hierarchy of Needs.

Physiological Needs

Maslow's most basic needs revolve around the physiological – food to provide fuel and support, clothing and shelter for protection, and rest to allow the body to build strength. Until these most basic needs are met, more social and psychological needs are not even identified, let alone realized. For the academic recovery student (and perhaps many traditional college students as well), these most basic needs may be in doubt. In fact, the quest to satisfy these basic needs may be an underlying cause for academic issues. Students who need to work full time to provide for rent, food, utilities, and clothes for themselves or their family will likely have a difficult time prioritizing classroom attendance. Until students are comfortable that these specific needs have been met, they are likely unable to address their next set of needs seriously. Advisors are well positioned and should be able to discuss campus and community resources such as food banks, shelters, and the Dean of Students or similar offices. Talking about graduation plans with a student who is not yet certain where they are staying that night will be frustrating to both the student and the advisor.

Security and Safety Needs

The next level of needs according to Maslow deal with security and safety. In general terms, this level includes protection from the elements, freedom from fear, and a sense of security and order. These needs can be addressed with inclusive classrooms, gender-inclusive facilities, and freedom from microaggressions. For the academic recovery student, safety and security often begin with the transparency and openness of the academic recovery process. Language and working of websites, of paperwork, and of even the appointment process can help a student feel secure enough to open up to an advisor about the realities of academic issues. For some students, feeling unconnected to a major can create feelings of doubt and insecurity. Helping students explore majors and find opportunities that relate to their strengths, values, and goals can help the academic recovery student find a sense of academic security. Introducing the student to student-affairs resources such as food pantries and legal services, as well as creating connections with counselors or life coaches, can also increase feelings of safety and security.

Belonging Needs

Maslow's third level includes the need to belong. Behavior becomes motivated by the desire to affiliate with a group, create attachments, and build interpersonal relationships. In general, these needs can be satisfied by forming close friendships, joining a social organization, creating an identity as a member of a profession, or simply registering to vote under a particular political party. At the university level, advisors need to be proactive in providing connection to first-generation programs or mentoring programs for students who may be unfamiliar with how colleges and universities work.

An academic recovery student's need to belong is a strong a motivator for behavior. On the most surface level, the academic recovery student is seeking to belong to the institution, to still identify as a college student. Students build relationships with their advisors, and the relationship moves them toward the next level of the model. Sometimes the relationship is based on identification: The student connects with an advisor who shares a goal (such as the student's success), or perhaps the advisor has a characteristic the student would like to strengthen. Often, the student simply finds the advisor easy to talk to. On a deeper level, identifying with students who have overcome similar obstacles; observing or communicating with professionals who earned degrees in the same major; joining an academic or social program on campus; and building appropriate relationships with a variety of university staff, students, and professors all evidence a student's fulfillment of belonging.

Esteem Needs

In Maslow's (1943, 1954, 1962) work, esteem was divided into two categories: personal and social. Personal esteem motivates people toward achievement, independence, mastery, and dignity. Social esteem leads to status and prestige. For the college student, this level of motivation involves grades, social integration, academic honors, and respect from self and from others. While guiding students through the esteem level, advisors are helping students identify strengths, capitalize on academic and personal success, and become leaders in the college setting. This process, too, is part of the guided autonomy mentioned earlier. Students become their own architects at this level, creating and building themselves with a vision of success, an understanding of strength, and a value for independence laced with interdependence. The advisor helps the student recognize and understand that independent does not mean alone. Esteem is built through teams that support and facilitate growth, mastery, persistence, and success. The advisor is very likely the initial part of the team that will show students the next level, acknowledge their readiness to move forward, and congratulate them on the success they have created.

Self-Actualization Needs

In motivational psychology, *self-actualization* refers to the desire for self-fulfillment: "The tendency might be phrased as the desire to become more and more what one is, to become everything that one is capable of becoming" (Maslow, 1943). For the academic recovery student, self-actualization comes as the student strives to become the ideal college student – blending academic success with social identity and a developing professional vision of the future. Transitional advising meetings involve conversations about the future, about building on strengths and success, about ideals and how to achieve them.

Practical Strategies for Academic Recovery Advising

Knowing the theories relevant to advising lays the foundation for advising the academic recovery student. Putting those theories into action takes some guidance … and practice. Each theory relates to steps and conversations to engage the academic recovery student during advising appointments. While no two appointments look or flow the same, having a set of strategies can help frame the semester.

An important first step is engaging the student in a conversation about persistence in terms of mindset and grit. The student plans to persist and likely has completed multiple steps to do so. From either reenrolling or possibly the reapplication process to meeting outside requirements such as community college courses to perhaps writing an essay or enrolling in an academic strategies course, the student has shown perseverance to continue with the academic journey. The effort aspect of grit is evident. Even so, many first meetings with students after academic probation or even academic suspension result in the student concentrating on past failures and offering simplistic statements of change such as, "I'll study more" or "I know this semester will be different" without truly delving into the issues that helped create the situation. An initial advising meeting with an academic recovery student should focus on how to change previous behavior to change the outcome. Otherwise, behaviors and results are likely to mirror the previous attempts.

One way to assist with identifying barriers to success is to use a checklist or survey of common roadblocks (see the Appendix). One used in the author's department breaks down obstacles into broad categories such as free time obstacles, academic/study-skills obstacles, personal obstacles, and work-related obstacles, among others. Students complete this checklist prior to meeting with an advisor. Completing the list in advance gives the student time to reflect, to consider, and to be honest. The list also includes referrals to the student counseling center and student disability services should the obstacles be more personal than the student chooses to discuss with an advisor. This list also helps the advisor identify those first-level motivational needs such as food insecurity or financial concerns to better provide resources and assistance at the first meeting.

Identifying the barrier is only the first step, however. Identifying how the barrier affects academics is essential. The discussion on grit earlier in this chapter showed that students reported less effort on the grit survey if advising focused on less academic topics. The advisor who understands that academic focus is essential to grit can take the conversation to new depths and explore the key attitudes and behaviors complicating academic success, adding the academic component that makes grit effective for the academic recovery student. For academic recovery students to put forth the effort to succeed academically, advising needs a decidedly academic focus.

In keeping with Dweck's (2006) mindset, the conversation moves from what did not work to how to make it work. Finding paths around barriers, looking for success in the face of failure, and identifying challenges to patterns of thought all combine to help create a more malleable mindset. Failure is no longer a given and a stopping point. Failure simply becomes a result of a behavior that does not work. Other behaviors can work, and the student begins to recognize that failure is not an end but a beginning of a new thought process. Rhetoric cannot be stressed enough here. Advisors should take the opportunity to reframe academic struggles into terms or experiences students understand. One person mentioned changing mistakes (failure) to mis-takes (the second or third takes in a film), thereby changing failure into a learning process. I explained once to a student athlete in my class that a low grade on a test is very much like walking the first batter in an inning. The right answer is to shake it off, evaluate, and change the process and then deliver a different result.

The second step in academic recovery advising involves a combination of prescriptive and developmental advising to create a stronger sense of self-efficacy for the student. Prescriptive advising can be an essential component of academic recovery advising due largely to the institutional requirements for the student either to gain readmission or to retain current admission. Completing steps for financial aid, retaking failed courses, and registering for academic support courses may all be requirements for the academic recovery student. Prescriptive advising is essential in this situation. The student has tasks to perform and may not be aware of all that is involved. The advisor prescribes the next steps, the course enrollment, and even the frequency of advising appointments. In this case, the advisor is not facilitating student success. The advisor is outlining what absolutely must happen according to institutional policy. This part of the interaction is wholly prescriptive and completely essential to the student's ultimate success, for without these steps, the student may not move forward at all.

Follow-up meetings become full-range advising, a combination of prescriptive and developmental advising approaches. Talking through successes and challenges since the last meeting helps build a relationship and afford the student an opportunity to guide the conversation. The advisor listens, encourages, and engages in a more developmental approach. Putting the student in charge with questions such as, "What resources would help you perform better in that math class?" or "What changes have you seen in your study habits in the last week?" helps the student develop a sense of academic self-efficacy but also a sense of trust in the advising relationship. Advisors will also identify key steps to be completed before the next meeting (prescriptive advising) – financial aid applications, for example, or other institutional policies or program requirements.

Creating a goal for the following meeting is essential to all advising but especially for the academic recovery student. Many institutions require that students in academic jeopardy show academic progress at the end of the term to remain enrolled. Having weekly or biweekly goals helps the student maintain continuity of thought and behavior throughout the semester and to maintain focus on academic success. The goal may be to attend campus-provided tutoring for a particular subject or to begin studying five days in advance of a test in history. Initially, the advisor may need to create the goal (a more prescriptive practice), but eventually the student will become the architect of the next week or two and will rely on the advisor to provide support for the goal instead of the goal itself, moving to a much more developmental relationship.

These follow-up meetings are also instrumental in helping the student to create an enhanced academic self-efficacy. Remember from the earlier discussion on self-efficacy, motivation can come from three different types of behavior: mastery, performance approach, or performance avoidance. Each of these motivation points will either build or diminish a student's academic self-efficacy.

The academic recovery student very likely has at least one class with a failing grade. Advisors often suggest the student retake the class with an F to improve GPA. The student's natural motivation factor, as mentioned earlier, is complete avoidance of this course. It has already proven to be a problem course. Taking it a second (or third) time opens the student up to those negative responses to stress and negative situations. However, retaking the course is essential, so the advisor may calculate GPA with and without the grade replacement or grade forgiveness option. Success in the course this next time will almost certainly move the student steps closer to good standing and then to graduation than would allowing the grade to stand.

While repeating the course makes sense in every way possible, the student's primary motivation may still be avoidance. To build a student's self-efficacy, the advisor can help the student create short-term goals that lead to mastery – earn at least 80% on homework this week or create a chapter outline – so the student reaches milestones. Perhaps attending tutoring or office hours becomes part of the two-week plan. Initial success will create more success, and the student then becomes motivated to complete the class (mastery) instead of avoiding it. Those intermediate, short-term goals are essential to building mastery.

Another strategy to build mastery in a troubled area is by using the student's strength in another area. This strengths-based approach works by taking mastery in one area – writing, for example – and using the success, knowledge, and skills in that subject to create successful practice in the trouble area. For our writing aficionado who struggles in math, creating a poem or an essay or a simple outline may help to contextualize a forgotten formula.

The advisor serves as a mentor by providing self-efficacy motivation opportunities. Mastery experiences – opportunities to show what has been learned – are likely the most significant motivator for academic self-efficacy. For the academic recovery student, mastery experiences may seem few. However, almost certainly the advisor will find an area in which the student excels (cooking, math, offering advice to friends) that can lay a foundation for success in another field. Talking through prior successes can help the student visualize future success (social persuasion) and provide a self-efficacy boost.

Simply telling students they have what it takes to succeed will do some good, but to really help the student, the advisor needs to create a series of mastery experiences through a full range of advising strategies as well as an understanding of the student's current motivational level. What is also needed is a series of structured activities that bring on that success through self-improvement and improved skills. In academic recovery advising, that means helping a student create obtainable short-term goals while working toward the long-term academic standing goal and the longer-term graduation goal.

A Case for Institutional Support

One could make the argument that the prescriptive, intrusive, full-range advising practice central to promoting academic success with at-risk students is also central to promoting academic success with all students. Ensuring that advisor caseloads are small enough to allow for meaningful, recurring engagement is central to impactful academic advising, whether that advising is with students who need skill development or those who would benefit from mentoring. Academic advising requires professional development that includes coaching strategies, mentorship, academic skill development, and campus resource engagement. The next chapter in this book provides excellent information on coaching, which can greatly affect the advising support a student receives. Academic advising professional development should include teaching academic skills or academic preparedness courses, and above all, it requires time. To develop a growth mindset in students, to foster mastery experiences and a sense of belonging, and to build the physical, social, and emotional environment to support success, academic recovery advisors need time to develop relationships with these students. More time means fewer assigned students. With growing enrollments, the equation quickly distills to more academic advisors or student-support teams.

Adding advising staff can seem expensive to the university. However, consider the cost of losing these students. The cost to the university simply to recruit a student to fill this spot is more than the cost of a new advisor. The cost to the community in terms of an educated workforce makes even stronger a case for additional support. The difference in lifetime earning potential between a high school graduate and an associate's degree earner is over $400,000. The difference between a high school graduate and someone with a bachelor's degree is almost $1 million (APLU Factsheet, n.d.). Then there is the cost to the student, a person whose dreams, whose goals, whose contributions, and whose future can and will be forever changed.

The simple matter to the institution is that attrition costs money. It costs in unrecovered tuition, athletic fees, housing, food, bookstore purchases, and other expenditures, which can be estimated at well over $100,000 per student (Raisman, 2013). Calculating the loss of 100 students moves the revenue loss to $10 million. Adding additional advising support nets the university a significant savings. The return on investment cannot be overstated.

Conclusion

If the academic recovery program begins with the end in mind, then retention and persistence should be at the forefront of program development (Nutter, 2017). Creating an advising program for students in academic distress cannot be single-faceted, nor can it be a pure replication of a major-specific advising program simply with more interactions. The needs of the student are different, and so must be the process to address those needs. The one factor all researchers seem to agree on is that the academic advisor has the most impact on the success of the program. Higher involvement, even if the meetings are mandatory, had a significantly higher impact on student success, as measured by academic standing and GPA (Nutter, 2017). As Kirk-Kuvawe et al (2001) explained,

> advisors and administrators should not assume that aggressive involvement alienates students who are in academic difficulty. In fact, high-involvement intervention may be a positive outcome regardless of eventual academic performance: Students may feel that the people in the institution care enough to reach out during their times of difficulty. (p. 45)

If we combine all that has been considered, we have an intensive, intrusive, grit-creating academic advising practice that includes multiple structured conversations with students about goals, academic skills, mindset, and motivation. We have reached out to students (developmental advising) in academic distress. In our initial meeting, we addressed barriers to success (grit, mindset, prescriptive academic advising, motivational level) and helped create strategies to address those obstacles (prescriptive advising, developmental advising, self-efficacy). We may have created a contract that includes reduced enrolled hours, limited extracurricular activities (prescriptive advising), and specific tutoring/resource engagement (engagement and inclusion, mindset, grit). We may even have the assigned academic advisor teaching an academic strategies class. Our follow-up meetings (full-range advising, grit, mindset, engagement) will include discussions of plans and strategies to enhance those plans (prescriptive, developmental, mindset, grit). All told, we have created an advising plan that is proactive, responsive, student-centered, and goal-oriented.

References

APLU Fact Sheet. (n.d.) *How does a college degree improve graduates' employment and earnings potential?* https://www.aplu.org/projects-and-initiatives/college-costs-tuition-and-financial-aid/publicuvalues/employment-earnings.html

Baloul, F. M., & Williams, P. (2013, August). Fuzzy academic advising system for on probation students in colleges of applied sciences—Sultanate of Oman. In *Computing, Electrical and Electronics Engineering* (ICCEEE), 2013 International Conference on (pp. 372–377). IEEE.

Bandura, A. (1977). Self-efficacy: Toward a unifying theory of behavioral change. *Psychological Review, 84*(2), 191–215.

Bandura, A. (2008). An agentic perspective on positive psychology. *Positive psychology, 1,* 167-196.

Bandura, A. (2010). Self-efficacy. In I. B. Weiner & W. E. Craighead (Eds.), *The Corsini Encyclopedia of Psychology.* 1-3. https://doi.org/10.1002/9780470479216.corpsy0836

Barbuto, J. E., Jr., Story, J. S., Fritz, S. M., & Schinstock, J. L. (2011). Full range advising: Transforming the advisor–advisee experience. *Journal of College Student Development, 52*(6), 656–670.

Bazelais, P., Lemay, D. J., & Doleck, T. (2016). How does grit impact college students' academic achievement in science?. *European Journal of Science and Mathematics Education, 4*(1), 33–43.

Beasley-Fielstein, L. (1986). Student perceptions of the developmental advisor–advisee relationship. *NACADA Journal, 6*(2), 107–117.

Bolkan, S., Pedersen, W. C., Stormes, K. N., & Manke, B. (2021). Predicting 4-year graduation: Using social cognitive career theory to model the impact of prescriptive advising, unit load, and students' self-efficacy. *Journal of College Student Retention: Research, Theory & Practice, 22*(4), 655–675.

Boswell, S. S. (2012). "I deserve success": Academic entitlement attitudes and their relationships with course self-efficacy, social networking, and demographic variables. *Social Psychology Education, 15,* 353–365.

Bouffard, T., Boisvert, J., Vezeau, C., & Larouche, C. (1995). The impact of goal orientation on self-regulation and performance among college students. *British Journal of Educational Psychology, 65*(3), 317–329.

Campbell, S. M., & Nutt, C. L. (2008). Academic advising in the new global century: Supporting student engagement and learning outcomes achievement. *Peer Review, 10*(1), 4.

Crookston, B. (1972). A developmental view of academic advising as teaching. *Journal of College Student Personnel, 13,* 12–17.

Crede, M. (2018). What shall we do about grit? A critical review of what we know and what we don't know. *Educational Researcher, 47*(9), 606–611.

Crede, M., & Niehorster, S. (2011). Adjustment to college as measured by the student adaptation to college questionnaire: A quantitative review of its structure and relationships with correlates and consequences. *Educational Psychological Review, 24,* 133–165.

Doubleday, J (2013, December 2). Under pressure to hit learning goals, colleges amp up advising. *The Chronicle of Higher Education.* http://chronicle.com/article/Under-Pressure-to-Hit-Learning/143303/

Drake, J. K. (2011). The role of academic advising in student retention and persistence. *About Campus, 16*(3), 8–12. https://doi.org/10.1002/abc.20062

Duckworth, A. (2014). *Grit: The power of passion and perseverance* [Video]. TED: Ideas worth Spreading. https://www.ted.com/talks/angela_lee_duckworth_grit_the_power_of_passion_and_perseverance?language=en

Duckworth, A., & Gross, J. J. (2014). Self-control and grit related but separable determinants of success. *Current Directions in Psychological Science, 23*(5), 319–325.

Duckworth, A. L., Peterson, C., Matthews, M. D., & Kelly, D. R. (2007). Grit: Perseverance and passion for long-term goals. *Journal of Personality and Social Psychology, 92*(6), 1087-1101.

Duckworth, A. L., & Quinn, P. D. (2009). Development and validation of the Short Grit Scale (GRIT-S). *Journal of Personality Assessment, 91*(2), 166–174.

Dweck, C. S. (1986). Motivational processes affecting learning. *American Psychologist, 41*(10), 1040-1048.

Dweck, C. S. (2000). *Self-theories: Their role in motivation, personality, and development.* Psychology Press.

Dweck, C. (2014). *The power of believing that you can improve* [video]. TED Conferences. https://www.ted.com/talks/carol_dweck_the_power_of_believing_that_you_can_improve?language=en

Dweck, C. S. (2006). *Mindset: The new psychology of success.* Random house.

Dweck, C. S., Chiu, C. Y., & Hong, Y. Y. (1995). Implicit theories and their role in judgments and reactions: A word from two perspectives. *Psychological Inquiry, 6*(4), 267–285.

Dweck, C. S., & Yeager, D. S. (2019). Mindsets: A view from two eras. *Perspectives on Psychological Science, 14*(3), 481–496.

Eskreis-Winkler, L., Duckworth, A. L., Shulman, E. P., & Beal, S. (2014). The grit effect: Predicting retention in the military, the workplace, school and marriage. *Frontiers in psychology, 5*, 36.

Fielstein, L. L. (1994). Developmental versus prescriptive advising: Must it be one or the other? *NACADA Journal, 14*(2), 76–79.

Frost, S. H. (1993). Developmental advising: Practices and attitudes of faculty advisors. *NACADA Journal, 13*(2), 15–21.

Fosnacht, K., Copridge, K., & Sarraf, S. A. (2018). How valid is grit in the postsecondary context? A construct and concurrent validity analysis. *Research in Higher Education, 60*(6), 803–822. https://doi.org/10.1007/s11162-018-9524-0

Gifford, D. D., Briceno-Perriott, J., & Mianzo, F. (2006). Locus of control: Academic achievement and retention in a sample of university first-year students. *Journal of College Admission, 191,* 18–25.

Gordon, V. N. (1994). Developmental advising: The elusive ideal. *NACADA Journal, 14*(2), 71–75.

Gordon, V., & Grites, T. J. (2001). NACADA Journal authors: 20 years of contributions. *NACADA Journal, 21*(1–2), 70–76.

Grites, T. J. (2013). Developmental academic advising: A 40-year context. *NACADA Journal, 33*(1), 5–15.

Hong, Y. Y., Chiu, C. Y., Dweck, C. S., Lin, D. M. S., & Wan, W. (1999). Implicit theories, attributions, and coping: a meaning system approach. *Journal of Personality and Social psychology, 77*(3), 588-599.

Hsieh, P., Sullivan, J. R., & Guerra, N. S. (2007). A closer look at college students: Self-efficacy and goal orientation. *Journal of Advanced Academics, 18*(3), 454–476.

Kannangara, C. S., Allen, R. E., Waugh, G., Nahar, N., Khan, S. Z. N., Rogerson, S., & Carson, J. (2018). All that glitters is not grit: Three studies of grit in university students. *Frontiers in Psychology, 9,* Article 1539.

Karp, M. M. (2011). *Toward a new understanding of non-academic student support: Four mechanisms encouraging positive student outcomes in the community college.* CCRC Working Paper No. 28. Assessment of Evidence Series. Community College Research Center, Columbia University.

Kirk-Kuwaye, M., & Nishida, D. (2001). Effect of low and high advisor involvement on the academic performances of probation students. *NACADA journal, 21*(1–2), 40–45.

Laskey, M. L. & Hetzel, C. J. (2011). Investigating factors related to retention of at-risk college students. *Learning Assistance Review, 16*(1), 31–43. eric.ed.gov/?id=EJ919577

Lotkowski, V. A., Robbins, S. B., & Noeth, R. J. (2004). *The role of academic and non-academic factors in improving college retention.* ACT Policy Report. http://files.eric.ed.gov/fulltext/ED485476.pdf

Maddi, S. R., Matthews, M. D., Kelly, D. R., Villarreal, B., & White, M. (2012). The role of hardiness and grit in predicting performance and retention of USMA cadets. *Military Psychology, 24*(1), 19-28.

Maslow, A. H. (1943). A theory of human motivation. *Psychological Review, 50*(4), 370-96.

Maslow, A. H. (1954). *Motivation and personality.* New York: Harper and Row.

Maslow, A. H. (1962). *Toward a psychology of being.* Princeton: D. Van Nostrand Company.

Mottarella, K. E., Fritzsche, B. A., & Cerabino, K. C. (2004). What do students want in advising? A policy capturing study. *NACADA Journal, 24*(1–2), 48–61.

National Student Clearinghouse Research Center. (2016). *Snapshot report: Yearly success and progress rates.* https://nscresearchcenter.org/wp-content/uploads/SnapshotReport20-YearlySuccessandProgressRates.pdf

Nutter, C. (2017). *Academic probation and suspension students: Perspectives on academic advising and grit.* [Doctoral dissertation, Texas Tech University]. Texas Tech University Libraries Electronic Theses and Dissertations. https://ttu-ir.tdl.org/handle/2346/73139

Schreiner, L. A. (2017). The privilege of grit. *About Campus, 22*(5), 11–20.

Shelton, E. N. (2003). Faculty support and student retention. *Journal of Nursing Education, 42*(2), 68–76.

Swecker, H. K., Fifolt, M., & Searby, L. (2013). Academic advising and first-generation college students: A quantitative study on student retention. *NACADA Journal, 33*(1), 46–53.

Tinto, V. (1987). *Leaving college: Rethinking the causes and cures of student attrition.* University of Chicago Press.

Tinto, V. (1998). Colleges as communities: Taking research on student persistence seriously. *The Review of Higher Education, 21*(2), 167–177.

Swecker, H. K., Fifolt, M., & Searby, L. (2013). Academic advising and first-generation college students: A quantitative study on student retention. *NACADA Journal, 33*(1), 46–53.

Vander Shee, B. A. (2007). Adding insight to intrusive advising and its effectiveness with students on probation. *NACADA Journal, 27*(2), 50–59. https://doi.org/10.12930/0271-9517-27.2.50

Warren, J. M., & Hale, R. W. (2020). Predicting grit and resilience: Exploring college students' academic rational beliefs. *Journal of College Counseling, 23*(2), 154–167.

Young-Jones, A. D., Burt, T. D., Dixon, S., & Hawthorne, M. J. (2013). Academic advising: Does it really impact student success? *Quality Assurance in Education, 21*(1), 7–19.

CHAPTER TWO

Appendix - Academic Success Workbook

(permission granted from University Advising, Texas Tech University)

Free Time Obstacles
- [ ] Too much social life
- [ ] Overextended in outside activities
- [ ] Too much TV

Financial Obstacles
- [ ] Worried about money
- [ ] Financial Aid Requirements
- [ ] Inadequate financial aid
- [ ] Spouse not working
- [ ] Too many debts
- [ ] Time limit on school funds

Work Related Obstacles
- [ ] Working too many hours
- [ ] Problems with the boss
- [ ] May lose job
- [ ] Conflicts with job
- [ ] No part-time work available
- [ ] Must work to survive

Obstacles with Major
- [ ] Selecting a major
- [ ] Major-entry requirement
- [ ] GPA requirements
- [ ] Classes unavailable

- [ ] Major not offered
- [ ] Not happy with major

Academic/Study Obstacles
- [ ] Learning disability
- [ ] Poor study habits
- [ ] Poor time management
- [ ] Poor study environment
- [ ] Ineffective studying
- [ ] Inadequate study time
- [ ] Inferior academic preparation
- [ ] Inadequate reading skill
- [ ] Inadequate writing skill
- [ ] Inadequate math skill
- [ ] Inadequate science skill
- [ ] Inadequate subject knowledge
- [ ] Poor Note taking skills
- [ ] Poor concentration
- [ ] Unhappy with instructor
- [ ] Instructor impersonal
- [ ] Poor academic advising
- [ ] Unclear educational goals

Obstacles with Fear of
- [ ] Failure
- [ ] Not being Perfect

- [ ] Accomplishments
- [ ] Pressures
- [ ] Success
- [ ] Commitment
- [ ] Making decisions
- [ ] Making mistakes
- [ ] Difficult Tasks

Personal Obstacles
- [ ] New Independent status
- [ ] Roommate problems
- [ ] Relationship worries/ breakup
- [ ] Loneliness
- [ ] Socially uncomfortable/shy
- [ ] Housing problems
- [ ] Value conflicts
- [ ] Dislike TTU
- [ ] Demanding church calling
- [ ] Dislike college & studying
- [ ] High anxiety
- [ ] Previous failure
- [ ] Negative attitude
- [ ] Parental pressure
- [ ] Lack of sleep

Other Obstacles
- [ ] _____
- [ ] _____

Sensitive Obstacles

If your academic obstacle is found among the following obstacles, mark the category heading but not the specific obstacle. You are strongly encouraged to seek services from professionals such as the University Counseling, University Career Services Student Disability Services, the Student Wellness, your Physician, etc.

- ☐ Anxiety/Stress
- ☐ Depression
- ☐ Divorce/Separation
- ☐ Emotional Abuse
- ☐ Family Health problems
- ☐ Family Issues/Concerns
- ☐ Health/Medical worry
- ☐ Illness/Death
- ☐ Learning Disability
- ☐ Marriage/Relational Issues
- ☐ Physical Abuse
- ☐ Pregnancy
- ☐ Rape/Assault
- ☐ Substance Abuse or Use

FREE TIME SOLUTIONS
Set Goals
Use a Planner
Use To-Do List Daily
Say 'NO' to Distractions
Manage Time Better
Other_____

FINANCIAL SOLUTIONS
See Financial Planner
Consider Independent Study
Contact Study Financial Aid
(Loans/Grants)
Other_____

WORK RELATED SOLUTIONS
Reduced Work Hours
Locate a job
Position Change within Job
See University Career Services
If Possible don't Work
Other_____

SOLUTIONS RELATED to MAJOR
Career/Interest Assessment
Internship Possibilities
Career Counseling
Computer-assisted Career Counseling
Consider a Career Workshop
Other_____

ONLINE CAREER ASSISTANCE:
www.bls.gov for the
Occupational Outlook Handbook
www.twc.texas.gov for
Texas Workforce Commission
www.onetonline.org for
O*Net Interest Profiler
Error! Hyperlink reference not valid. for
My Next Move (Assessment)

STUDY SKILLS SOLUTIONS
Visit the Writing Center
Acquire Tutoring
Speak with Professors/Instructors
Visit Academic Advisor Regularly
Consider a Study Group
Consider Changing Study Environment
Visit Student Disabilities Services
Other_____

SOAR LEARNING CENTER:
www.depts.ttu.edu/soar/lc/ for
Academic Tutoring
Online Academic Tutoring
Academic Coaching

ACADEMIC LIFE COACHING:
www.depts.ttu.edu/provost/success/
coaching/ http://www.depts.ttu.edu/
provost/success/coaching/ for

Organization	Goal Setting
Accountability	Work Life Balance
Communicating	Handling Conflict
Self Confidence	Self Efficacy
Commitment	Social Engagement

SOLUTIONS RELATED to PERSONAL ISSUES
Consider Personal Counseling
Consider Group Counseling
Acquire Problem Solving Skills
Stress Management Help
Other_____

STUDENT COUNSELING CENTER:
www.depts.ttu.edu/scc/ for
Personal Counseling

FAMILY CONCERNS
OFFICE of the DEAN of STUDENTS:
www.depts.ttu.edu/dos/ for
Student and Family Concerns

Texas Tech University

 University Advising

My Academic Obstacles

Obstacle	How does this obstacle interfere with your academic success?
1.	
2.	
3.	
4.	

Possible Solutions to My Obstacles

Obstacle	Solution #1	Solution #2	Solution #3	Solution #4
1.				
2.				
3.				
4.				

Pick four of the solutions above you will try, then list and balance them below.

Balancing my Solution Choices

Solution to Try	How Will This Solution Help Me? (i.e., Which obstacle will it confront?)	What Additional Problems May Result? (i.e., Will using it be worth the cost?)

Achieving My Goals

To achieve my goals, using the solutions I picked, I will do the following by:

1. _____

   By: _____

2. _____

   By: _____

3. _____

   By: _____

4. _____

   By: _____

CHAPTER THREE

Academic Coaching and Supporting Students on Academic Probation

Claire Robinson

Every year many colleges and universities across the country boast they have enrolled the best and brightest incoming first-year class. As such, thousands of first-year college students arrive on campus confident they will easily transition to their new collegiate environment given their previous high school success. AP credit, perfect GPAs, and high ACT/SAT scores accompany thousands of students on their first day of class. Yet despite impressive pre-enrollment credentials, study habits and academic routines that worked well in high school or earlier do not ensure success in college. New college students often experience "academic culture shock," and many end up on academic probation after their first or second semester (Moore, 2006). Furthermore, academic difficulty is not unique to the first year or the transition from high school to college, and students can, and do, experience challenge at multiple points in the undergraduate experience. Individualized support is essential when retaining a student who is on academic probation. Establishing a way for students to develop a personal connection to the university is a key strategy when designing strategic academic recovery programming.

Academic/success coaching (or academic coaching) is a popular and relatively new strategy aimed at student retention. In addition to traditional academic advising, tutoring, counseling, and mentoring, many institutions invest in developing coaching programs designed to retain students on academic probation. Research supports this individualized approach. Astin (1993) and Tinto (1982, 1988, 1993) suggested that "personal interactions" are linked to higher retention rates and degree attainment. Undergraduate students who experience frequent one-on-one interactions with institutional representatives show positive outcomes on measures of motivation, social integration, and academic integration. Specifically, the needs and characteristics of first-year students and academically underprepared students make it likely that they will benefit from this type of personalized coaching support. This chapter highlights coaching strategies for working with students on academic probation and offers guidance on how coaching can aid in academic recovery.

Definition of Terms

The term "coaching" assumes a variety of definitions and connotations both inside and outside higher education. From athletics coaching to executive talent planning, the coaching field has grown exponentially over the last three decades (International Coaching Federation, 2018). The business sector often defines coaching as "a partnering of two people, one client and one coach, who together create an alliance which is designed to deepen the client's learning of themselves and supports them in forwarding their learning to action" (Vansickel-Peterson, 2010, p. 1). In addition to exploring definitions, the relationship between *academic coaching* and *academic advising* must be explored and the two models must be differentiated. While academic advising has a long history in higher education, academic coaching is still working to identify its uniqueness.

One significant difference between advising and coaching is that the academic coaching model "deemphasizes the need for students to receive permission from the coach (as an advisor) to enroll, or change courses, and instead creates a relationship that provides guidance and support at multiple interactions, both formal and informal" (Neuhauser & Weber, 2011, p. 48). According to Brock (2008), coaching is a "a goal-directed, results-oriented, systematic process in which one person facilitates sustained change in another individual or group through fostering the self-directed learning and personal growth of the coachee" (p. 147). Academic coaches generally carry a smaller caseload and can often provide more high-touch, intensive intervention and support to students on academic probation than the student's assigned academic advisor can. Coaches exist at the intersection of several unique support services – answering questions, providing resources, and making referrals. When considering the unique needs of college students on academic probation, perhaps the best definition of academic coaching is

> the individualized practice of asking reflective, motivation-based questions, providing opportunities for formal self-assessment, sharing effective strategies, and co-creating a tangible plan. The coaching process offers students an opportunity to identify their strengths, actively practice new skills, and effectively navigate appropriate resources that ultimately results in skill development, performance improvement, and persistence. (Robinson, 2015, p. 125)

Reasons for Establishing Academic/Success Coaching Programs

Considering the unique needs of students on probation, it appears the inception of many academic coaching programs were developed to support and retain academically deficient students. In 2014, the author conducted a national survey of higher education institutions to identify the catalyst(s) for establishing a coaching program (Robinson, 2015). Participants were asked, "Why was your coaching program first established?" Survey responses were submitted from 160 participants and are included in Table 3.1 in order of frequency.

Since respondents could mark more than one reason, results in Table 3.1 are organized by total respondents/participants in the survey ($n = 160$) and total responses to selections provided ($n = 372$). Over 55% of individual respondents indicated their coaching program was created to increase retention. The answer "To work with academic deficient students/ students on academic probation" was selected by 60 distinct institutions or 38% of all respondents, which was the second highest response rate. Several responses to "other" reasons included an intent to serve special populations and to complement and enhance academic advising. As discussed by Nutter in Chapter 2 of this volume, academic advisors may lack the capacity to provide the support necessary for students in academic recovery. When academic advising is inadequately resourced and staffed, institutions likely see these specialized staff as a necessary supplement to meet the needs of students on probation.

Table 3.1.

Catalyst for Creating Coaching Program as Indicated by Top Three Reasons

Reason established	Frequency	Percent total responses (n=372)	Percent total respondents (n=160)
Increase retention	89	23.9	55.6
Support academically deficient students	**60**	**16.1**	**37.5**
Unique service (please specify)	52	14.0	32.5
New service	46	12.4	28.7
Special student population (please specify)	45	12.1	28.1
Enhance academic advising	33	8.9	20.6
Current service (please specify)	22	5.9	13.7
Replace old title	10	2.7	6.3
Other #1	15	4.0	9.4
Total	372	100	-

Academic/success coaching aims to foster meaningful conversations and interactions with students. As Trumpy (2006) stated, struggling students, "through active faculty and staff support, are wise to make both personal and academic skills development major priorities of their … experience" (p. 30). Thus, academic/success coaches have a unique and important opportunity to work with probationary students to provide outreach, ongoing support, and a personalized plan to decrease the likelihood of students feeling marginalized. When working with students on academic probation, this customized, ongoing, and intentional collaboration between a coach and student is a key to satisfaction, connectedness, and ultimately persistence to earning a college degree. Tools such as engagement planning, experiential learning, and reflection are used in coaching sessions to help students develop a deeper connection to their institution.

Coaching Students to Success

Given the breadth and depth that effective coaching programs employ, it is no surprise academic coaching is often seen as a go-to strategy for institutions looking to retain and recover students on academic probation. Higgins (2003) defined academic probation as "an academic warning for students whose academic performance falls below an institution's requirement of good standing" (p. 1). Academically deficient students fall below GPA criteria for a certain school or college. Outlining the complexity of student academic success, Higgins cited research on factors that contribute to student attrition, including "peer culture, academic major, college environment, faculty contact, work, career choice, personal motivation, organization, study habits, quality of effort, self-efficacy, and perceived control" (Higgins, 2003, para. 3). Three types of traditional institutional interventions that have a positive effect include 1) instruction in academic skills, 2) advising and counseling, and 3) comprehensive support programs. Specifically, within advising, intrusive techniques tend to have the greatest impact on retention. Practical intrusive strategies include setting short- and long-term goals, developing a plan, and following up on status. Effective academic/ success coaching programs encompass all three strategies (i.e., academic skill development, advising/counseling, and a comprehensive, holistic approach to student success). Because of the unique role of coaches and their position at the intersection of several unique services, academic coaches can offer a blend of intrusive advising, academic strategy development, and comprehensive student support.

Coaching as a Comprehensive Support Model for Students on Academic Probation

Many of the qualities and characteristics that define coaching are intertwined with related professions in higher education. Historically, students in need of academic recovery support may be referred to a variety of offices because no one office or service feels equipped to handle the majority of the students' needs. However, this segmented thinking about student success may lead to more harm than good. Certainly, advising, tutoring, counseling, and mentoring advertise expertise in a particular area, and this specialization serves an important purpose. However, students on the verge of leaving the institution may find a ping-pong approach to academic recovery overwhelming and time consuming. Furthermore, institutions who subscribe to this nuanced staffing strategy may lead a student through expensive bureaucracy and unnecessary red tape.

Many offices and student services boast they are a "one-stop shop," but one must examine the truth in this claim. Tutors refer to advisors, advisors refer to counselors, counselors refer to academic support, and so on. Academic coaching, if designed and resourced correctly, can offer a more holistic solution to segmented student success. True academic coaching offers students on academic probation one expert-level professional who is well versed in a variety of strategies that include academics, curriculum, college success, mentorship, and basic counseling. Academic coaches can draw on basic tactics from the various professions by prioritizing breadth over depth. For example, rather than asking a student on probation to attend multiple meetings with multiple seemingly fragmented offices, a coach can reduce this approach and refer (or more specifically "navigate") students only to the most essential offices based on each student's unique need (such as finances).

Figure 3.1 illustrates how academic coaching pulls strategies from closely related professions in higher education to offer students a single point person for comprehensive support. The outer ring includes qualities that can be easily applicable to advising, counseling, mentoring, tutoring, and coaching, such as goal setting, reflection, motivation, questioning, supportive, individualized, referrals, and collaboration. Tutors, mentors, advisors, counselors, and coaches often ask students to set a goal, reflect on their motivation, ask questions, provide students support in a one-on-one environment, and make referrals. These standard approaches are not unique to any one profession.

Figure 3.1. Academic Coaches' Skill Versatility.

Moving inward in Figure 3.1, the professions take on a bit more specialization, such as academic advising's focus on curriculum, counseling to address emotional concerns, tutoring students on course content, and mentors serving as role models. This specialization leads to institutions investing in unique positions within focused areas of student support. Certainly, academic coaches cannot possess full expertise in all these related professions. However, as illustrated in Figure 3.1, it is feasible for coaches to offer basic strategies in multiple areas supporting student success.

Academic Coaching and Organizational Contexts

In thinking about designing or enhancing academic coaching programs to support students on probation, perhaps one of the most confusing aspects about academic coaching in higher education is identifying the profession and campus role most closely aligned with coaching. Some institutions position the role of academic coaches to focus on study skills, skill development, and learning assistance. Other coaching programs are an extension of academic advising. Both the Global Community for Academic Advising (NACADA) and the Association for the Coaching and Tutoring Profession (ACTP) have devoted communities of practice to "academic coaching." For example, NACADA's Coaching Interest group stated,

> More than an informative role, academic advising is based around the relationship between the advisor and their advisees. Advisors often incorporate coaching methods into their practice in order to address the whole student. Academic Coaching is an advising approach that pushes the student to reflect and act on the range of goals, interests, and passions available in higher education. (https://nacada.ksu.edu/Resources/Clearinghouse/Academic-Coaching.aspx)

There are also many examples of this organizational variety at the institutional level. In a 2014 national survey conducted on academic/coaching (Robinson, 2015), approximately 160 institutions were asked, "In which division/unit/department is your coaching program held?" The distribution is represented in Table 3.2.

Table 3.2.
Division/Unit/Department in Which Coaching Program Is Housed

Division/Unit/Department (Check all that apply)	Frequency	Percent total responses (n=190)
Student-success cntr/learning asst/ac support	52	27.4
Academic affairs	51	26.8
Student affairs	38	20.0
Athletics	3	1.6
Other (Please specify)	11	5.8
Nonresponse	35	18.4
Total	190	100

Results show a nearly identical frequency of the organizational location of coaching programs within learning assistance centers and academic affairs. The third most frequent organizational structure was student affairs. Clearly this variety shows no one clear leader in placement of coaching programs, and this placement may have implications for the way coaching is positioned and performed on individual campuses. Placement of coaching programs within existing organizational structures may influence the tools and strategies that coaches use.

These results may be indicative of the need for a broader conversation about student support in general and academic recovery programs in particular. To offer true and meaningful comprehensive support to students on academic probation, an effective academic coach should possess broad-based knowledge and skill sets that span multiple roles and campus units while using a variety of theoretical approaches to best address students' varied needs. To accomplish this, a coach's knowledge base must include curricular knowledge (i.e., academic advising) and skill development, career aspirations, and academic interests. To practice only one strategy is a myopic approach to the complications that often surround academic recovery. Arguably, academic/success coaching is not an offshoot of the tutoring, mentoring, or advising professions. Rather, academic/success coaching, when done correctly, is a combination of multiple professions. For example, at Florida Atlantic University, the academic coaching program is an extension of the university advising office. FAU's Academic Coaching and Career Enhancement for Student Success (ACCESS) is an example program that "offers a comprehensive approach to student success that focuses on academic coaching/ advising, tutoring, career counseling and developing a meaningful connection to Florida Atlantic University, all of which lead to student retention" (https://www.fau.edu/access/).

Training Considerations

If academic coaching is to draw on multiple professions, coaches must synthesize multiple approaches to meet the variety of students needs. Academic coaching positions are not entry-level positions. Work with students on probation requires a professional who has a passion for working one on one with students to learn their strengths and passions as individuals and who is driven to learn curriculum, skill development, and quality mentorship.

Perhaps the danger in suggesting a comprehensive approach to student success through a semi-singular source is the risk of compromising quantity with quality. For example, counselors in higher education often need years of training, certification, and licensure to offer the authorized psychological support required by many college students. Coaches are not expected to be certified counselors. However, if academic coaches are to offer both breadth and depth of student support though multiple appointments, coaches must possess a wealth of knowledge from multiple areas. This knowledge base is not easy or quick to obtain. Given the novelty of academic coaching, much of the empirical evidence and research is lacking in this field. Students may not inherently understand the purpose or purview of "academic coaching" programs or whether it truly is a different experience than others their campus provides. Furthermore, coaches themselves may find it difficult to truly master multiple professions. It takes time to truly develop into an effective coach who offers high-level support in multiple facets of campus.

Training considerations are also a critical component to the success of any coaching program. As mentioned, coaches must possess a multilayered skill set and maneuver their approach based on student need. Many academic coaching programs use the appreciative advising (Bloom et al., 2008) framework Disarm, Discover, Dream, Design, Deliver, and Don't Settle as the foundation for their coaching programs. Based on the 2014 national survey of coaching programs, appreciative advising/inquiry was the most frequently used conceptual framework, used at nearly 34% of the participating institutions (Robinson, 2014).

Theoretical frameworks such as appreciative advising provide coaches with an approach to synthesizing the various strategies when working with students on probation. Specifically, you can see theory to practice in self-assessment (discover), academic planning (design), student engagement/involvement (deliver), and ultimately, successful academic recovery (don't settle).

Table 3.3.
Type of Conceptual Frameworks Used for Coaching Service Delivery

Framework	Percent total respondents (*n* = 56 institutions)
Appreciative advising/inquiry	33.9
Intrusive/proactive advising	12.5
Student development theory	7.1
Motivational interviewing/models	5.4
Bloom's taxonomy	3.6
GROW coaching model	3.6
Self-regulated learning	3.6
Life coaching/Life bound	3.6
Developing own	3.6
Isolated response – coach specific	7.1
Isolated response – non-coach specific	37.5
Multiple (coaching program employs two or more frameworks)	23.2

Coaching Strategy 1: Academic Advising and Curricular Knowledge

College students on academic probation often need options. As McClellan and Moser (2011) stated, "once a solid list of options has been identified, coaching models suggest the coach assist the student in the evaluation and selection of options that can be crafted into a plan for moving forward" (para. 12). Perhaps a student's "Plan A" major is not feasible, so the student needs a "Plan B" major, and sometimes a "Plan C" major. Consider a sample student, Jim, who is pursuing a degree in business administration. Jim arrives on campus, finds difficulty in the transition to college, realizes he is not strong in mathematics, and feels distant from his professors because of large classes. Jim eventually ends up on academic probation and has one semester to pull up his GPA. Should Jim continue to pursue business? Perhaps not. Jim needs to be presented with different majors and curricular options in a meaningful way. An academic coach must be well versed in multiple majors, disciplines, and curricula. Critical information such as course sequencing and balancing, course selection, time to graduation, and other academic requirements should be shared with Jim so he makes an informed decision. Omitting curricular conversations when working with students on probation is a significant deficit to an academic recovery program. Furthermore, this information is likely best presented and discussed in a one-on-one format to offer students dedicated time to fully understand and reflect on their options. This individualization is a hallmark strategy of an effective academic coaching session.

As such, comprehensive academic coaching builds on the foundation of academic advising and curricular knowledge. Academic advising integrates students' academic and career goals by providing individualized, accurate information on majors, courses, general education, degree requirements, out-of-class activities, institutional policies/procedures, and appropriate referral to academic and nonacademic resources (Robinson, 2015). Some academic advisors posit they incorporate coaching techniques into their advising sessions with students (McClellan & Moser, 2011). In these instances, semantics and connotations play a role. Are advisors coaching? Or, do coaches advise? Either way, students on academic probation need a higher-education professional well versed in curriculum, majors, and academic information. When accompanying this skill set with strengths, self-assessment, study skills and strategies, and other more noncurricular items, we begin to enter coaching techniques.

Coaching Strategy 2: Academic Planning and Success Strategies

While quality conversations and holistic advising serve as the foundation for coaching students on probation, it is also essential that students leave the coaching session with a clear and strategic personalized plan. After a coaching session(s), students should be able to answer the question, What are the next steps to my success? Identify them. Define them. Demystify them. Write them down. Set deadlines. Follow up. Academic planning and campus engagement planning are two critical components for coaching students on academic probation. Academically, students must understand their current GPA status, requirements for probation removal, progression standards within their major, course selection, and other academic parameters.

The University of South Carolina (UofSC) created a nationally adopted academic plan (see Figure 3.2) that encompasses many of these strategies. At UofSC, all first-year students on academic probation must meet with an academic coach within the first 6 weeks of the subsequent semester to avoid a registration hold. As part of this process, all first-year students on probation complete a 10-page academic plan that includes self-assessments, GPA projections, strategies for meeting with professors, and identification of campus resources. Ideally, first-year probationary students meet with their same academic coach three times within the same semester. Multiple meetings allow for the student and coach to revisit and refine their academic and/or engagement planning.

Academic Plan*

Page 1

*By creating my Academic Plan, I will self-assess, reflect, and determine what it takes for me to be a successful student at the University of South Carolina.

Complete Before Appointment

1 My Academic Plan Involves

1. Personalized Academic Planning & Strategies
2. Strengths Identification
3. Navigating Campus Resources

2 My Academic Coaching Appointments will be

Session 1 _____ DATE _____ TIME

Session 2 _____ DATE _____ TIME

Session 3 _____ DATE _____ TIME

3 Academic Plan Student Agreement
(Check all boxes)

☐ I agree to use the strategies I have mapped out in my Academic Plan.

☐ I have a clear understanding of what I need to do to be academically successful at USC.

☐ If I have any questions or need further assistance, I will contact my Academic Coach.

4 Student Name Printed _____   USC ID# _____

Student Signature _____   Date _____

5 Student Preparation/Response
(Complete at time of **first** appointment)

I arrived to my appointment on time.   ☐Yes ☐No ☐Time _____

I completed Academic Plan (pages 1-5) prior to my appointment.   ☐Yes ☐No ☐N/A

I brought my Self-Assessment scores to my appointment.   ☐Yes ☐No ☐N/A

I was receptive to strategies /session.   ☐Yes ☐No ☐Moderate

ACADEMIC COACH USE ONLY

Academic Plan certified as complete.

Academic Coach Name Printed _____

Academic Coach Signature _____   Date _____

University **Advising** Center
University of South Carolina

✉ advising@sc.edu
☎ 803-777-1222
➤ Close Hipp, Suite 381

UNIVERSITY OF
SOUTH CAROLINA

sc.edu/**advising**/ace

Figure 3.2 continues on page 74

Figure 3.2 continued from page 73

3 Difficulties Experienced/Concerns
(Check all that apply)

- ☐ Academically Under-prepared
- ☐ Alcohol
- ☐ Drugs
- ☐ Changing Major
- ☐ Difficulties with Professors
- ☐ Failed to Attend Class
- ☐ Family Crisis
- ☐ Financial Concerns
- ☐ First Generation College Student
- ☐ Homesickness

- ☐ Documented Learning Disability
- ☐ Over Involvement in Activities
- ☐ Poor Time Management Skills
- ☐ Relationship Problems
- ☐ Took too Many Credits Hours
- ☐ Transfer Student
- ☐ Adult Student
- ☐ Victim of Crime
- ☐ Worked too Many Hours
- Other _____

4 I have used the following resources at the University of South Carolina...
(Check all that apply)

- ☐ Academic Advisor
- ☐ Academic Coaching
- ☐ Exploratory Advising
- ☐ Career Center
- ☐ Counseling & Psychiatry
- ☐ Student Disability Resource Center
- ☐ Student Health Center
- ☐ Financial Aid

- ☐ Professor's Office Hours
- ☐ Financial Literacy
- ☐ Library
- ☐ Supplemental Instruction (SI)
- ☐ Tutoring
- ☐ Withdrawal Services
- ☐ Writing Center
- Other _____

Page 3 | About Me   Complete Before Appointment

5 Answer the Following Questions in Detail

It is helpful to reflect on your personal experience as you begin to develop a clear plan for academic success at the University of South Carolina.

① I was motivated to pursue a college degree because...

② How I plan on using my college degree after graduation...

③ Things I find challenging in college include...

④ What has been your best experience as a student at the University of South Carolina?

Figure 3.2 continues on page 75

Figure 3.2 continued from page 74

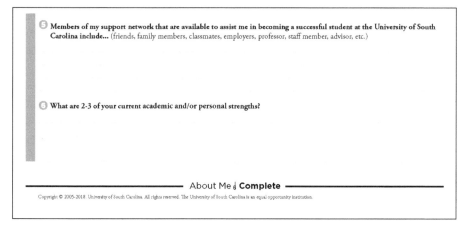

Figure 3.2. University of South Carolina Academic Plan Components.
(University of South Carolina, n.d.a., *Academic Plan.* Shared with permission from the University Advising Center at the University of South Carolina.).

Coaching Strategy 3: Self-Assessments and Strengths Identification

In their research on *Strengths-Based Advising*, Shriener & Anderson (2005) cited Gallup poll research and stated,

> Individuals who focus on their weaknesses and remediate them are only able to achieve average performance at best; they are able to gain far more – and even to reach levels of excellence – when they expend comparable effort to build on their talents. This discovery is of enormous import to higher education as a whole, but it has particular application to the relationships of advisors and students. (p. 21)

When working with students on probation, strengths-based coaching is a central strategy to build confidence and motivation. This ability – helping students to identify their true and unique talents and strengths – may be the forefront of all coaching strategies and of particular use when coaching students on academic probation or in the process of academic recovery.

Subscribing to the essential nature of the strengths-based approach of coaching, academic coaches also take into account several special considerations when evaluating individual student's transition to college, mental health, and well-being. Several studies have reinforced the need for sensitivity surrounding students' adjustment. For example, Lee et al. (2009) evaluated first-year and transfer college students' adjustment to a large, public four-year institution. Citing the research, the authors assert that college students may experience significant distress, adjustment difficulties, depression, feelings of worthlessness or inadequacies, and other transitional issues at these critical junctures in the educational pipeline. The authors also differentiated between academic counseling and general counseling and the effects on retention. Variables explored in the study include the counseling experience, precollege academic performance, service types, number of sessions, college academic performance, and retention. The study compared two groups' performance: counseled students versus non-counseled students, and the results "indicated that counseling experience is significantly associated with student retention: students receiving counseling services were more likely to stay enrolled in school" (p. 305).

Koydemir and Sun-Selışık (2016) explored well-being and the developmental challenges in college students between the ages of 18 and 25. First-year students are the most psychologically at risk because of the unique challenges they face during the transition from high school into a college environment. The authors asserted, "Among the most evident challenges experienced by first-year students are homesickness and friend-sickness, loneliness and social dissatisfaction, managing interpersonal conflicts, health problems such as low-quality sleep, and dealing with various academic difficulties. The psychological well-being of individuals is known to be threatened as they start to university" (p.434). The findings suggest that higher education must develop strategies to combat potential emotional and behavioral problems while offering supportive environments to facilitate well-being.

Given the mental health concerns many students face, an important coaching strategy is one of strengths identification. Rather than entering a conversation from a deficit standpoint, academic coaches should begin by asking reflective, narrative inquiry-based questions that solicit a student's story and talents. Narrative inquiry has been adapted in the appreciative advising framework as an essential means of student's ability to storytell (Bloom et al., 2008). As stated, "stories teach more about students than other methodologies. Therefore, Appreciative Advising strategies focus on the questions that will elicit stories from students" (p. 44). Sample narrative-based questions include

1. Tell me a story about a time you positively impacted another person's life.

2. Who are your two biggest role models? Why are they your role models, and what about them do you hope to emulate?

When asking these questions, students must respond with a story. There can be no one-word answers. Students must reflect and share something positive, enabling the coach to build on the student's strengths.

Coaching Strategy 4: Engagement Planning and Campus Involvement

Another proven and key retention strategy is the degree to which students are engaged and involved within their campus community. Research demonstrates that students who participate in high-impact practices and/or meaningful campus involvement opportunities find a sense of belonging within the university community and college life (Kuh et al., 2005). As Kuh et al. (2005) stated, "some [students] are fortunate to become involved early with an activity that morphs into a lifeline to persistence, graduation, and a rich harvest of learning" (p. 269). However, students on academic probation may feel like the only aspect of their undergraduate experience in which they should focus is academic.

The reciprocal relationship between campus engagement and academic success is an essential component of coaching students. For example, high-impact practices (HIPs) such as undergraduate research, internships, peer leadership, and service learning have demonstrated positive effects on college student success and learning (Kuh, 2008). As Grabsch et al. (2021) stated, "Most HIPs can have a transformative influence on students' personal development and educational growth. Research has shown persuasively that HIPs improve the quality of students' experience, learning, retention, and success, particularly for underserved students" (p. 89). Students who participate in campus activities, HIPs, and other engagement opportunities often find tremendous value in their experiences because they are developing new skill sets, meeting new people, and finding purpose in their work.

Quality coaching helps the student identify and participate in meaningful engagement opportunities as part of academic recovery. The Student Engagement Inventory shown in Figure 3.3 was developed at the University of South Carolina as part of a coaching program. Students can quickly indicate if they have an interest in various engagement/involvement opportunities.

Coaching questions:

- When you are not in class, how do you like to spend your time?
- What opportunities are you looking for at the University/College?
- When was the last time you were really excited about something? What was exciting about it?

After students indicate their level of interest in participating in engagement opportunities on campus, the coach can then assist the student in making appropriate connections to the offices. Students on probation may especially benefit from these experiences if they feel a lack of belongingness to their institution. Through involvement, leadership, and campus participation, students going through academic recovery may find these experiences reinvigorating.

As you fill out this inventory, reflect on your college experience thus far. The goal is to be intentional and selective with your engagement experiences, so they have the greatest impact and meet your individual needs over time. Please circle the appropriate number in regard to each category using the following scale:

	Unfamiliar	No Interest	Some Interest	Interested	Participating
Working with my professors outside of class.	0	1	2	3	4
Participating in a practicum, internship, field experience, co-op, or clinical assignment	0	1	2	3	4
Doing research in my field of study	0	1	2	3	4
Participating in study abroad, volunteering abroad, or an internship opportunity or foreign language immersion experience	0	1	2	3	4
Serving as a peer leader/ peer educator on-campus (e.g., resident mentor, U101 peer leader, orientation leader, academic tutor)	0	1	2	3	4
Participating in community service opportunities (e.g., Service Saturdays, MLK Days of Service, or AmeriCorps programming)	0	1	2	3	4
Finding employment both on or off campus (e.g., work-study, internships)	0	1	2	3	4
Participating in a student organization.	0	1	2	3	4
Other engagement opportunities of interest:	0	1	2	3	4

Figure 3.3. University of South Carolina Student Engagement Inventory.

(University of South Carolina, n.d.b., *Student Engagement Inventory.* Shared with permission from the University Advising Center at the University of South Carolina.)

Coaching Strategy 5: Navigating Campus Resources

Johnson, Walther, and Medley (2018) researched advising of high-achieving college students and found a critical theme, building connections and referral networks. Connection with campus resources is also critical for students on academic probation. However, advisors and campus professionals often fall short in making effective referrals. All too often a referral is a simple mention of another office and a few words of encouragement. If there is time, an appointment can be made with the partner office. While these techniques are better than none, simple referrals do not necessarily set the student up for success. Coaching goes beyond referral. Rather, coaches help students navigate campus resources by demystifying partner offices.

Consider two different scenarios: Approach A (a typical referral) and Approach B (coaching navigation). Approach A encourages the student to attend a counseling appointment and talk through concerns or seek guidance. An appointment is scheduled for next Wednesday, and the student agrees to go. In Approach B, everything occurring in Approach A occurs; however, the coach continues the conversation and delves into the resource. Coaches will walk a student through what to expect, using coaching communication such as that shown here regarding navigating resources (beyond referral):

> When you go to the _____ center you'll want to enter the building and go up to the sixth floor. Let's put the office number in your cell phone now in case you need it later on. When you arrive to your appointment next Tuesday at 2pm, you will check in to the front desk, and you'll need your student ID card. Then, you will meet with a licensed professional for 60 minutes. The meeting will be confidential, but you can ask for notes should you want them. Let's brainstorm two or three things you may want to discuss during the meeting and write them down. Do you have any questions you would like answered? Let us make a note on what you hope to get out of your _____ session, and you can take these ideas with you when you go. Let us think about what you hope to accomplish. How will you know if the session achieved what you hoped it would? (What does success look like?) Finally, when you are done with your _____ appointment, you can decide if you'd like a return appointment. You'll have [e.g., five] free sessions, so if you want more regular meetings, you'll want to think about how you can fit those into your schedule.

Referrals are often quick, with surface-level mentions that students may or may not act upon. Navigating resources takes the guesswork out of the partner office, which may increase the likelihood a probationary student will take advantage of additional support. However, for a coach to offer true navigation, that coach must venture over to partner offices, get to know the partner department, understand the office operation, attend a training or experiential opportunity, and ask for specific resources or talking points that can be shared with students. Navigating campus resources takes effort and intentionality. This added layer of effort and expertise differentiates the coaching service from an ordinary referral.

Conclusion

Given the rising costs of higher education, today's college students need clear guidance and transparency to aid in their academic endeavors. Miller and Murray (2005) argued that because today's bachelor's degree is equivalent to "a high school diploma 100 years ago," many students within the current generation may not be fully equipped to attend college but do so out of necessity for today's workforce. Citing research conducted by the Association of American Colleges and Universities, the authors quoted, "53% of students entering our colleges and universities are academically underprepared, i.e., lacking basic skills in at least one of the three basic areas of reading, writing, or mathematics (Tritelli, 2003, as cited in Miller & Murray, 2005)." Given this increase in stress and unpreparedness, students can potentially benefit from increased one-on-one attention and resources to help them integrate into the university. Academic coaching programs, intentionally designed, can serve as one of these principal resources.

In addition to these ethical obligations to student success, colleges and universities are ranked on their performance based on a series of metrics. U.S. News and World Report identified 16 performance indicators, including retention rate and graduation rates (Burnsed, 2011). These ranking often lead to increased financial support. As Trumpy (2006) recommended, "Coupled with the predominance of undergraduate attrition occurring during the freshman year of college, institutions would be wise to employ programs and strategies likely to positively impact rates of first-year retention, GPA, and credits earned, simultaneously" (p. 2). Rayle and Chung (2008) stated, "In the 21st century, it seems that mattering to others still matters to first-year college students. In response, colleges may want to develop intervention programs and services to try to aid first-year students in their transition to university life in an effort to retain these students" (p. 34).

In conclusion, when considering the unique needs of students on academic probation, perhaps one of the most compelling arguments for retaining this population is the essential need for holistic support, rather than fragmented services that required one student to meet with multiple higher-education professionals. Large universities are notorious for designing boutique programs based around a specialist paradigm. Students on the verge of leaving the university may not have the time, energy, or wherewithal to meet with multiple offices and retell their story in multiple contexts. The student's and university's time would be better spent diving into a deeper relationship with one individual who is well versed in a multitude of university policies, procedures, curricula, strengths, and proven-effective support strategies.

Yet, to offer authentic, comprehensive academic coaching to aid in academic recovery, institutions must invest in dedicated staff who gain expertise in both the breadth and depth of their campuses. Coaches must have low caseloads, enabling them to have capacity to meet with students on probation multiple times throughout the semester and offer follow-up and outreach. Coaches should be considered the most senior-level academic advisors, renowned mentors, tutors of academic success strategies and, perhaps most important, deeply devoted to the individual success of each of their students.

References

Astin, A. W. (1993). *What matters in college? Four critical years revisited.* Jossey-Bass.

Bloom, J., Hutson, B., & He, Y. (2008). *The appreciative advising revolution.* Stipes Publishing.

Brock, V. G. (2008). *Grounded theory of the roots and emergence of coaching* [Doctoral dissertation, International University of Professional Studies]. ProQuest. https://libraryofprofessionalcoaching.com/wp-app/wp-content/uploads/2011/10/dissertation.pdf

Burnsed, B. (2011). Liberal arts colleges with lowest student-faculty ratios. *Yahoo News.* https://news.yahoo.com/news/liberal-arts-colleges-lowest-student-faculty-ratios-152033558.html

Grabsch, D. K., Webb, S., Moore, L. L., & Dooley, K. E. (2021). A Qualitative Study Exploring the Decision-Making Experiences to Participate in High-Impact Practices. *College Student Affairs Journal, 39*(1), 88-102.

Higgins, E. M. (2003). *When expectations and reality collide: Working with students on probation.* NACADA Clearinghouse. https://nacada.ksu.edu/Resources/Clearinghouse/View-Articles/Advising-students-on-probation.aspx

Johnson, M., Walther, C., & Medley, K. J. (2018). Perceptions of advisors who work with high-achieving students. *Journal of the National Collegiate Honors Council, 19*(1), 105–124.

Kinzie, J. (2012). High-impact practices: Promoting participation for all students. *Diversity and Democracy, 15*(3). https://www.aacu.org/publications-research/periodicals/high-impact-practices-promoting-participation-all-students.

Koydemir, S., & Sun-Selışık, Z. E. (2016). Well-being on campus: testing the effectiveness of an online strengths-based intervention for first-year college students. *British Journal of Guidance & Counselling, 44*(4), 434–446.

Kuh, G. D., Kinzie, J., Schuh, J. H., Whitt, E. J., & Associates. (2005). *Student success in college.* Jossey-Bass.

Kuh, G. D. (2008). *High-impact educational practices: What they are, who has access to them, and why they matter.* Association of American Colleges and Universities.

Lee, D., Olson, E. A., Locke, B., Michelson, S. T., & Odes, E. (2009). The effects of college counseling services on academic performance and retention. *Journal of College Student Development, 50*(3), 305–319.

McClellan J., & Moser, C. (2011). *A practical approach to advising as coaching.* NACADA Clearinghouse. https://nacada.ksu.edu/Resources/Clearinghouse/View-Articles/Advising-as-coaching.aspx

Miller, M. A., & Murray, C. (2005). *Advising academically underprepared students.* NACADA Clearinghouse. https://nacada.ksu.edu/Resources/Clearinghouse/View-Articles/Academically-underprepared-students.aspx

Moore, R. (2006, Fall). Do high school behaviors set up developmental education students for failure? *The Learning Assistance Review, 11*(2), 19–32.

Neuhauser, C., & Weber, K. (2011). The student-success coach. *New Directions for Higher Education, 2011*(153), 43–52.

Rayle, A. D., & Chung, K.-Y. (2008). Revisiting first-year college students' mattering: Social support, academic stress, and the mattering experience. *Journal of College Student Retention: Research, Theory & Practice, 9*(1), 21–37.

Robinson, C. E. (2015). *Academic/Success coaching: A description of an emerging field in higher education* [Doctoral dissertation, University of South Carolina – Columbia]. Scholar Commons. https://scholarcommons.sc.edu/etd/3148/

Schriener, L. A., & Anderson, E. (2005). Strengths-based advising: A new lens for higher education. *NACADA Journal, 25*(2), 20–29. https://doi.org/10.12930/0271-9517-25.2.20

Trumpy, R. J. (2006). *The impact of an academic recovery program on underperforming first-year college students' retention, grade point average, and credits earned* [Doctoral dissertation, Seattle University]. ProQuest Dissertations & Theses Globa https://www.proquest.com/pqdtglobal/docview/304934984/4D5B07C6F6524D16PQ/1?accountid=13965

Tinto, V. (1975). Dropout from higher education: A theoretical synthesis of recent research. *Review of educational research, 45*(1), 89-125.

Tinto, V. (1982). Limits of theory and practice in student attrition. *Journal of Higher Education, 53*(6), 687–700.

Tinto, V. (1988). Stages of student departure: Reflections on the longitudinal character of student leaving. *Journal Of Higher Education, 59*(4), 438–55.

Tinto, V. (1993). *Leaving college: Rethinking the causes and cures of student attrition* (2nd ed). University of Chicago Press.

Tritelli, D. (2003, Winter). *From the Editor.* Association of American Colleges and Universities. http://www.aacu.org/peerreview/pr-wi03/pr-wi03editor.cfm

University of South Carolina. (n.d.a.). *Academic coaching plan.* Columbia, SC: University of South Carolina

University of South Carolina. (n.d.b.). *Student engagement inventory.* Columbia, SC: University of South Carolina

Vansickel-Peterson, D. L. (2010). *Coaching efficacy with academic leaders: A phenomenological investigation.* [Doctoral dissertation, University of Nebraska]. https://www.proquest.com/docview/818744187?pq-origsite=gscholar&fromopenview=true

CHAPTER FOUR

Early Alert and Academic Intervention

Michael T. Dial and Paige McKeown

To this point, this book has explored policies related to probation, suspension, and reinstatement as well as advising and coaching practices aimed at supporting students on probation. We turn our attention here to early-alert initiatives aimed both to prevent major academic consequences like probation and to be used as a tool to monitor and support students on probation. Early-alert programs, as defined by Cuseo (n.d.) are "formal, proactive, feedback system[s] through which students and student-support agents are alerted to early red flags." Tampke (2013) went a bit further, defining early alert as a "systematic method of recording and communicating student behaviors that contribute to student attrition" and "effective intervention at the first indication of academic difficulty" (pp. 523–524). Early-alert initiatives are designed to recognize and support students at risk of attrition before their challenges are too much to overcome (Simons, 2011). Often these programs rely on faculty to submit alerts that notify student-support professionals about students' risk status. In this chapter, we argue for the inclusion of a wider range of academic interventions, such as the identification of students falling below ideal enrolled credit hours or those not registered for upcoming terms, to be included in the definition of early-alert initiatives. In that vein, we provide an overview of different methods for identifying student risk of attrition and tailoring interventions according to institutional contexts and needs.

At-risk students have been informally monitored and supported likely since the beginning of higher education, or at least since the beginnings of the student-affairs profession. Compared to more hallmark programs, though, such as new-student advising and first-year seminars, early-alert programs are relatively new to higher education. According to Simons (2011), at the time, 68% of early-alert initiatives nationwide had been in existence less than 5 years. However, other intervention efforts existed on campuses long before formal early-alert programs were established.

Historically speaking, faculty were more deeply ingrained in the lives of college and university students in the early 20th century than they are today. In the early years of American higher education, the college-going population also tended to come from more homogenous cultural, racial, and socioeconomic backgrounds. Although a variety of federal legislation actions broadened access to a college degree, the massification of higher education made the work of identifying at-risk students during the academic term more difficult. In the late 1980s and early 1990s the proliferation of technology, including campus networks and the internet, made mass communication between faculty and student-support staff significantly more efficient. Concurrently, the term "early alert" began appearing in the academic lexicon. The idea gained prominence in recent decades with the advent and proliferation of several for-profit student retention platforms that seek to be the next panacea for student attrition. Technological advances over recent decades further led to the widespread adoption of early-alert programming at most institutions.

Today, the existence of early-alert programs pushes back against academic Darwinism, the idea that it is a natural given that a certain percentage of students are incapable of persisting in specific academic programs. In fact, high-touch, high-impact interventions model the care promised to students and families throughout the admissions and orientation processes. High-quality early-alert programs monitor all students, not just those who enter with an at-risk indicator.

Several national surveys (Barefoot et al., 2012; Estrada & Latino, 2019; Simons, 2011) have pointed to the widespread use of early-alert programs to meet student success and retention goals. Most recently, the 2017 National Survey on The First-Year Experience (Keup, 2019) identified early-alert systems as the second most commonly cited first-year experience program or intervention (reported by 79% of responding institutions), behind only first-year advising (80.4%) and ahead of 20 other first-year initiatives, including preterm orientation (75.4%) and first-year seminars (73.5%). The 2017 National Survey on the First-Year Experience also asked campus representatives to identify the types of students who are monitored through early-alert systems. At 76.0% of responding institutions, all first-year students are monitored. Only 6.9% of institutions specifically identified students on probation as a population that was monitored through early-alert initiatives. According to Barefoot et al. (2012) on an earlier survey that sought similar information, all sophomores were monitored by early-alert programs at 57.0% of the surveyed institutions, all juniors at 53.1% of the institutions, all seniors at 53.8% of the institutions, and 56.4% of colleges and universities said they monitor all new transfer students. Smaller campuses are more likely than their larger peers to monitor all students through early-alert systems. Although institutions don't specifically report monitoring students on probation at high rates, if early-alert programs are monitoring all students, students on probation will be included in these efforts.

Theoretical Approaches Relevant to Early Alert and Intervention

As evidenced, early-alert programming is nearly universal in higher education. Because of this ubiquitous nature, programs run the risk of being created haphazardly, with little theoretical grounding. Although the literature is scant on philosophies and theories directly related to academic intervention, several other theoretical approaches can be applied to these efforts. The majority of this chapter is dedicated to the administration of early-alert programming. To ground that discussion, we turn to theoretical approaches that undergird the interventions facilitated by staff with at-risk students.

Intrusive Intervention

All early-alert programs rely on some form of intrusive intervention (Earl, 1988). Intrusive advising/intervention is an action-oriented model that relies on identifying students at points of crisis and reaching out with appropriate resources that may aid in their success. Of course, for students on academic probation, exhibiting signs of attrition-risk behaviors during the term would serve as a point of crisis. Being able to connect these students with appropriate resources may be vital to their ability to persist through academic recovery. In fact, the literature suggests that meaningful interactions with campus faculty and staff plays a significant role in students' decision to stay on campus and strive to persist (Chickering & Gamson, 1987; Heisserer & Parette, 2002). Intrusive advising is grounded in three postulates (Earl, 1988):

- Faculty and staff can be trained to recognize students at crisis points.
- Students respond to direct contact in which their worries are acknowledged and support is offered.
- Deficiencies in a student's sense of belonging and ability to succeed can be treated.

Students on academic probation benefit from being monitored by early-alert systems. In fact, where academic recovery programs do not require students to engage with institutional support, students on academic probation may get caught in institutional early-alert efforts.

The Transtheoretical Model of Human Behavior Change

A theoretical model not often attributed to the general college student explains student reluctance to seek help and change behaviors. Originally designed and used in healthcare settings to explain patient hesitancy to engage in a variety of positive health-related action plans, the transtheoretical model (TTM) of human behavior change (Prochaska & DiClemente, 1983; see Figure 4.1), posits that behavior change "involves a process that occurs in increments and that involves specific and varied tasks" (cited in Miller & Rollnick, 2002, p. 201). The model defines stages that individuals pass through on the way to making intentional behavior changes.

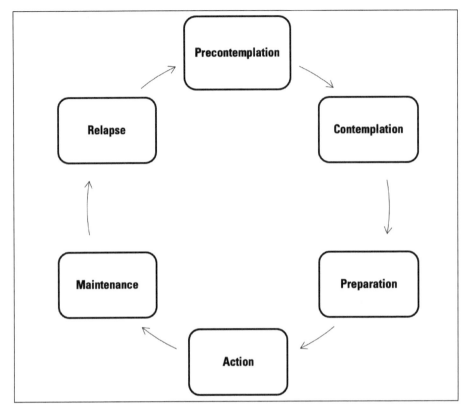

Figure 4.1. Stages of Change from the Transtheoretical Model of Human Behavior Change (Miller and Rollnick, 2012).

The TTM begins in a stage of precontemplation, in which students are not yet considering making changes to their behavior for a host of reasons to be explored later in this chapter. Following precontemplation, students enter the contemplation stage, in which they begin to acknowledge deficits in current behavior or ways of thinking and, for the first time, consider making changes. At this stage, students may be able to envision where they would like to be but do not have the means or the awareness of resources to make a change at present. As students move into the preparation stage, they begin to seriously consider making changes and start to make plans for doing so. Specifically, in the preparation stage, students may begin reaching out to campus professionals in search of support. In the action stage, students begin to put change plans into motion. However, it should be noted that a commitment to change does not automatically mean that plans will be effective or that the change will be successful in the long term. As changes become quasi-permanent, students enter a maintenance stage in which they attempt to sustain new behaviors. Students may, at times, unfortunately relapse and revert to old behaviors and modes of thinking. According to the TTM, these relapses are only partial setbacks and should not be viewed as abject failures. When relapse occurs, students, with the help of peers and campus support professionals, may find themselves back at the precontemplation stage or at the preparation stage, reevaluating prior results and recommitting or making new plans for successful change (Miller & Rollnick, 2002).

Most student-services offices on campus are designed for students in the preparation stage, students who acknowledge their need for support and seek it out. Through intrusive outreach to students presenting problematic behaviors (e.g., attendance concerns, failing exams, registering in too few credit hours), the intervention agent can help to nudge the student through the stages of change more rapidly than they might have otherwise done alone.

Identifying Red Flags

We get the idea of "red flags" as a key component of effective intervention – the signals that alert us to a student who needs additional support to be successful – from the Cuseo (n.d.) definition of early intervention. Early intervention can be described as the set of systems that alert the necessary actors to these red flags, but what are the red flags themselves? They are going to differ from campus to campus based on the needs of the student population or subpopulations as well as the capacity of those involved with the work of early intervention.

Because these red flags need to be tailored to the situation of each campus, the first step in effective early intervention programming must be to identify these potential bottlenecks in the student experience. Valuable questions to ask, which help to identify the key "crisis points" in the student experience, can be used as touch points for launching effective early intervention, which we will consider later in this chapter. Any of these questions could be adapted specifically to monitoring and supporting students on academic probation and should be addressed among practitioners with those students' unique needs in mind.

How do we know what factors are going to lead to the most informative red flags or identifiable crisis points? It is beneficial to start from a success-oriented, as opposed to an insufficiency, mindset, á la Estrada and Latino (2019): "The key to early intervention is to identify the behaviors that contribute to success, and then implement a systematic method for intervening when students fall short of those behaviors" (p. 53). With this in mind, a valuable question with which to begin might be, "What factors are predictive of overall student success and retention on your campus?" By considering these issues on a macro level, practitioners can determine which populations will be best served by intervention initiatives and in what ways. One might consider course completion overall, key progression courses for different curricula, GPA, timely course registration, class attendance, and ideal credit-hour enrollment at a particular campus. Later in this chapter we detail intervention beyond faculty as referral agents, and we dive into some of these specific red flags more in depth with examples.

After identification of those hallmarks of student success, it is valuable to pivot to identifying the roadblocks that stop students from achieving success. Are the students unaware of dates, policies, and procedures, and would systematic outreach to communicate this information be of benefit? Or would smaller groups of high-need students be better served with high-touch interventions to determine why they're not registering for classes? These factors will differ from situation to situation and can be used to determine the answers to additional questions: Who would identify students at these crisis points, and who would conduct outreach? What outcomes do you hope to see from addressing these crisis points, and how will you demonstrate that the intervention is successful? These questions are important to ask and answer to close the loop on determining the effectiveness of red flags and the intervention to conduct based on what will ultimately most benefit the student population of interest.

After identifying the appropriate red flags, the next step in effectively supporting students is to determine whether the suitable intervention should be proactive, reactive, or, potentially, both. Proactive interventions may be geared toward historically at-risk populations and may work to preempt initial acclimation challenges and support students through them. Most early interventions are reactive, based on some sort of referral or alert of concerning behavior. Intervention as it relates to probation could take either slant – proactive by pre-identifying subpopulations who are vulnerable to probationary status (certain majors, first-generation students) or reactive by determining the needs and roadblocks of students once they have been placed on probation. All these approaches are completely valid intervention strategies as long as they serve the target population and address students in identified points of crisis.

Challenges

Effective early intervention is not without its challenges. As vital as this work is in supporting student populations, including students on probation, there are roadblocks that must be considered in advance for the efforts expended by student and academic affairs professionals to be as successful as possible. One initial challenge arises in how to best identify the red flags that are barriers to student success on a particular campus or for a specific student population and what the effective intervention will be to respond to those flags. Because many red flags that prompt intervention responses come from classroom behavior or performance, faculty referrers are a key component in the cycle and process of intervention as early, intensive, and continuous (Seidman, 2012). However, getting faculty buy-in for intervention practices can be a struggle.

One component to consider in this process is whether an institution's power to enact change in practice comes from the top down or arises from grassroots initiatives. A top-down structure is seen when the president, provost, or deans embrace an idea and faculty automatically buy in. Grassroots looks more like getting a small but influential group of faculty members committed and allowing word of mouth to spread. This can be most challenging when it comes to convincing faculty to embrace novel technologies, some of which are often necessary or incredibly beneficial for effective intervention. Starting with small instances of proof of concept is essential. One way to ensure the success of early intervention efforts and buy-in from faculty occurs is to make certain that the communication loop is closed between referrers and intervention agents. Faculty have often remarked that it is frustrating to act as a caring referrer and then never to hear back on whether contact was made with the student or anything was done (Estrada & Latino, 2017). A few simple actions on the part of the intervener to communicate and confirm with the referral agent can go a long way in gaining faculty members as champions of intervention initiatives.

Finally, challenges that absolutely must be attended to in order to do this work effectively and efficiently, with the greatest payoff for students, are addressing duplication and avoiding communication fatigue. Mission creep and duplication of efforts are prevalent phenomena in higher education, and that is especially clear in the work of early intervention that has no "perfect" professional home. This occurs regularly and is detrimental, particularly for students who are already struggling, do not know where to seek help, and, when faced with an excessive number of resource choices, get overwhelmed and retreat (Thaler & Sunstein, 2008). It is essential that institutions examine this phenomenon on a micro and macro level and determine with some level of oversight who is best suited to intervene in any given area and minimize duplication where possible.

The Role of Technology in Academic Intervention

As with most modern initiatives on college campuses, the role of technology in early intervention is one to closely consider and regularly evaluate. In the 2017 National Survey on the First-Year Experience (Estrada and Latino, 2019), the prevalence and use of technology in intervention was described on a scale of 1 to 7, with 1 being entirely technology-based and 7 being entirely human-based. Unsurprisingly, nearly a quarter of institutions report a score somewhere in the middle, at a 4. Perhaps a bit more surprising, however, is that over 30% of institutions share that their intervention initiatives score a 7, indicating that technology does not play a role at all. Although the aspect of human connection and an established relationship is crucial to the success of intervention, the efficient use of technology platforms can streamline communication, simplify data collection, and reveal valuable patterns for analysis that can lead to more effective and impactful intervention initiatives.

To attain the ideal use of technology in early-alert interventions, we must determine the data that is needed, can be generated efficiently, and used regularly to make the intervention effective. Precollege metrics, student self-reports (such as survey responses), faculty reports, and learning management system (LMS) exports are just a few examples of the valuable data that can be generated and used in early-alert intervention strategies. Having the right data easily at hand is crucial to identify the appropriate red flags that will trigger intervention efforts.

Technology can also play a critical role in effective early-alert communication. Closing the loop on interventions with all parties involved is key to its success and technology platforms can play a significant role in making that achievable. The proper technology platform can streamline the process of gathering student contacts for outreach, documenting that outreach, and responding to the initial red flag that precipitated the intervention. Technology can also make it easier to reach students by providing multiple forms of communication in one place. We know, for instance, that the method of communication that a student is least likely to respond to is the most commonly used communication method used by staff – email (Loveland, 2017). Technology platforms can provide intervention agents the ability to email students for documentation purposes, but also replicate that message or nudge the student with, for instance, a text message or other type of instant message.

In essence, technology can provide valuable resources for intervention work, streamline workflow, and potentially increase the likelihood of student response. However, an appropriate balance between "tech versus touch" is critical to that success: "In other words, sending up a red light isn't likely to influence retention. But, if that red light leads to advisors or tutors reaching out to students and providing targeted support, we might see bigger impacts on student outcomes" (Karp, 2014, para. 5). In short, the technology system alone is not what makes intervention effective, but the right system used the right way can be a key component.

Who Is Best Suited to Intervene With At-Risk Students?

As one of the most cited programs used to support student-success goals, early-alert efforts rank with hallmark programs like advising, first-year seminars, and new-student orientation (Keup, 2019). Interestingly though, unlike its peer programs, early-alert initiatives lack a perfect professional home on many campuses and in the national organizations. At the national level, NACADA is clearly the natural home of academic advising research and best practice, orientation information is housed under the auspices of NODA, and practitioners across the world look to the National Resource Center for the First-Year Experience and Students in Transition for best practices related to the first-year seminar. Furthermore, on campuses, early-alert and academic intervention programs may be housed in individual colleges, academic success centers, academic advising units, or central retention offices.

This issue of programmatic "ownership" begs the question of who should intervene with at-risk students. According to the 2017 National Survey on the First-Year Experience, at approximately 90% of institutions, early-alert programs are a partnership between faculty and academic advisors (see Figure 4.2). Other common administrative models for this intervention include academic support personnel (68.4%), student-affairs staff (64.0%), athletics department staff (54.8%), counseling and other health services staff (43.6%), residence life staff (41.8%), peer mentors (22.7%), information technology staff (15.1%), and finally other individuals (9.4%). Student retention is certainly everyone's responsibility, but when it comes to intervening with students who have exhibited behaviors that tend to lead to an at-risk status, it appears that certain staff may be better suited and organizationally positioned than others to act.

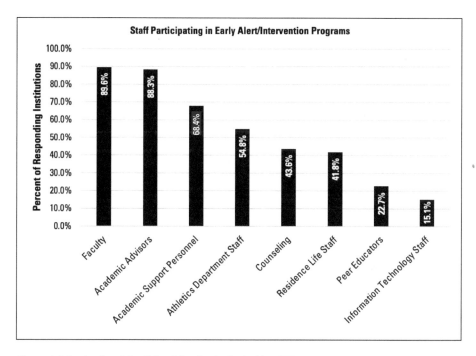

Figure 4.2. Institutional Staff Participating in Early Alert Efforts.

Note. Data from the 2017 National Survey of the First-Year Experience (NSFYE) (Estrada & Latino, 2019).

Academic Advisors

Lynch-Holmes, Trory, and Ramos (2012) suggested that the most successful interventions are intrusive and individualized. To accomplish truly individualized interventions, early-alert outreach and interventions should be conducted by institutional professional staff with the closest affiliation to the affected student. It can reasonably be assumed that students who perceive a connection to the person providing the intervention may be more likely to respond to their outreach attempts. In the case of a general student or a student on probation with no other affiliations, the student's academic advisor is likely best suited to reach out to intervene when the student displays predictive behaviors. Academic advisors should already be providing an elevated level of care to the students on academic probation in their caseload, as described by Nutter in Chapter 2 of this book. When outreach comes from a name that a student on probation already recognizes and from whom they are receiving continued support, they may be more likely to respond positively.

Beyond these pre-existing relationships, Dial and McKeown (2020) offered several reasons why academic advisors are best suited to reach out to students in academic distress. When caseloads are appropriately sized at or lower than 300:1, advisors can stratify their students into tiered categories based on their level of risk. Most of an advisor's caseload will perform adequately under normal circumstances and require minimal support throughout the semester. Because of this, advisors can use active caseload management to direct their time and attention to their rising-risk (15% of population) and high-need (5% of caseload) students. This tiered intervention model is based on the response to intervention (RTI) model often practiced in K–12 education settings (The IRIS Center, 2008). Furthermore, because advisors are positioned in the academic units in which they advise, they are primed to support students "when the issues that arise manifest as academic" (Dial & McKeown, 2020, para. 9). Advisors have a comprehensive knowledge of the curricula, can work with students to ensure that they are in majors and courses that align with their strengths and interests, and can make appropriate individualized referrals to help students overcome the distal factors behind their proximal signs of distress. This, of course, assumes that institutional academic advising is adequately staffed and funded. In the cases where it is not, these efforts may fall on the shoulders of full-time academic coaches or other central retention-focused staff. However, students may be less likely to respond to central early-alert staff with whom they have no name recognition.

For students associated with specific programs, their outreach is likely best suited coming from their honors, athletics, or other program advisor. These secondary advisors often carry smaller caseloads than the typical academic advisor and are likely in more frequent contact with affected students. Students are more likely prepared to respond to outreach from these staff with whom they have an existing relationship (Simons, 2011). Eimers (2000) suggested that early alert, when possible, should be "less formal, more frequent, less intimidating" (p. 13) and closely linked with faculty. This reiterates the case for relation-based intervention in early alert.

Peers

Given everything known about the impact peers have on student success, it is surprising that peers are less involved in academic intervention as responders (Barefoot, Griffin, and Koch, 2012; Estrada & Latino, 2019). Over 40 years of research supports the idea that peer groups are the primary forces influencing college student development. In fact, many studies have supported the notion that the most impactful teachers on a college campus are other students (Astin, 1993; Chickering, 1969; Newton & Ender, 2010). Students who benefit from the work of peer leaders gain increased familiarity with campus resources and use them more, develop mature relationships, receive support in coping through transitions, show enhanced academic skills, and exhibit greater persistence to degree (Cuseo, 2010; Latino & Ashcraft, 2012; Shook & Keup, 2012; Keup, 2016). Why then do so few institutions use peer leaders as intervention agents in early-alert initiatives?

There are likely several reasons why institutions are less likely to lean on peers for this type of student support. First, students likely lack one-on-one relationships with the specific peer leaders performing early-alert outreach. Given the significant role that name recognition plays in at-risk student response to outreach, this is problematic. In fact, under the best-case scenario they would not know the peer leader reaching out and under the worst-case scenario the peer assigned to their case could be in their social group, a fellow student whom they would prefer not have access to their academic information. Peer leaders are also often associated with specific programs and are hired and trained on a semester-by-semester basis. As such, they may be early in their own academic careers and are therefore less informed about services of which they have not availed themselves and those that are housed outside the offices for whom they work. Given these facts, it would be difficult for a peer leader to provide a student on probation the individualized attention required for high-quality early alert and intervention.

Many institutions also likely take the Federal Educational Rights and Privacy Act (FERPA) into consideration and deem that undergraduate students should not have access to the sensitive educational academic records of their peers. According to the Educational Advisory Board (EAB, 2019), the creators of Navigate, one of the largest tech platforms for early alert today, "students should have limited access to students' personal information in the advising system (p. 17)." This could include access to records indicating students' experiences of academic distress.

Academic Intervention Beyond Faculty Referrals

Particularly for students on probation, and for the work done to prevent probationary status, intervention should be based on factors other than looking at what is happening in the classroom, or classic faculty referral. While teaching faculty play an incredibly valuable role in raising the red flags that lead to intervention, these are not the only alerts that should be relied upon to notify an intervention agent that a student may be struggling. Academic advisors or other professional staff intervention agents are also primed to implement interventions based on data available in forms other than direct referral (Dial & McKeown, 2019). Intrusive outreach can be based on a number of predictive factors that often reveal the root causes of student struggles, often more so than classroom performance alone, and can lead to holistic intervention.

Some opportunities for gathering stand-alone data and conducting interventions look at factors such as credit-hour enrollment, registration holds, and nonregistration for upcoming terms. Credit-hour completion can be a critical signal in a student's likelihood to persist and graduate on time or to be retained in a particular degree program. It may seem too simple a factor on its own on which to conduct intervention, but it can be one of the most effective ways to "catch" a student who might not have exhibited any other early risk factors (Venit, 2017). Many concerns, such as scholarship retention, time to degree, and major persistence, can arise from diminished credit-hour enrollment and may lead to other factors that exacerbate students' ability to succeed.

Intervention to support students related to credit-hour enrollment has been demonstrated effective on the institutional level. In 2012, the University of Hawaii launched a campaign to impart to their students the significance of completing 15 credits per semester in relation to four-year graduation. Examples include avoiding unnecessary semesters of student debt and income sacrificed from not yet being employed. Within one year of starting this outreach, the rate of new students at the flagship campus enrolled in 15 credits per semester increased from 38% to 64%. The system campuses of the University of Hawaii saw similar results (Nietzel, 2019).

Nietzel (2019) noted that similar "15-to-finish" initiatives have been rolled out in more than half the states in the country and hundreds of institutions. In Hawaii, after controlling for high school GPA, students earn better grades and are more likely to be retained if they complete 30 credits per year. In both two- and four-year public colleges in Nevada, students who enrolled in 15 or more hours consistently were more likely to pass critical math courses. Finally, when many universities have combined the emphasis on 15 credits with intrusive advising approaches and appropriately staffed academic advising, the share of completed credits counting toward degree requirements also increases.

Though registration holds that prevent students from adding or dropping classes may seem menial in and of themselves, a hold placed on a student's account, if the student lacks the tools and feedback to resolve it in a timely manner, can lead to a downward spiral that creates significantly greater negative results. Holds could be placed by a variety of campus offices or individuals, such as the bursar's office, student health, or student conduct. Advisors notifying students of holds prior to deadlines for course registration changes and being present to support students can enable those students to resolve holds before more significant consequences arise, such as delayed registration, which leads to missing or inappropriate courses, academic difficulties, increased time to degree, increased financial burden, and ultimately attrition when the student's resources are tapped.

Outreach to students who have not yet enrolled for the upcoming semester but are eligible to do so can be considered a light-touch intervention that can have a huge impact and address a number of distal factors that may affect students' motivation to persist. Hutt (2017) described the value of a simple, 34-word email that can be sent from advisors to nonregistered students asking, "Is there anything I can do to help?" The original campaign, conducted by Hutt while serving as the assistant vice president for academic advising at Kennesaw State University, was sent to 4,000 students with 3.0 or higher GPAs. Over 35% of students responded to Hutt's outreach, many within a few days, to describe registration barriers that they were facing and were therefore able to be assisted and retained. This further enforces Whitcomb and Mathews' (2014) study that advisors cannot rely solely on metrics of academic success to determine whether students will benefit from intervention.

Beginning in 2016, the University of South Carolina has run a similar intervention termed the "non-registered initiative." A student's assigned academic advisor reaches out if the student is eligible to enroll in the upcoming semester and, by a certain point in time, are not registered for courses. This intervention is modeled off of Hutt's "nudge" and employs simple, supportive language to give students an open door to ask their advisor for help in returning to the institution. Rather than a central administrator, academic advisors can address the student's curricular needs, current circumstance, and personal reasons for nonenrollment. If the student communicates that they do not intend to re-enroll, the advisor documents that information for institutional retention personnel. Between the Fall 2020 and Spring 2021 semester at the University of South Carolina, 12% of eligible undergraduates were not registered in December 2020. Due in large part to this coordinated intervention, that number dipped to 3% by the time the deadline to add and drop classes had passed. This represents nearly 2,300 students who may have otherwise stopped out of their progression to degree.

Prioritizing Early-Alert Efforts

When time, fiscal, and personnel resources are limited, how do administrators and institutional leaders decide where to dedicate time and attention to early-alert efforts? In Figure 4.3, we present a prioritization model for choosing early-alert efforts on which to focus. The vertical axis expresses a continuum between intervention efforts that are passive and those that are intrusive. In passive efforts, an action is undertaken by a staff member, and the student can act when they find the information. In the model shown in the figure, we consider the placement of registration holds a passive (likely negative) measure. In intrusive efforts, an advisor or caring professional provides students important information at the first indication that they need it. Along the horizontal axis are the descriptors "negative," "informational," and "positive," which describe the nature of the messaging conveyed to students. Negative actions are punitive in nature and may discourage students from further engaging with the institution. Informational actions provide only the necessary facts and may be perceived as cold or uncaring. Positive messages are motivational and encourage students to take appropriate action and remind them that they have a support system to assist them in doing so. In Figure 4.3, early-alert efforts such as a minimum credit threshold outreach, a nonregistered initiative, and responding to faculty progress reports are examples of strategies that could be established as intrusive, positive efforts.

	Negative (punitive)	Informational (just the facts)	Positive (motivational)
Intrusive		Registration holds outreach Outreach to students on probation	Fewer than 15 credit hours Non-registered initiative At-risk progress reports
Passive	Registration holds	Probation outreach	Student kudos

Figure 4.3. Early Alert Prioritization Model.

This model may serve as both a prioritization structure and political mechanism. Institutional resources, including money, personnel, time, and staff capacity, are often limited. In an age of expanding technology adoption, leaders need to make decisions that compare the value of tech versus touch-based interventions. Finally, the matrix shown in Figure 4.3 may assist in timing decisions. If students have enough time to take action to correct their circumstances, institutions can draft messages that are positive in nature. If messaging is not sent until after the time has passed for a student to make course corrections (e.g., the add/drop deadline has passed), then any information shared with students will be negative or informational as they cannot act on the information provided.

Intervening With Undergraduate Students

Of interest relating to the advisors and staff intervening with students on probation and others through early-alert efforts, the TTM identifies four distinct types of precontemplators, those in the first stage of change (Miller & Rollnick, 2012; see Figure 4.4). These types reflect the reasons that students may be unwilling or not yet ready to make changes to their academic or social behaviors and/or seek help related to their studies or connection to the university.

The first type, *reluctant precontemplators*, lack awareness that a problem exists or may just not be ready to consider change. To support reluctant precontemplators, intervention agents should listen empathically and provide positive feedback. Because the reluctant precontemplator is not ready to consider making changes, staff need to be patient and stand by the student.

Rebellious precontemplators have knowledge that a problem exists but may be invested heavily in the problem behavior. These precontemplators are not interested in being told what to do and are set on making their own decisions. These are often students whose academic struggles are tied to alcohol or other substance use and late nights. Years ago, I (Dial) worked with a student in academic recovery who was incredibly intelligent but was missing classes and not turning in work. After weeks of interactions, the student finally shared that when he got home from classes, and sometimes, in the mornings before class, he smoked marijuana. I knew that I wasn't going to get the student to stop smoking and that maybe that wasn't my role anyway. With that in mind, I presented the student with three options: 1) Keep doing what you're doing and get the results you've been getting, 2) stop smoking entirely, or 3) make a plan to get your work done prior to engaging in the recreational use of marijuana. Because the student had options and wanted to succeed, he chose the third option. His grades improved, and he made plans to transfer to another institution to major in agriculture with a business minor.

Resigned precontemplators, on the other hand, lack both energy and investment. These students have given up on the possibility of turning things around. We encounter many students on probation who exhibit these traits. Over the winter break they were notified that they were not meeting the standards of membership in the academic community and have just done poorly on their first exam. They may begin to feel like their challenges are insurmountable. Intervention agents can best support these students by helping them find hope in their current circumstances. Staff can accentuate the positive academic experiences the student has achieved in other college classes or even having been accepted to the institution. Acknowledging resigned precontemplators' prior successes helps them to build self-efficacy (Bandura, 1977).

Finally, *rationalizing precontemplators* believe they can beat the odds. They are also often likely to blame others for their current state of affairs. They may appear to have all the answers and are likely not considering change because of personal risk. In the population of college students, these students may blame an instructor's pedagogical approach or a real or perceived language barrier on their own struggles. Staff can support rationalizing precontemplators by encouraging them to lay out a balance of pros and cons related to maintaining their present course and making positive behavioral changes (Miller & Rollnick, 2012).

Precontemplator type	Hallmarks	Intervention/Motivation strategies
Reluctant	Lack of knowledge	Be patient
	Do not want to consider change	Listen and provide empathic feedback
Rebellious	Aware of the problem	Providing options and allow them to choose for themselves.
	Often invested in the problem/problem behavior	Redirect rebellious energy into positive energy focused on change.
	Invested in making their own decisions – "don't tell me what to do"	
Resigned	Lack of energy or investment	Instill hope and help them explore and identify the barriers to their change.
	Given up on the possibility of change	Accentuate their positive steps – acknowledging their successes will help build self-efficacy.
	Overwhelmed by the problem	Assure them that relapse is common and does not have to be final.
Rationalizing	Appears to have all the answers	Empathy and reflective listening.
	Not considering change because of personal risk	Help the student lay out a decisional balance of pros and cons to remaining in the course and/or behavior change.
	May believe their problems are someone else's fault	

Figure 4.4. Precontemplator Types Identified in the Transtheoretical Model of Human Behavior Change (Miller & Rollnick, 2012).

The challenge for practitioners lies in the fact that many of today's student-support offices are designed for the student who both recognizes they are experiencing a challenge and is ready to make the effort to adjust their conditions. The probationary student is often unaware of or potentially even invested in the problem behavior(s) that resulted in their present circumstances and therefore is not actively seeking the support that our institutions offer. An understanding of the TTM and the stages in which students exist, and identification of a student's precontemplator type, may help practitioners to provide the appropriate support and resources to students on probation who exhibit risky behaviors.

Conclusion

Early-alert programs provide systematic means of monitoring and tracking student behaviors, sending up alerts to caring professionals, and individualizing interventions for at-risk students. The value and effectiveness of interventions increases accordingly the closer they occur to the moment a student begins displaying warning signs (Rienks & Taylor, 2009; Seidman, 2012). These systems portray an institutional ethic of care, commitment to student success, and intentionality while assisting students in overcoming common challenges. While intervening with at-risk students is not new in higher education, the formal adoption of early-alert systems is relatively recent. Programs vary across institutional contexts as evidenced in scholarly and best-practice literature (Barefoot et al., 2012; Estrada & Latino, 2019). Common and promising practices call on early-alert system administrators to identify the student populations to be monitored, delineate processes for intervention and follow-up, and consider technological needs up front (Estrada & Latino, 2019; Lynch-Holmes et al., 2012; Simons, 2011).

With regard to students on academic probation, early-alert systems can be used by institutions both to reduce the number of students who fall on probation as a major academic consequence and to further identify and support probationary students. Most institutions do not specifically monitor their students on probation through these systems; however, students on probation can be engaged in these efforts, which often monitor high-enrollment and historically difficult classes. Advisors and academic coaches with students on probation in their caseload should pay special attention to alerts generated through these systems. As they already have more frequent contact with their advisees in this high-risk group, these advisors and coaches have name recognition, and students will be more likely to respond (Simons, 2011).

The literature on early-alert systems is limited. These are truly emergent programs bolstered by advances in technology and commercial applications over recent decades. Early-alert programs may be key to creating formal, systemic networks across campus joining disparate offices in the work of connecting students to appropriate campus resources. These systems also have the potential to foster greater collaboration among faculty, professional advisors, and units on campus by aligning faculty and administrators as specialists in their own realms of student success. As partners in the work of connecting students to appropriate resources and encouraging positive academic behaviors (e.g., attendance, study skills, time management), faculty, advisors, and other professionals can approach collaboration with common language, aims, and outcomes.

References

Astin, A. W. (1993). *What matters in college? Four critical years revisited.* Jossey-Bass.

Bandura, A. (1977). Self-efficacy: toward a unifying theory of behavioral change. *Psychological Review, 84*(2), 191-215.

Barefoot, B. O., Griffin, B. Q., & Koch, A. K. (2012). *Enhancing student success and retention throughout undergraduate education: A national survey.* John N. Gardner Institute for Excellence in Undergraduate Education. https://static1.squarespace.com/static/59b0c486d2b857fc86d09aee/t/59bad33412abd988ad84d697/1505415990531/JNGInational_survey_web.pdf

Chickering, A. W. (1969). *Education and identity.* Jossey-Bass.

Chickering, A. W., & Gamson, Z. F. (1987, March). Seven principles for good practice in undergraduate education. *AAHE Bulletin,* 3–7.

Cuseo, J. (n.d). *Red flags: Behavioral indicators of potential student attrition* [White paper]. http://listserv.sc.edu/wa.cgi?A0=FYE-LIST

Cuseo, J. (2010). Peer power: Empirical evidence for the positive impact of peer interaction, support, and leadership. *E-Source for College Transitions, 7*(4), 4–6.

Dial, M., & McKeown, P. (2020, December). Academic early alert and intervention: Why academic advisors are best suited to intervene at at-risk students. *Academic Advising Today, 43*(4). https://nacada.ksu.edu/Resources/Academic-Advising-Today/View-Articles/Academic-Early-Alert-and-Intervention-Why-Academic-Advisors-Are-Best-Suited-to-Intervene-with-At-Risk-Students.aspx

EAB. (2019). *Mentor support guide: Recruitment and training.* https://attachment.eab.com/wp-content/uploads/2019/10/36998-AAF-Recruitment-Training-and-Mentor-Support-Guide.pdf

Earl, W. R. (1988). Intrusive advising of freshmen in academic difficulty. *NACADA Journal, 8*(2), 27–33.

Eimers, M. T. (2000). *Assessing the impact of the early-alert program.* [Paper presentation]. Association for Institutional Research (AIR) Annual Meeting 2000, Cincinnati, OH. https://eric.ed.gov/?id=ED446511

Estrada, S., & Latino, J. (2019). Early-alert programs. In D. Young (Ed.), *2017 National Survey on the First-Year Experience: Creating and Coordinating Ctructures to Support Student Success* (pp. 53–61). University of South Carolina, National Resource Center for The First-Year Experience & Students in Transition.

Hutt, C. (2017, November 24). Breaking down barriers to retaining students. *The Chronicle of Higher Education.* https://www.chronicle.com/article/Breaking-Down-Barriers-to/241814

Heisserer, D. L., & Parette, P. (2002). Advising at-risk students in college and university settings. *College Student Journal, 36*(1), 69–83.

Keup, J. K. (2016). Peer leadership as an emerging high-impact practice: An exploratory study of the American experience. *Journal of Student Affairs in Africa, 4*(1), 33–52.

Keup, J. (2019). Institutional attention to and integration of the first-year experience. In D. Young (Ed.), *2017 National Survey on the First-Year Experience: Creating and Coordinating Ctructures to Support Student Success* (pp. 53–61). University of South Carolina, National Resource Center for The First-Year Experience & Students in Transition.

Latino, J. A., & Ashcraft, M. L. (2012). *The first-year seminar: Designing, implementing, and assessing courses to support student learning and success: Vol IV. Using peers in the classroom.* University of South Carolina, National Resource Center for the First-Year Experience and Students in Transition.

Loveland, E. (2017). Instant generation. *The Journal of College Admissions, 235,* 34-38.

Lynch-Holmes, K., Troy, A. B., & Ramos, I. (2012). *Early alert & intervention: Top practices for intervention* [White paper]. http://info.connectedu.com/Portals/119484/docs/early_alert_white_paper_final.pdf

Miller, W. R., & Rollnick, S. (2012). *Motivational interviewing: Helping people change.* Guilford Press.

Newton, F. B., & Ender, S. C. (2010). *Students helping students: A guide for peer educators on college campuses.* Jossey-Bass.

Nietzel, M. T. (2019). The 15-To-Finish campaign: Putting the "four-year" back in four-year degrees. *Forbes.* https://www.forbes.com/sites/michaeltnietzel/2019/03/04/the-15-to-finish-campaign-putting-the-four-year-back-in-four-year-degrees/#:~:text=In%202012%2C%20the%20University%20of,having%20a%20full%2Dtime%20job

Prochaska, J. O., & DiClemente, C. C. (1983). Stages and processes of self-change of smoking: toward an integrative model of change. *Journal of Consulting and Clinical Psychology, 51*(3), 390-395.

Rienks, J., & Taylor, S. (2009, June). *Attrition and academic performance of students identified as at-risk using administrative data alone.* [Paper presentation]. First Year in Higher Education Conference 2009. Brisbane, Australia. https://unistars.org/past_papers/papers09/content/pdf/1B.pdf

Seidman, A. (2012). Taking action: A retention formula and model for student success. In A. Seidman (Ed.), *College student retention formula for student success* (pp. 267–284). Rowman & Littlefield.

Simons, J. (2011). A national study of student early alert models at four-year institutions of higher education (Doctoral dissertation). *Retrieved from ProQuest Dissertations and Theses datebase.* (UMI No. 3482551).

Shook, J. L., & Keup, J. R. (2012). The benefits of peer leader programs: An overview from the literature. *New Directions for Higher Education, 157,* 5–16.

Tampke, D. R. (2013). Developing, implementing, and assessing an early-alert system. *Journal of College Student Retention: Research, Theory & Practice, 14*(4), 523–532.

The IRIS Center. (2008). *RTI (part 5): A closer look at Tier 3.* https://iris.peabody.vanderbilt.edu/module/rti05-tier3/

Venit, E. (2017, August 21). *Why even C students should consider taking 15 credits their first semester.* https://eab.com/insights/blogs/student-success/why-even-c-students-should-consider-taking-15-credits-their-first-semester/

Whitcomb, H., & Mathews, S. (2014, December). Exploring the relationship between student understanding of degree requirements and academic performance. *Academic Advising Today,* 37(4). https://nacada.ksu.edu/Resources/Academic-Advising-Today/View-Articles/Exploring-the-Relationship-between-Student-Understanding-of-Degree-Requirements-and-Academic-Performance.aspx

Young, D. G. (2019). *2017 National Survey on the First-Year Experience: Creating and coordinating structures to support student success.* University of South Carolina, National Resource Center for The First-Year Experience and Students in Transition.

CHAPTER FIVE

First-Year Seminars for Students on Academic Probation

Dan Friedman, Stephanie M. Foote, and Dottie Weigel

Academic success in the first college year, or lack thereof, is influenced by a range of variables that span from a lack of academic skill development or preparation to social and/ or emotional issues (Upcraft et al., 2005). Although it is not possible to account for all influences on student success, it is important to create experiences that support all students while drawing on students' strengths or assets. Historically, many programs for students on academic probation were developed with the assumption that these students lacked the academic skills to be successful in college-level courses, and as a result, the focus was on skill development through workshops, courses (often noncredit bearing), or meetings with academic advisors or coaches. As this chapter illustrates, many efforts aimed at supporting students on academic probation, namely first-year seminars, are evolving to focus on aspects of motivation, sense of belonging, and support.

According to James and Graham (2010), "these interventions are offered in a variety of forms such as meetings or workshops and occasionally courses. Their design varies in terms of time commitment, requirements (mandatory vs. voluntary participation), and level of intrusiveness" (p. 74). Hamman (2014) noted that

> some institutions find that offering course for credit, most often developmental, is a more attractive option because students tend to take it more seriously, and those working with the students have a captive audience. Most often this coursework is focused on assisting students with developing study strategies and helping them develop a personalized plan for success. (p. 30)

Thus, a credit-bearing, graded course provides a hook and motivation for students to engage in the type of work, conversations, and reflections necessary for growth. This makes a first-year success course an ideal vehicle for helping students placed on academic probation after their first semester in college.

Overview of First-Year Seminars

First-year seminars have long been used to foster student success. According to Hunter and Linder (2005), a first-year seminar is

> a course designed to assist students in their academic and social development and their transition to college. A seminar, by definition, is a small discussion-based course in which students and their instructors exchange ideas and information. In most cases, there is a strong emphasis on creating community in the classroom. (pp. 275–276)

These seminars have been part of the higher-education landscape for over 100 years. While the first appearance of such a credit-bearing course is thought to be Reed College in 1911 (Fitts & Swift, 1928), the current resurgence is part of the larger first-year experience movement that began in 1972 at the University of South Carolina (Morris & Cutright, 2005).

According to research by the National Resource Center for the First-Year Experience and Students in Transition, it is estimated that between 73% and 90% of colleges and universities across the United States now offer some form of first-year seminar (Young, 2019; Young & Hopp, 2014). In the most recent survey of first-year seminars and programs, 96% of first-year seminars were offered for credit, and slightly over half (51.8%) of responding institutions required all first-year students to take the course (Young, 2019). Moreover, of institutions that did not require the seminar for all students, 19.5% noted that the course was required specifically for students on academic probation.

Hunter and Linder (2005) described several potential rationales for first-year seminars, including enhancing student persistence, increasing academic performance and degree attainment, assisting with academic and social integration, encouraging and intrusively demanding active student involvement in learning, helping students transition to a new learning environment and community, and transmitting the culture and expectations of the institution. According to the latest survey of first-year seminars (Young, 2019), the five most common objectives of these seminars were academic success strategies; connection with the institution; knowledge of campus resources; analytical, critical thinking, or problem-solving skills; and introduction to college-level academic expectations.

First-year seminars have typically been associated with greater student persistence to the second year; increased academic performance; and greater likelihood that students will connect with their peers, use campus services, be satisfied with their experience, and become involved and engaged outside of class (Barefoot et al., 1998; Porter & Swing, 2006; Tobolowsky et al., 2005). Furthermore, Porter and Swing (2006) found that students who took a first-year seminar were less likely to be placed on academic probation. In addition to benefiting a wide population of students, first-year seminars are also likely to have a greater impact on students who may struggle in their transition to college, such as first-generation, Pell recipients, students of color, and those with lower academic motivation (Culver & Bowman, 2020; Pittendrigh et al., 2016).

Seminars for Students on Academic Probation

While a wealth of evidence speaks to the outcomes of first-year seminar participation on the transition and success of students in general, there is also evidence that this type of curricular intervention is effective in supporting students on academic probation. McGrath and Burd (2012) found that a one-credit success course required of all first-year students on academic probation at a large public university was associated with a higher rate of returning to good academic standing (49% compared to 9%) and higher levels of persistence (60% vs. 22%) and graduation rates (25% vs. 2%) when compared with the prior year's cohort that did not take the course. Lipsky and Ender (1990) found that a voluntary one-credit study-skills course designed for academically at-risk students was associated with higher GPAs over two years following the course. Moreover, research conducted by Kamphoff, Hutson, Amundsen, and Atwood (2007) at the University of North Carolina at Greensboro found that a required success course for students on probation that focused on motivation and empowerment was associated with higher academic achievement when compared with the previous year's cohort that did not receive this approach. Furthermore, in a study of 100 undergraduates on academic probation at Mount Saint Vincent University in Canada (Bowering et al., 2017), enrollment in a success course that focused on learning strategies and motivation was associated with an increase in motivation and cognitive strategies as well as a decrease in test anxiety and procrastination.

Although much of the existing research on seminars for students on academic probation is positive, it is worth noting this is not always the case. In a doctoral dissertation, Shea (2018) studied a program designed to increase the GPAs of first- and second-year students on academic probation at Copper University. In comparing participants to nonparticipants, multiple regressions revealed that course participation was not a significant predictor of semester GPA. Mellor, Brooks, Gray, and Jordan (2015) studied a seminar course that focused on practical academic skills at a large four-year public university in the Northeast United States and found that the course had a modest positive effect on retention and academic self-efficacy but not on grades. Offering first-year seminars for students on academic probation can also be problematic in terms of timing. Specifically, some institutions do not place students on probation until the end of the first year, and in these instances, students may not have the opportunity to take the course until the beginning of their second academic year. The findings of both Shea (2018) and Mellor et al.'s (2015) research suggest that careful consideration should be given to the content and timing of seminars, underscoring the importance of designing these courses so they can be flexible enough to meet the diverse needs of students on academic probation.

Considerations When Designing a Seminar for Students on Probation

Align Course Goals With Needs of This Student Population

Whether designing an entire course or section(s) of an existing seminar dedicated to serving students on academic probation, consideration should be given to the extent to which the course focuses on skill development, goal setting and motivation, self-efficacy, belonging, and engagement. A review of the literature and existing institutional examples of first-year seminars shows many different models and philosophies for the focus of these courses. Moreover, there is no clear answer whether any particular approach works better than another. Specifically, in a single institution study at a public comprehensive institution, Ryan and Glenn (2004) found that seminars focused on learning strategies were more successful than socialization-focused seminars in fostering one-year retention rates. However, according to an unpublished study at a large public research university (Padgett & Friedman, 2010), the strongest predictor of a student's persistence to the second year as a result of taking the first-year seminar was the extent to which the course fostered a sense of belonging.

As the review of literature indicated, there is a range in both content and approach to first-year seminars for students on probation. For example, one course at a large public university enrolled first-year probationary students in a one-credit success course during their second semester (McGrath & Burd, 2012). This course focused on "five core areas: student development; test-taking and notetaking strategies; campus policies and procedures; exploration of different majors; and engagement with faculty members, advisors, and other student resources on campus" (p. 46). Conversely, a required course for students on probation at the University of North Carolina at Greensboro (Kamphoff et al., 2007) focused less on developing specific study strategies and more on developing motivation and empowerment. Moreover, Albion College in Michigan offered a credit-bearing academic success course for students on probation (Lorenzetti, 2009). Given that their student population was generally academically capable, this course prioritized effort and ambivalence. An administrator responsible for the course stated that "effort is more important than strategy. I think that appropriate effort can make up for a lack of strategy and limited skills. Good strategy doesn't compensate well for a lack of effort" (p. 3). The Academic Recovery section of University 101 at the University of South Carolina focuses the majority of the course instruction on motivation, mindset, and confidence-building, rather than skill development. This explicit focus has resulted in gains in the areas of constructive use of time and positive identity, measured, pre- and post-course, by the Appreciative Advising Inventory (M. Dial, personal communication, December 9, 2019). In each of these instances, the course was found to be successful in helping students recover from academic probation; thus, both the student population and institutional context are important drivers of what is covered in these courses.

To ensure positive outcomes, the purpose of the seminar should be aligned with the reasons that students struggle. The appropriate ratio of this content would be institution specific, driven by specific student population, institutional context, and the reasons students ended up on academic probation. Several approaches can be used to determine the reasons students struggle. First, educators could collect survey and/or interview data from students who are on probation or those who have successfully achieved good academic standing. Second, faculty and staff working with students on academic probation might collect student information before the course begins through a confidential survey. The intent of a beginning-of-course survey, which could be administered before the course begins, is to provide instructors with "microdata about their [students'] individualized needs" (Pacansky-Brock, 2020, n.p.). For example, the survey could include questions about preferred name and pronouns, personal goals and commitments, examples of things they are good at, and feelings or beliefs about the course (Killpack & Melón, 2020). Third, it is possible to mine existing institutional data that reflect student performance and progression to identify points of concern and challenge.

However, it is important to remember that the course should be designed to respond to individualized student needs as well as address common challenges for students on academic probation. Humphrey (2005) addressed this need for flexibility of approaches when working with this population:

> The design of the program is both structured enough to offer a shared experience to students in different groups yet open enough to allow individualized interactions for the participants. Such a program design reflects the belief that there are some issues basic to academic success such as good time management and effective study skills while, at the same time, not generalizing that all probationary students are the same. (p. 49)

Student Learning Goals. Learning goals and outcomes are "goals that describe what students will be able to do as a result of a learning experience" (Suskie, 2018, p. 41). While the terms "outcomes" and "goals" can be used interchangeably, learning goals describe the *intended or expected* learning that will take place and outcomes describe the *actual* outcome or result (Suskie).

Seminar instructors must design learning in such a way that it advances students' abilities beyond memorizing information to more advanced capabilities such as synthesizing and critically evaluating information (Bloom et al., 1956). Banta and Palomba (2015) suggested the tasks being measured should demonstrate the learning directly related to the nature of the discipline in which students are engaged, and Gahagan, Dingfelder, and Pei (2010) emphasized the importance of developing learning goals that are measurable. They indicate this step, when done well, "guides our methodology but also dramatically improves our work with students in and beyond the classroom" (p. 6). Much of this can be accomplished through carefully designing student learning goals that are meaningful and measurable.

Fink (2013) offered a taxonomy of significant learning that "goes beyond understand-and-remember and even beyond application learning" (p. xii). Fink suggested, "Individuals and organizations involved in higher education are expressing a need for important kinds of learning [such as] learning how to learn, leadership and interpersonal skills, ethics, communication skills, character, tolerance, and the ability to adapt to change" (p. 29). In Fink's taxonomy, significant learning is represented by (a) *foundational knowledge* – students develop a basic understanding that can be used for other kinds of learning; (b) *application* – students are able to apply what they have learned to a new form of action (intellectual, physical, or social); (c) *integration* – students see and understand connections between different things; (d) *human dimension* – students learn something important about themselves or others that helps them function or interact more effectively; (e) *caring* – students' learning experiences change the way they care about something; and (f) *learning how to learn* – students learn about the process of learning itself so that they can continue to do so in the future with greater effectiveness.

The Structure of the Learning Goal. All learning goals have a common format: subject–verb–object (Gahagan et al., 2010). In the academic recovery seminar context, the subject is the student on probation. The learning goal is written in such a way that, as a result of engaging in a particular educational practice, the student will be able to do or accomplish a particular skill or educational outcome. In light of Fink's (2013) taxonomy, designing learning outcomes with impactful learning in mind, the verb used in the learning goal requires careful thought and reflection in planning. Saying a student will be able to identify where a student-success center is located on campus is very different than a student who employs strategies they learned. A student who can describe where student-success coaches are located and what services they offer is very different from a student who *engages personally* in an academic success coaching session and is able to justify the importance for their own success. This student is making personal connections, practicing positive academic behaviors, and applying their learning.

Align Course Goals With Institutional Goals

In addition to aligning academic recovery courses with the needs of students, seminars designed to support students on probation should have goals which align with institutional priorities. In *Student Success in College: Creating Conditions that Matter*, Kuh, Kinzie, Schuh, Whitt, and associates (2010) suggested students are most likely to achieve success in institutions with collaborative environments with alignment among program goals and institutional values. Hutchings (2016) emphasized the importance of alignment to improve student learning, especially for students who "swirl through multiple institutions, stop out and return" (p. 3). This is particularly relevant when addressing the needs of students on academic probation, who could benefit from a counter-fragmentation (Hutchings, 2016). A curriculum map is an excellent tool to ensure learning goals are achieving their designed purpose (Suskie, 2018). The curriculum map sample (see Figure 5.1) illustrates an Academic Recovery section of the first-year seminar at the University of South Carolina, designed to improve student learning and engagement for students who are academically at risk. The course is offered to students who received grades lower than C in a fall section of UNIV 101 or were placed on academic probation following their first semester (Foster, 2019). The course aims to "foster a sense of belonging, promote engagement in the curricular and cocurricular life of the university, develop critical thinking skills and help to clarify purpose, meaning and direction" (University of South Carolina, n.d., para. 1). This is achieved through three overarching goals for students: (a) foster academic success; (b) discover and connect with the University of South Carolina; and (c) promote personal development, well-being, and social responsibility (University of South Carolina, n.d.-b.).

Ideally, the broad institution-wide goals of the curriculum map will demonstrate a clear connection to department goals and specific learning goals for students. The first column of Figure 5.1 includes institution-wide goals or outcomes, followed by course goals, and individual learning goals for students. In the assessment planning process, the goal is to align each of these categories, and it begins with the overall institution-wide drivers. As an example, the University of South Carolina currently has nine strategic priorities as documented through the strategic plan for the university. These strategic initiatives connect back to the institutional mission to "educate the state's citizens through teaching, research, creative activity, and community engagement" (University of South Carolina, 2010, para. 1) and guide specific departmental goals and outcomes. Highlighting the connections among institutional, departmental, and course goals is an important step in planning and setting student learning goals. Taking time to reflect on the institutional mission and goals and how they relate to the course is a critical part of the course planning process.

The assessment grid is not only beneficial for demonstrating alignment between institutional goals, course goals, and specific learning goals for students. It also includes measures, targets, and a timeline that serve as key performance indicators.

College or university goals	First-year seminar course goal	Academic recovery first-year seminar learning goals	Measure/ method to gauge achievement of expected results	Target/ Indicator	Timeline/ Collection
Provide the highest quality of rigorous instruction and student-centric educational experience to all students	Foster academic success	Students will: Apply appropriate academic strategies to their courses and learning experiences (through engaging 1:1 in an academic coaching appointment through the University Advising Center)	2- to 3-page graded reflection paper	90% of students will score a 4 or higher on the grading rubric	End of spring semester
Provide the highest quality of rigorous instruction and student-centric educational experience to all students	Discover and connect with the University of South Carolina	Students will: Engage in "safe" discussion in order to create a sense of belonging	End-of-course evaluation	90% of students will agree or strongly agree that course discussions with peers helped facilitate a sense of belonging on the end-of-course evaluation	End of spring semester

Figure 5.1 continues on page 111

Figure 5.1 continued from page 110

College or university goals	First-year seminar course goal	Academic recovery first-year seminar learning goals	Measure/ method to gauge achievement of expected results	Target/ Indicator	Timeline/ Collection
Provide the highest quality of rigorous instruction and student-centric educational experience to all students	Promote personal development, well-being, and social responsibility	Students will: Establish and work toward the attainment of personal and professional goals.	Final course presentation	90% of students will score a 4 or higher on the grading rubric	End of spring semester

Figure 5.1. Example Curriculum Map.

Allow Space for Affirmation and Validation

Another important benefit of a first-year seminar is that the discussion about college-related topics tends to create a sense of validation and affirmation about what students are experiencing. It becomes a place where students can share their challenges, successes, and questions. During a check-in activity, such as "highs or lows" (an exercise that involves asking students to reflect on and share highs and lows for the day or week), students can disclose that they are homesick, struggling in a particular course, or feeling stressed about their workload. Hearing that other students feel the same way provides an important validation of the experience and normalizing these common issues. As such, creating a safe space that allows for this type of communication is likely to help students overcome their challenge more readily. If students feel they are the only one struggling, they may be more likely to disengage or give up. Validation and support from peers and the instructor underscore the importance of having a dedicated class with other students experiencing similar challenges. Furthermore, in a qualitative doctoral dissertation, Barouch-Gilbert (2015) found that the self-efficacy of students on academic probation was helped by encouragement (social persuasions) and learning/ guidance from others (vicarious experiences).

For example, students on academic recovery at the University of North Carolina at Greensboro enroll in an asynchronous, online course, ARS 100, that include weekly modules on "university policies, academic and campus resources, time management, personal wellness, and goal setting [personal and academic]" ("Academic Recovery FAQs," n.d.), as well as GPA calculation. While the content is offered in a self-paced format, throughout their experience in the course, students receive guidance and affirmation from an academic recovery specialist in the Students First Office.

Incorporate Other Institutional Probationary Requirements Into the Seminar

First-year seminars for students on academic probation can be ideal as they provide opportunities for students to receive dedicated support that is appropriate to their specific needs. Students who may lack the college knowledge needed to be successful at the institution or those who need social, emotional, or academic support can receive or be connected to institutional programs and services, through the context of the course, that provide these forms of support. For example, at Chaffey College, students on academic probation must complete five visits to the success center for help with reading, writing, and math (Scrivner et al., 2009). At Albion College, students in their academic success course are required to attend three 2-hour study sessions each week (Lorenzetti, 2009). These types of requirements could be integrated into the success course so that students get credit for attending, thus providing an even greater hook and support to complete the additional probationary requirements. It is also important to incorporate academic and career advising, counseling services, financial aid, and academic support or success services in the development and delivery of first-year seminars for students on academic probation to ensure that institutional requirements and various forms of services are embedded in the context of the course. The extent to which these services are incorporated should again be determined by student needs.

Engage Students on Academic Probation in Integrative Learning

In *Mapping the Terrain*, Huber and Hutchings (2004) defined integrative learning as "connecting skills and knowledge from multiple sources and experiences; applying theory to practice in various settings; utilizing diverse and even contradictory points of view; and, understanding issues and positions contextually" (p. 13). Integrative learning experiences provide opportunities for students on probation to address real-world problems; adapt their intellectual skills; and understand and develop individual purpose, values, and ethics (Rhodes, 2010). Many students can intellectually address real-world problems and grow in their intellectual capacities but miss a key ingredient of their learning – reflection. Several theoretical models provide context and can serve as guides for promoting learning and reflection and have several important considerations for students on academic probation.

The Experiential Learning Model. Kolb's (1984) experiential learning model demonstrates how to weave reflection into the learning experience to help students deduce meaning. In an optimal learning environment, students would engage each of the stages, building off of what they have learned. However, the reality for academically at-risk students is that they are likely to miss out on one or more of these stages. With this context in mind, in the first stage of Kolb's model (concrete experience), students who neglect to engage this stage would struggle to describe how the experience made them feel, why they reacted the way they did, and the overall purpose of the activity (reflective observation). Perhaps they would engage an assigned reading and lecture on a particular topic of interest (abstract conceptualization), but they would likely fail to make connections. Finally, academically at-risk students may be less likely to apply and integrate concepts learned (active experimentation). Ideally, students will engage all of the stages to experience the greatest gains. When planning learning activities using the experiential model, educators must be conscientious of academically at-risk students' needs (e.g., building trust) and avoid assumptions (e.g., assuming all students have achieved the time management skills necessary to be successful).

The Four Cs. McCoy (2018) emphasized the importance of self-reflection in promoting student learning and engagement for students on academic probation. McCoy stated, "Self-reflection is a skill that can help them beyond college, and institutions can help support its development. [Self-reflection] can help students become well informed, able to self-regulate, and more likely to be successful" (para. 9). Eyler, Giles, and Schmiede (1996) suggested using *Four Cs* when planning and facilitating reflection:

Continuous – Incorporate reflection throughout the learning experience – before, during, and afterward.

Connected – When reflection is "connected," students can integrate their beyond-the-classroom learning with theories and concepts from class. Reflection activities aim to help students connect the abstract to the concrete. In some cases, students can connect their learning to other life experiences.

Challenging – Ask students to think critically. Reflection questions go beyond the surface and stretch students' thinking. Students may be asked to develop alternative explanations for what they thought and observed initially.

Contextualized – Connect reflection activities to overall goals of the learning experiences. Furthermore, make those experiences appropriate and meaningful and ask students to reflect beyond the current moment or activity.

In the classroom setting, reflection prompts and activities can be used as practical ways to promote reflection. The following are a few examples:

Letter to Myself – Students write a letter to themselves, describing their hopes and fears before engaging in the learning experience. How do they define and measure their own academic success? Are their expectations self-imposed or expectations that others have placed upon them? Having a record of what they thought as they approached a task can show how far they have come and be a powerful learning tool at the end of the semester or after the learning experience.

Three-Part Journal – A journal entry is divided into thirds (i.e., description, analysis, application). In the first section, students describe a beyond-the-classroom learning experience (e.g., academic coaching session, advising appointment). In the second section, they analyze how course content relates to the experience. In the application section, students write about how they can apply the experience and course content to their personal or professional life (Bringle & Hatcher, 1999).

Exit Cards – Students turn in a note card at the end of the class period. On the front, they reflect on disciplinary content and class discussion and write one thing they learned during the period. On the back, they write a question that still lingers about the topic. This informal assessment effort provides an easy way to consistently gauge student progress.

Case Studies – Given a scenario that addresses content from class and a real-world context, students gather in small groups and discuss ways to address the issue presented.

Jacoby (2011) offered a reminder that reflection is "not a neat and tidy exercise that closes an experience with a nice, tidy, little bow. Rather, reflection is ongoing, it's often messy, and it provides more openings than closings" (para. 1). Ideally, students will become more comfortable with ambiguity as they progress in their education, and creating an atmosphere of trust is critical to each student's ability to reflect well. This is particularly important for students on academic probation. McCoy (2018) indicated, "Providing the opportunity for struggling students to develop relationships with peers, staff, or faculty in the capacity of mentorship and advising can help students increase their sense of belonging – to a major, department, peer group, or campus—while addressing academic skills" (para. 7). By creating safe spaces for students to learn and reflect, educators are better equipped to move students along in the learning process.

Conclusion

Supporting first-year students on academic probation can present a variety of challenges in both the design and the delivery of programs and courses for this particular student population. To that end, careful consideration must be given to the specific content and approach associated with these experiences, and there is no exception for first-year seminars that are designed for students on academic probation. While first-year seminars in general are pervasive in American higher education, there are far fewer instances of these courses for students on academic probation. Despite this fact, numerous evidence-based institutional examples of first-year seminars have had positive effects on the persistence and success of students on academic probation. For this reason, we purport that seminars or sections of existing first-year seminars should be designed and offered specifically for students on academic probation. These courses or sections of courses should be developed in ways that provide maximal opportunities for academic skills development, as needed, while fostering meaningful engagement and support, both in and beyond the classroom. Ultimately, these courses should support, affirm, and provide requisite challenge, through personal reflection and goal setting, to motivate students who enroll.

References

Academic Recovery FAQs. (n.d.). University of North Carolina at Greensboro. https://studentsfirst.uncg.edu/academic-recovery/academic-recovery-faqs/

Barouch-Gilbert, A. (2015). *Self-efficacy beliefs of former probationary students* [Doctoral dissertation, Washington State University]. Research Exchange https://rex.libraries.wsu.edu/esploro/outputs/doctoral/SELF-EFFICACY-BELIEFS-OF-FORMER-PROBATIONARY-STUDENTS/99900581530901842

Barefoot, B. O., Warnock, C. L., Dickinson, M. P., Richardson, S. E., & Roberts, M. R. (Eds.). (1998). *Exploring the evidence: Reporting the outcomes of first-year seminars* (Vol. II, Monograph No. 25). University of South Carolina, National Resource Center for The First-Year Experience and Students in Transition.

Bowering, E. R., Mills, J., & Merritt, A. (2017). Learning how to learn: A student success course for at-risk students. *The Canadian Journal for the Scholarship of Teaching and Learning, 8*(3). Article 4

Culver, K. C., & Bowman, N. A. (2020). Is what glitters really gold? A quasi-experimental study of first-year seminars and college student success. *Research in Higher Education, 61*(2), 167-196.

Eyler, J., Giles, D., & Schmiede, A. (1996). *A practitioner's guide to reflection in service-learning: Student voices and reflection.* Nashville, TN: Vanderbilt University.

Fink, L. D. (2013). *Creating significant learning experiences: An integrated approach to designing college courses.* John Wiley & Sons.

Fitts, C. T., & Swift, F. H. (1928). The construction of orientation courses for college freshmen. *University of California Publications in Education, 1897–1929, 2*(3), 145–250.

Gahagan, J., Dingfelder, J., & Pei, K. (2010). *A faculty and staff guide to creating learning outcomes.* Columbia, SC: University of South Carolina, National Resource Center for The First-Year Experience and Students in Transition.

Hamman, K. J. (2014). *An examination of support programs for students on academic probation in the Pennsylvania state system of higher education* [Doctoral dissertation, Indiana University of Pennsylvania]. Semantic Scholar. https://www.semanticscholar.org/paper/An-examination-of-support-programs-for-students-on-Hamman/a4a0c9c3eb0ab64c6b34339dfcbc31f16d986743

Huber, M. T., & Hutchings, P. (2004). *Integrative learning: Mapping the terrain.* Washington, DC: Association of American Colleges & Universities and The Carnegie Foundation for the Advancement of Teaching.

Humphrey, E. (2005). Project success: Helping probationary students achieve academic success. *Journal of College Student Retention: Research, Theory & Practice, 7*(3), 147–163.

Hunter, M. S., & Linder, C. (2005). First-year seminars. In M. L. Upcraft, J. N. Gardner, & B. O. Barefoot (Eds.), *Challenging and supporting the first-year student: A handbook for improving the first year of college* (pp. 275–291). Jossey-Bass.

Jacoby, B. (2011, May 11). Critical reflection adds depth and breadth to student learning. In M. Bart, *Faculty Focus.* Retrieved from http://www.facultyfocus.com/articles/instructional-design/critical-reflection-adds-depth-and-breadth-to-student-learning/

James, C. L., & Graham, S. (2010). An empirical study of students on academic probation. *Journal of the First-Year Experience & Students in Transition, 22*(2), 71–92.

Kamphoff, C. S., Hutson, B. L., Amundsen, S. A., & Atwood, J. A. (2007). A motivational/empowerment model applied to students on academic probation. *Journal of College Student Retention: Research, Theory & Practice, 8*(4), 397–412.

Kolb, D. A. (1984). *Experiential learning: Experience as the source of learning and development* (Vol. 1). Englewood Cliffs, NJ: Prentice Hall.

Lipsky, S. A., & Ender, S. C. (1990). Impact of a study-skills course on probationary students' academic performance. *Journal of the Freshman Year Experience, 2*(1), 7–15.

Lorenzetti, J. P. (2009). Facing ambivalence helps students on probation bounce back. *Recruitment and Retention in Higher Education, 23*(10), 3–4.

McCoy, M. R. (2018, March). Holistic approaches to advising students on academic probation. *Academic Advising Today, 41*(1). Retrieved from: https://nacada.ksu.edu/Resources/Academic-Advising-Today/View-Articles/Holistic-Approaches-to-Advising-Students-on-Academic-Probation.aspx

McGrath, S. M., & Burd, G. D. (2012). A success course for freshmen on academic probation: Persistence and graduation outcomes. *NACADA Journal, 32*(1), 43–52.

Mellor, D. T., Brooks, W. R., Gray, S. A., & Jordan, R. C. (2015). Troubled transitions into college and the effects of a small intervention course. *Journal of College Student Retention: Research, Theory & Practice, 17*(1), 44–63.

Morris, L. V., & Cutright, M. (2005). University of South Carolina: Creator and standard-bearer for the first-year experience. In B. O. Barefoot, J. N. Gardner, M. Cutright, L. V. Morris, C. C. Schroeder, S. W. Schwartz, M. J. Siegel,& R. L. Swing (Eds.), *Achieving and sustaining institutional excellence for the first year of college* (pp. 349–377). Jossey-Bass.

Pacansky-Brock, M. (2020). *Humanizing visual guide.* https://brocansky.com/humanizing/infographic2

Padgett, R., & Friedman, D. B. (2010). *Relationship of FYI factors and persistence.* University of South Carolina. https://sc.edu/about/offices_and_divisions/university_101/research_and_assessment/research_reports/index.php

Pittendrigh, A., Borkowski, J., Swinford, S., & Plumb, C. (2016). Knowledge and community: The effect of a first-year seminar on student persistence. *The Journal of General Education, 65*(1), 48–65.

Porter, S. R., & Swing, R. L. (2006). Understanding how first-year seminars affect persistence. *Research in Higher Education, 47*(1), 89–109.

Ryan, M. P., & Glenn, P.A. (2004). What do first-year students need most: Learning strategies instruction or academic socialization? *Journal of College Reading and Learning, 34*(2), 4–28.

Shea, E. (2018). *Intervening with students on academic probation: The effectiveness of a student success course* [Unpublished doctoral dissertation, Alfred University]. https://aura.alfred.edu/handle/10829/8163

Tobolowsky, B. F., Cox, B. E., & Wagner, M. T. (Eds.). (2005). *Exploring the evidence: Reporting research on first-year seminars* (Vol. III, Monograph No. 42). University of South Carolina, National Resource Center for The First-Year Experience and Students in Transition.

University of South Carolina. (n.d.-a.). *For South Carolina: A path to excellence.* https://sc.edu/about/our_leadership/president/strategic_plan/index.php

University of South Carolina. (n.d.-b.). Courses. Retrieved from: https://sc.edu/about/offices_and_divisions/university_101/courses/index.php

Upcraft, M. L., Gardner, J. N., & Barefoot, B. O. (2005). *Challenging & supporting the first-year student: A handbook for improving the first year of college.* Jossey-Bass.

Young, D. G. (Ed.). (2019). *2017 National Survey on The First-Year Experience: Structures for supporting student success* (Research Reports on College Transitions No. 9). University of South Carolina, National Resource Center for The First-Year Experience and Students in Transition.

Young, D. G., & Hopp, J. M. (2014). *2012–13 National Survey of First-Year Seminars: Exploring high-impact practices in the first college year* (Research Reports on College Transitions No. 4). University of South Carolina, National Resource Center for The First-Year Experience and Students in Transition.

CHAPTER SIX

Assessing Student Probation and Academic Recovery Initiatives

Dallin George Young and Dottie Weigel

The previous chapters have outlined a strong case for why we should be paying attention to students who find themselves in academic distress and the ways in which the policy and practice environment can be structured to support them and provide pathways to academic success. However, simply offering or creating conditions to help students achieve their academic goals is insufficient. Institutions and the educators who work in them must monitor the ongoing viability and effectiveness of such efforts. Assessment and evaluation of student probation and academic recovery initiatives can ensure that success is achievable for students on academic probation.

Carrying out the assessment of probation and recovery policies and programs has many challenges. As the authors of the previous chapters have demonstrated, academic probation and recovery is a complex collection of antecedents, experiences, and institutional responses, which means that the successful implementation and use of any assessment activity must account for this complexity. Furthermore, rising college costs and equitable access continue to be causes for concern at many institutions, and the pressure to develop effective learning outcomes that serve diverse student populations can be challenging. Challenges are compounded for faculty and staff who are already stretched thin with the growing demands of supporting student success (Greenfield et al., 2013; Jankowski et al., 2018). Thus, higher educational professionals may find it difficult to find time and energy necessary to intentionally devote efforts toward successful assessment practices (Baker et al., 2012).

Notwithstanding the challenges, high-quality, thoughtful, and purposeful assessment can help colleges and universities engage in organizational learning and ultimately deliver on the promises made to students (Young, 2018). Gathering data can help to answer questions such as, "How well are students learning what they need to succeed in their future endeavors? If students are not learning those things, what is the college or program doing to improve learning? ... Is the college or program operating efficiently as well as effectively?" (Suskie, 2018, pp. 90–91). Assessment also encourages higher educationalists to investigate the "primary causes for students' lack of success" (Greenfield et al., 2013, p. 208). This requires those with stewardship over student success to engage in double-loop learning (Argyris & Schön, 1996; Boyce, 2003; Young, 2018) and to operate under the assumption that an ounce of prevention is worth a pound of cure – especially when it comes to students who find themselves on academic probation.

This chapter is structured to highlight the issues that are unique to assessing student probation and academic recovery initiatives and to provide practical recommendations for those who have stewardship over them. First, we describe how the complexity of probation and academic recovery has an impact on assessment approaches. Second, we turn to a discussion of describing success and identifying appropriate assessment objectives and outcomes. Third, we provide a framework for deciding on approaches to gather data and assess probation initiatives. Then, we turn to the importance of understanding assessment of academic probation as organizational learning. Finally, we conclude the chapter with some recommendations.

Assessment Must Respond to the Complexity of Academic Probation and Recovery

As discussed in previous chapters, advising, academic coaching, early-alert programs, and first-year seminars can be used to address the academic recovery needs of students on academic probation, and assessment provides a valuable way to measure the effectiveness of these practices. However, before outlining any of the traditional trappings of approaches to assessment, we stop to reflect on what the previous chapters have revealed about the nature of academic probation and recovery.

Probation and Recovery Are Multifaceted, Multiphased, and Multilocational

A review of the chapters on probation and academic recovery policies and programs reveals that they are multifaceted, multiphased, and multilocational. Probation and academic recovery are *multifaceted* in that they represent a variety of causes (e.g., academic motivation, preparation, internal to the student, structural at the institution), potential solutions (e.g., intrusive, appreciative, direct, programmatic, academic, affective, cognitive), and philosophical orientations (e.g., where responsibility for recovery lies, what share of the effort lies with which stakeholder, what recovery should entail). Time plays an important role in the nature of the efforts aimed at academic success: to prevent, define, or respond to probation. Thus, the collection of probation and academic success policies and initiatives are *multiphased*, or attempting to intervene at multiple points in time. In addition, due to the multifaceted nature of probation and recovery, many stakeholders and offices are involved. These efforts are *multilocational*, as the array of services, programs, and other offerings to students are likely both organizationally and geographically separated. The multifaceted, multiphased, and multilocational nature of probation and recovery initiatives has an impact on assessment approaches.

A Typology of Student Probation and Academic Recovery-Related Initiatives

To illustrate and make sense of how the multifaceted, multiphased, and multilocational nature of probation and recovery initiatives influence assessment, we present a typology of these policies, programs, and services. The typology includes five groupings of probation and recovery initiatives first organized by the temporal dimension (multiphased): before, determining, and after probation. The next organizing level is grouping them by their general approach (multifaceted). The final dimension, that of location, is attended to through examples of how different stakeholders play roles in the types of probation and recovery programs. This typology organizes probation and recovery initiatives in five general categories: (a) campuswide approaches to student success, (b) academic and curricular gateways, (c) probation-prevention initiatives, (d) policies and procedures defining probation and recovery, and (e) academic recovery initiatives. As the scope and purpose of this chapter is on assessment, we provide only a brief description of each of these with the focus on how they might illustrate pathways to gathering data, interpreting it, and making improvements to the academic success landscape on campus.

Campuswide Approaches to Student Success

This type of probation initiative refers to the overall campus approach to support student success. It covers the overall institutional ethos to supporting student success and, as a result, must be conceptualized as an antecedent to student probation. This grouping includes such initiatives as institutional student-success committees, retention schemes, first-year experience, and student-success approaches based in undergraduate general education.

Academic and Curricular Gateways

Similar to campuswide approaches, academic and curricular gateways represent the academic mindset toward success in and across individual courses, departments, colleges, or institutions. Additionally, these approaches represent the pathways to success or the barriers that can trip up an individual or large numbers of students. Included in this type are gateway courses or other courses with high rates of students earning grades of D, F, W, or I (Greenfield et al., 2013). As a result, these most frequently fit temporally before academic probation; however, they may also serve as a challenge after probation and make recovery difficult.

Probation-Prevention Initiatives

As the name implies, these initiatives are designed to explicitly intervene before students encounter academic situations that would place them on probation. Probation-prevention programs include early alert, student-success and academic coaching, academic advising, and credit-momentum initiatives (e.g., 15-to-finish).

Policies and Procedures Defining Probation and Recovery

Temporally, the policies that define probation, in particular, represent an inflection point as they are both proactive and reactive in nature. As was expressed in Chapter 1, academic probation policies are multifaceted, as the interpretation of what constitutes probation – and by extension, what is required to return to good academic standing – may vary by program, department, and institution.

Academic Recovery Initiatives

This group is defined explicitly by the temporal dimension: The student has been placed on probation, and initiatives are implemented to help the student to recover to the same academic state as before probation. As illustrated in previous chapters, academic recovery initiatives can be located within other student-success programs on campus, including advising, first-year seminars, and academic coaching.

Importance of Understanding Types of Probation and Recovery Initiatives for Assessment

At this point, it should be clear that jumping into a discussion of assessment without establishing the complexity of the institutional landscape of probation and recovery would have ignored important features of these initiatives and processes. Now that we have established an understanding of the range of programs, services, and other offerings related to probation and recovery, we can outline some of the common features of assessment and how they might be applied. The following sections provide insights toward identifying the objectives of the different policies, programs, and initiatives for probation and recovery; deciding on assessment approaches; and engaging in organizational learning across the complexity of these multifaceted, multiphased, and multilocational initiatives.

Defining and Describing Objectives and Outcomes of Probation and Recovery

With the complexity of what causes probation, what engenders recovery, and the variety of approaches designed and employed to support student success, a logical place to start is by determining the objectives and outcomes of academic probation and recovery initiatives. A review of assessment models confirms this, as identifying objectives and outcomes is nearly universally named as the first step in any assessment cycle (Friedman, 2012;

Maki, 2004; Suskie, 2018; Volkwein, 2010). In this section, we present three perspectives related to defining objectives and describing success for assessment of probation and recovery initiatives: (a) acknowledging the complexity and aligning the objectives, (b) defining procedural and learning outcomes, and (c) considering multiple dimensions of outcomes.

Acknowledging the Complexity and Aligning the Objectives

The complexity of the different approaches that institutions take to support or forestall students on academic probation illuminates points of view important to defining objectives and outcomes of these initiatives. For example, as probation and recovery programs and policies are multifaceted and multilocational, it is possible (and likely) that each has its own definition of what success looks like for both the student and the office responsible for the effort. This is not necessarily bad. The autonomy of the office to chart its own course allows it to be responsive to student needs. However, as Kuh et al. (2010) suggested, students are most likely to achieve success in institutions with collaborative environments with alignment among program goals and institutional values. Moreover, alignment can improve student success, especially for students who "swirl through multiple institutions, stop out and return" (Hutchings, 2016, p. 3), which is more likely for students on probation who are counseled to enroll at another institution as a form of academic recovery (Versalle, 2018). Therefore, steps should be taken to understand how the different objectives for each component of the overall institutional approach to probation and recovery work together to create a coherent approach to understanding student outcomes through assessment.

Defining Procedural and Learning Outcomes

Learning objectives and outcomes are "goals that describe what students will be able to do as a result of a learning experience" (Suskie, 2018, p. 41). While the terms "outcomes," "objectives," and "goals" can be used interchangeably, learning goals or objectives describe the *intended* or *expected* learning that will take place and outcomes describe the *actual* outcome or result (Suskie, 2018). Elaborating on the variety of student success outcomes, Young (2018) made a further distinction between *procedural* and *learning and development* outcomes.

Procedural Outcomes

Procedural outcomes refer to the actions that students take to move them through institutional or curricular processes. They tend to be related to completion, persistence, and time to degree and include such tasks as credit-hour momentum, meeting with an academic advisor or coach, declaring or changing a major, or seeking academic assistance. These outcomes are an important part of a student's relationship with the institution and their progress toward completion of an academic program; "they are at best signals for deeper learning and engagement" (Young, 2018, p. 51). Some procedural outcomes specific to probation and recovery programs might include

- Progress through early-alert programs, such as the successful completion of an academic coaching session
- Student change of major following a conversation with academic advisor
- Participation in a supplemental instruction section connected to a gateway course
- Completion of a certain number of credit hours with a satisfactory grade, including a recovery section of a first-year seminar

In addition, many program-level outcomes are procedural. These include effective communication of probation and expectations for recovery, successful tracking of student progress through early-alert programs, effective collaboration among departments partnering in early-alert or academic recovery initiatives, positive perceptions of student-success staff and participating faculty by the student in recovery (Greenfield et al., 2013).

Learning and Development Outcomes

Learning and development outcomes, on the other hand, refer to the interpersonal, intrapersonal, and cognitive growth that comes as the result of participating in an educationally purposeful activity. Banta and Palomba (2015) suggested the tasks being assessed should demonstrate the learning directly related to the nature of the discipline in which students are engaged. Moreover, learning outcomes tend to be specific and outline a particular competency we want a student to accomplish (Bresciani et al., 2009). Probation and recovery learning and development outcomes might include

- Improved forms of engaged learning following the successful completion of an academic coaching session
- Greater sense of purpose after meeting with an academic advisor
- Increased academic self-efficacy after meeting with faculty in gateway course
- Greater sense of belonging and community following participation in first-year seminar

It is important to determine and describe the procedural and learning and development outcomes at the heart of the probation and recovery initiatives on campus. An audit of the objectives and outcomes from this point of view can help decisionmakers understand whether they are focused primarily on simply moving students through the procedural aspects of their college experience or if they are also attending to their learning. When it comes to assessing the effectiveness of academic probation and recovery efforts, attention to the balance of both procedure and learning are key to success.

Considering Multiple Dimensions of Outcomes

When determining or describing the outcomes of probation or recovery initiatives in question, higher-education professionals would do well to think about outcomes along multiple dimensions. The first dimension we recommend is to look to scholarship on student transition and development to understand and develop language around students in academic recovery. For example, if a majority of students who are in academic recovery are sophomores, attending to issues facing students in the second year will provide an important guide for what kind of outcomes are developmentally appropriate and what might be the underlying causes that contribute to student performance issues (see Schreiner, 2018, for more information on sophomore student issues). The second dimension is the importance of disaggregating the measures of any of the outcomes by key student characteristics. This is especially critical for probation and recovery initiatives, given that students who find themselves on probation are overrepresented by racially minoritized, low-income, and first-generation groups. A failure to disaggregate outcomes along these dimensions, as well as others such as gender and ability, serves to erase the important information that could lead to improving the environment of success for these students and maintains the powerful forces of inequity that contribute to the persistence of these discrepancies in student success.

Using and Aligning Assessment Lenses to Define Success

Once objectives have been decided and outcomes measured, the question of interpretation of the results arises. What does the measure mean? What does it tell us about the effectiveness of the program? What does it tell us about student progress or learning? At the heart of all of these questions is "Have we been successful?" In this section, we present two viewpoints that assist in defining and interpreting successful activity in probation and recovery initiatives: employing lenses of assessment and aligning them with the type of initiative that is being assessed.

Lenses of Assessment

Data has been gathered, and it is time to understand and make sense of what it all means. Too often when assessment results are communicated, even when objectives and outcomes are clearly and carefully described and measured, momentum toward improvement is stalled as a result of disagreements over interpretation of the significance and implications of the findings. To assist in making sense of these results, Suskie (2004) outlined several perspectives or lenses (Friedman, 2012) that can be used to frame, define, and make meaning of assessment: (a) standards-based, (b) peer-referenced, (c) historical trends or longitudinal, and (d) value-added.

Standards-Based

The standards-based lens is concerned with how well students performed against a previously defined standard (Friedman, 2012; Suskie, 2004). These standards can have a local origin (are students meeting our own standards?) or an external standard (are students meeting standards set by another organization?). By its very nature, academic probation is a form of standards-based assessment because it is based on student performance against a predefined standard, such as maintaining a cumulative GPA higher than 2.0. When setting standards-based targets, it is ideal to express targets as percentages, not averages (Suskie, 2018). It is unlikely every student will be able to achieve the standard, but a high percentage creates a target that is challenging but also attainable. Finally, retention and persistence are standards-based measures of success, but these standards do not always allow educators to observe specific ways the learning has been effective.

Peer-Referenced

The peer-referenced lens compares the measured outcome to that of peers. This can happen internally, such as comparing a measure of a particular student's learning to a comparable group of students at the college or university (Suskie, 2004). Conversely, the results of assessment can be compared with those from external peer institutions. It is important that the comparator institution is similar enough in context to make the comparisons meaningful and interpretable. Many institutions have lists of peer and aspirant institutions. It might be unreasonable to use the aspirant institutions as a frame of reference, as they are likely to have meaningful differences in student profiles and resources. For recommendations on how to identify potential peer institutions, see Suskie (2004).

Historical Trend/Longitudinal

The historical trend or longitudinal lens allows institutions to answer the question, Is our program changing or improving over time? (Suskie, 2004). This can occur as programs look at changes in successive groups of students. To achieve this, educators compare current student outcomes against their peers from previous administrative cycles. It is important when evaluating historical trends to account for the changing context in which student progress is taking place and being measured. As a result, longitudinal assessment should contain as many points of data over time as are possible and practical and should be disaggregated to better understand the influence of changes in the environment and the composition of the student profile. This is particularly important when understanding academic probation: If the proportion of students on probation is decreasing, it is important to know how the academic and demographic profile of incoming students is changing before interpreting and claiming success of probation-prevention and student-success programs.

Value-Added

The value-added lens provides insight into whether students are improving because of participation in or exposure to probation or recovery initiatives (Friedman, 2012; Suskie, 2004). The benefits of the value-added lens are particularly relevant to academic recovery initiatives. Students who participate in academic recovery programs can demonstrate value-added outcomes in both procedural and learning domains. For example, an office can track the increase in the number of student-support services a student used (procedural) as well as gains in academic self-efficacy, comparing the levels before, during, and after academic recovery. However, Suskie (2004) recommended exercising caution in interpreting the improvement as a direct result of the intervention because it can occur as the result of a number of factors, including maturity, lessons learned from being put on probation, and any number of external sources of influence, such as family or influential members of the student's social network.

Aligning Assessment Lenses With Type of Probation and Recovery Initiative

These lenses of designing and interpreting assessment results are useful for framing evaluative activities for the multiple forms of academic probation and recovery programs. Table 6.1 provides examples of assessment approaches from each of the four lenses described by Suskie (2004), aligned with the five types of probation and recovery initiatives. It is important to note that the examples were constructed from the point of view of how to use assessment results to understand the effectiveness of the various probation and recovery initiatives. A variety of assessment approaches were included, including assessing procedural and learning outcomes, evaluating program effectiveness, and assessing the effectiveness of policy and procedure.

Table 6.1.

Example Approaches Using Various Assessment Lenses for Gathering Data and Assessing Student Probation and Academic Recovery Initiatives

	Student probation and academic recovery initiatives				
Lens of assessment	**Campuswide approaches to student success**	**Academic and curricular gateways**	**Probation-prevention initiatives**	**Policies and procedures defining probation and recovery**	**Academic recovery initiatives**
Standards-based	Counting the number of students who did not achieve a certain GPA or did not meet a threshold of credit hours earned	Measuring the percentage of sections of high-enrollment courses that have a predefined rate of students with grades of D/F/W	Measuring the per-centage of students in a particular cohort participating in a credit-completion program who have not earned the requisite number of credits	Review of policies describing proba-tion and recovery compared to profes-sional stan-dards from organiza-tions such as CAS or NACADA	Counting the num-ber of students who suc-cessfully achieve a grade of B or bet-ter in a recovery section of a first-year seminar
Peer-referenced	Comparing overall and disag-gregated student probation rates with peer and aspirant com-parison institutions	Comparing D/F/W rates across sections of gateway courses with historically high rates of student difficulty	Comparing messages sent from academic coaches at peer institutions to students who have triggered early alert to understand tone and focus of notifications	Analyzing academic probation and recovery policies from institutions with similar control, legal, and student enrollment environments	Comparing success rates for students moving from probation to good standing with other campuses' recovery programs that have similar features and student profiles

table continues on page 129

table continued from page 128

Lens of assessment	Student probation and academic recovery initiatives				
	Campuswide approaches to student success	Academic and curricular gateways	Probation-prevention initiatives	Policies and procedures defining probation and recovery	Academic recovery initiatives
Historical trend/ Longitudinal	Tracking long-term trend of student probation rates over time, disaggregated by student populations	The number of students over time who successfully complete gateway courses in an academic program	Examining student reflections and feedback over time on the effectiveness of academic coaching	An analysis of changes to interpretations and implementation of probationary procedures	Tracking the number and percentage of students who successfully complete a series of academic recovery coaching sessions for the past 5 years
Value-added	Measuring the incidence of higher-than-predicted retention, persistence, and graduation rates	Measuring gains in student confidence in material in gateway or notorious "weeder" courses using pre- and posttests	Comparing student engagement measures for students who participated in first-year academic advising initiative disaggregated by student demographics	Evaluating the impact on student persistence to graduation based on a change to the criteria for recovery to good academic standing	Measuring the extent to which students' academic commitment and sense of belonging have increased after participating in a recovery first-year seminar

Assessment as Organizational Learning: Collaboration in Interpretation and Implementation

Assessment of student learning does not by itself create increased student accomplishment or program effectiveness (Fulcher et al., 2014). In fact, evidence suggests that even among exemplars of "good assessment," very few institutions could document evidence of improved student learning (Baker et al., 2012; Banta & Blaich, 2011). For assessment and evaluation to improve effectiveness in higher education, colleges and universities must become learning organizations. Learning organizations define objectives for success, gather evidence about how well they are doing, and interpret evidence that leads to improved organizational action (Hussein et al., 2014). Assessment activities require institutions of higher education to constantly monitor the environment to improve their efforts and engage in organizational learning: creating, maintaining, and mobilizing knowledge or intelligence obtained by monitoring the organizational environment (Argyris & Schön, 1996; Kezar, 2005).

In this section, we offer two perspectives that will assist institutions in the organizational learning process, particularly as it relates to the interpretation of assessment results and the implementation of meaningful change. The first perspective is that the complexity of academic probation and recovery initiatives requires cross-functional collaboration. The second is the importance of involving students in the assessment process, particularly in the interpretation and implementation phases.

Complexity Requires Cross-Functional Collaboration

Again, we are back at the multifaceted, multiphased, and multilocational complexity represented in the responses designed to forestall and respond to academic probation. The connection between the complexity and assessment is perhaps most salient in the context of organizational learning. Banta and Kuh (1998) stated that "improving the quality of the undergraduate experience at any institution is so complex and multifaceted that it demands cooperation" (p. 42) among the multiple stakeholders on campus, including faculty members, student-affairs professionals, administrators, and students themselves (see also Young & Keup, 2019). Because probation does not come as a result of a single factor, the solutions that should become available to students must come from a collaborative approach, which means that the assessment and institutional meaning-making from assessment of students on probation must take place in a cross-functional manner in collaboration with or as part of student-success structures on campus, such as first-year experience, early alert, student well-being, or even behavioral intervention teams. The Council for the Advancement of Standards in Higher Education (CAS) has created a series of cross-functional frameworks that include standards for the structure, communication, operations, and assessment of these teams. These frameworks span organizational boundaries for student health and well-being, identification and response to behavior concerns, and the first-year experience. The standards and principles contained in the CAS cross-functional frameworks are all relevant to probation and academic recovery, as they represent different approaches to supporting some aspect of student probation.

Interpretation and implementation of assessment results and changes are improved and more effective when done as a collaborative process involving multiple departments and "integrated across multiple settings" (Suskie, 2018, p. 22). However, the multifaceted and multilocational aspects of academic probation and recovery initiatives mean that stakeholders will bring with them multiple perspectives and expectations of the assessment process (Jankowski et al., 2012; Suskie, 2018; Volkwein, 2010). It is important to keep in mind that different people need different information to inform different decisions (Suskie, 2018), and no one report, database, or website will meet the diverse needs of everyone (Jankowski et al., 2012). However, working together to identify priorities, sharing resources, distributing ownership, and communicating results and successes can result in more successful and effective collaborative approaches to interpreting and widescale implementation of institutional change.

Importance of Involving Students in the Assessment Process

It is easy to think of all the stakeholders on campus, such as faculty, staff, and administrators who have an interest in the success of academic probation and recovery initiatives without considering students. If assessment is organizational learning, educators should involve students in assessment as part of a learning-centered paradigm in which students are actively engaged in their learning and responsibility for the learning and the success of the programs that support it is shared among faculty and students (Weimer, 2013). Therefore, it is important to involve students in the design, interpretation, and implementation of the assessment process, especially students who have successfully participated in academic recovery.

Having a student who has successfully moved away from being on academic probation as a part of the assessment process provides a valuable voice in the development of goals and planning. Moreover, having at the table educators and students who can speak to the unique needs of academically at-risk students not only helps in planning assessment but also ensures the accurate use of results. This is useful in sharing the successes of academic recovery programs with students who are on probation and can be a clear way to signal that academic probation and recovery are not primarily punitive in nature, but developmental. When students are involved as stakeholders in the assessment process, the overall approach to improving student success on campus is more authentically connected to issues and barriers students face and enlightens paths to support and engender trust among students for the institution, particularly at a vulnerable time when trust in the institution might be low (Swing & Ross, 2016; Tschepikow, 2012).

Conclusion

In this chapter, we discuss ways to employ assessment as an effective practice to address the needs and future success of students on academic probation. Suskie (2018) indicated that successful assessment of student learning is accomplished through establishing learning goals, providing learning opportunities, assessing student learning, and using the results. When assessment is designed and performed effectively, at-risk students have more opportunity for success. Having a clear understanding of the unique needs of students on academic probation and establishing efforts to collaborate with others in addressing their needs is critical.

Establishing standards for success using multiple lenses is especially important, given the complex collection of stakeholders on campus who all create conditions that contribute to academic probation and recovery. Moreover, the discussion of how to assess these multifaceted, multiphased, and multilocational approaches to supporting academic recovery sheds light on important considerations for measuring student success and the ways, either wittingly or not, the initiatives, programs, and policies affect the students on probation, who are at the center of these activities.

The issue at play with students on probation is satisfactory academic progress, usually measured by the average number of grade points per (graded) credit earned, or GPA. Thus, academic probation and its signals are, at their core, part of an assessment process. They start with an objective, set a standard for that objective, use a measurement against the objective to signal an interpretation, and, in the best scenarios, lead to some sort of meaningful change toward improvement. However, multiple stakeholders are part of this assessment cycle – and the system is not a closed one. Academic committees and faculty set the standard, and individual faculty members measure and assign grades based on student performance in class. Furthermore, the signal of academic probation is received by multiple actors in the system, such as students, student-success centers, academic advisors, early-alert staff, academic departmental staff, maybe even student-affairs staff in such places as the residence halls and the career center. The organizational learning required to make meaningful change is centered on the student, who becomes the major stakeholder in this cycle. In fact, the institution's success in this example is contingent on the success of the student, who may have internalized the message communicated by the low grade (likely collection of grades) as a signal that they are unfit for the academic community and its practices.

It is incumbent on higher-education professionals who are responsible for the organizational learning and improvement of student success to engage in organizational learning that centers the responsibility for creating conditions for student success on the institution and institutional actors. Students are not absolved from their responsibility to put forth effort to learn and grow and meet academic standards, but their role shifts from being acted upon to having agency in their education. Such a shift is particularly important for students who have been historically marginalized in higher education, including racially minoritized, first-generation, and low-income students, who are more likely than others to find themselves on probation. Assessment and evaluation of academic probation and recovery initiatives thus have a role to play in creating environments that are either more inclusive and equitable or continue to disadvantage. With these guiding principles, we are more likely to ensure student success.

References

Argyris, C., & Schön, D. (1996). *Organizational learning II: Theory, method, and practice.* Addison-Wesley.

Baker, G. R., Jankowski, N., Provezis, S. & Kinzie, J. (2012). *Using assessment results: Promising practices of institutions that do it well.* University of Illinois and Indiana University, National Institute for Learning Outcomes Assessment.

Banta, T. W., & Blaich, C. (2011). Closing the assessment loop. *Change: The Magazine for Higher Learning, 43*(1), 22–27.

Banta, T. W., & Kuh, G. D. (1998). A missing link in assessment: Collaboration between academic and student-affairs professionals. *Change: The Magazine of Higher Learning, 30*(2), 40–46.

Banta, T. W., & Palomba, C. A. (2015). *Assessment essentials: Planning, implementing, and improving assessment in higher education.* Jossey-Bass.

Boyce, M. E. (2003). Organizational learning is essential to achieving and sustaining change in higher education. *Innovative Higher Education, 28*(2), 119–136.

Bresciani, M. J., Gardner, M. M., & Hickmott, J. (2009). *Demonstrating student success: A practical guide to outcomes-based assessment of learning and development in student affairs.* Stylus Publishing.

Friedman, D. B. (2012). *Assessing the first-year seminar.* University of South Carolina, National Resource Center for The First-Year Experience and Students in Transition.

Fulcher, K. H., Good, M. R., Coleman, C. M., & Smith, K. L. (2014, December). *A simple model for learning improvement: Weigh pig, feed pig, weigh pig* (Occasional Paper No. 23). University of Illinois and Indiana University, National Institute for Learning Outcomes Assessment.

Greenfield, G. M., Keup, J. R., & Gardner, J. N. (2013). *Developing and sustaining successful first-year programs: A guide for practitioners.* Jossey-Bass.

Hussein, N., Mohamad, A., Noordin, F., & Ishak, N. A. (2014). Learning organization and its effect on organizational performance and organizational innovativeness: A proposed framework for Malaysian public institutions of higher education. *Procedia – Social and Behavioral Sciences, 130,* 299–304.

Hutchings, P. (2016). *Aligning educational outcomes and practices.* (Occasional paper #26). University of Illinois and Indiana University, National Institute for Learning Outcomes Assessment.

Jankowski, N. A., Ikenberry, S. O., Kinzie, J., Kuh, G. D. Shenoy, G. F., & Baker, G. R. (2012, March). *Transparency & accountability: An evaluation of the VSA College Portrait pilot.* University of Illinois and Indiana University, National Institute for Learning Outcomes Assessment.

Jankowski, N. A., Timmer, J. D. Kinzie, J., & Kuh, G. D. (2018). *Assessment that matters: Trending toward practices that document authentic student learning.* University of Illinois and Indiana University, National Institute for Learning Outcomes Assessment.

Kezar, A. J. (2005). What do we mean by "learning" in the context of higher education? In A. J. Kezar (Ed.), *New Directions for Higher Education: No. 131. Organizational learning in higher education* (pp. 49–59). Jossey-Bass.

Kuh, G. D., Kinzie, J., Schuh, J. H., Whitt, E. J., and Associates (2010). *Student success in college: Creating conditions that matter.* Jossey-Bass.

Maki, P. L. (2004). *Assessing for learning: Building a sustainable commitment across the institution.* Stylus Publishing.

Schreiner, L. A. (Ed.). (2018). *Sophomore success: Making the most of the second year* [New Directions for Higher Education, No. 183]. Wiley.

Suskie, L. (2004). *Assessing student learning: a common sense guide.* Bolton, Mass., Anker Pub. Co.

Suskie, L. (2018). *Assessing student learning: A common sense guide.* Jossey-Bass.

Swing, R. L., & Ross, L. E. (2016). *Statement of aspirational practice for institutional research.* Association for Institutional Research. https://www.airweb.org/ir-data-professional-overview/a-statement-of-aspirational-practice-for-institutional-research

Tschepikow, W. K. (2012). Why don't our students respond? Understanding declining participation in survey research among college students. *Journal of Student Affairs Research and Practice, 49*(4), 447–462.

Versalle, G. L. (2018). *Understanding the experiences of students re-admitted after academic suspension as part of a university-initiated process: A qualitative study* [Doctoral dissertation, Western Michigan University]. ScholarWorks. https://scholarworks.wmich.edu/dissertations/3357

Volkwein, J. F. (2010). A model for assessing institutional effectiveness. In J. F. Volkwein (Ed.), *New directions for institutional research: No. 51. Assessing student outcomes* (pp. 13–28). Jossey-Bass.

Weimer, M. (2013). *Learner-center teaching: Five key changes to practice.* Jossey-Bass.

Young, D. G. (2018). Outcomes assessment and sophomore programs: How assessment as organizational learning can improve institutional integrity. *New Directions for Higher Education, 2018*(183), 47–57.

Young, D. G., & Keup, J. R. (2019). *CAS cross-functional framework for first-year experiences.* Council for the Advancement of Standards in Higher Education.

CASE STUDIES

To this point in this book, the authors have dedicated significant space to exploration of various policies and programs as they relate to students on probation. Chapters have blended author experiences as experts in their topical areas with theoretical grounding and short institutional examples to provide as much depth and breadth to each topic as is possible. We turn now to two longer institutional vignettes designed to provide a holistic and detailed overview of what effective support for students on probation can resemble.

Case Study 1, an example of institutional change at Cabrini University, highlights the importance of institutional willingness to shine a light inward, reflect critically, and embrace change to improve the experience of students on probation. This case study focuses attention on how the Center for Student Success at Cabrini University serves its most academically at-risk students who return to the university for a second semester with the intent to achieve good academic standing. Gebauer, DeRosa, Carney-Jones, and Boyd highlight an organizational restructure with the goal of better supporting students on academic probation through professional, intrusive advising. Through required meetings with a probationary counselor, Cabrini University has seen demonstrable gains in retention of its students on probation. The model presented at Cabrini University demonstrates the importance of institutional willingness to critically reflect and engage in change processes. The example highlights institutional policy, advising, and academic coaching. The authors discuss, in detail, how the conditional academic probation model at Cabrini University is structured to motivate rather than discourage students to get back "on track" and overcome their previous academic struggles. This example highlights the significance of institutional willingness to engage in the change process.

Case Study 2 examines the academic recovery section of the nationally recognized first-year seminar at the University of South Carolina, University 101 (UNIV 101). This special section of the course, offered as a supplement to institutional requirements for first-year students on probation, shares the learning outcomes of any general section of UNIV 101. However, this section is designed with students on probation in mind. Rea describes the theoretical perspectives that inform the design and facilitation of the course. While serving only a small population of students who opt into the experience, the course has proven successful at helping students in academic recovery to find their footing at the university.

Both models highlight the need to use psychologically attuned language (Waltenbury et al., 2018) when reaching out to students on probation. They also highlight the benefit students experience as a result of developing trusting relationships with a caring student-support professional (Arcand & Leblanc, 2011).

Discussion Questions

The hope is that these case studies provide examples and shine a detailed light on effective institutional practice in supporting students on probation. As you read the case studies and reflect on academic recovery policies and practices on your own campus, consider the following:

1. Does the institution collect and analyze data about the academic recovery process? If not, how would such a process begin? What data would be pertinent to access?

2. What stakeholder(s) on campus possess oversight of the academic recovery process? Does oversight fall to academic affairs, the faculty, student affairs, or some other person or group? How are data-driven changes implemented to the existing academic recovery process?

3. Are the staff resources (human capital) available and appropriate to mandate probation support meetings? If not, how might resources be prioritized?

4. Does the current academic recovery process include a partnership with academic and/or student life units to leverage support for the program?

5. How is the success of the academic recovery program evaluated? What does this program define as success?

Case Study 1
Cabrini University: Augmenting Academic Recovery Practices to Amplify First-Year Student Success

Richie Gebauer, Shana DeRosa, Julie Carney-Jones, and Kimberly L. Boyd

Institutional Profile

Cabrini University is a small, Catholic, liberal arts institution located in Radnor, Pennsylvania. This private four-year university is dedicated to academic excellence, leadership development, and social justice. The undergraduate student body is composed of approximately 1,450 students, with 441 first-time, first-year students enrolling in Fall 2018. For this cohort, the average high school GPA was 2.85 and the average SAT combined score was 1009 (as an SAT optional institution, only 47.8% submitted SAT scores). Gender distribution of Cabrini's student population is 33% male and 67% female. Of those reporting racial or ethnic makeup, 48.7% of students identify as White, 28.2% as Black or African American, 15.5% as Hispanic or Latino, 3.5% as bi- or multiracial, and 4.0% as other. Based on academic, social, and financial prematriculation data gathered via retention software, 40.9% of the cohort is classified as high or very high retention risk.

Academic Recovery Initiative

Supporting first-year students on academic probation is a complex process that challenges higher-education professionals to set a performance standard that either serves as a motivator to students to improve their academic performance or dissuades students from returning to the institution to climb the hill that lies ahead (Bénabou & Tirole, 2000). Prior to the 2017–2018 academic year, Cabrini University was unintentionally promoting the latter. Cabrini University recognized that each institution has the responsibility to examine and evaluate the conditions in place to promote student success and that, at times, structures, policies, and practices contribute to student failure (Mehaffy, 2017). Therefore, the university's Office of Academic Advising sought to identify inefficiencies in its academic recovery initiative to establish clear pathways to academic success.

This investigation of inefficiencies was driven by a shift in university admissions strategies that resulted in enrollment of undergraduate students with more varied levels of academic preparedness. It is important to note, when reviewing institutional pre-enrollment data at this institution, that there is a direct correlation between academic underpreparedness and race/ethnicity. Immediately following the shift, the University observed an increase in the percentage of first-year students failing to achieve good academic standing, as defined by achieving minimum term and cumulative GPAs. A further evaluation of the data suggested that a disproportionately high percentage of underrepresented minority students failed to achieve good academic standing. When these students were dismissed from the university with the opportunity to appeal their dismissal and return to campus, a low percentage actually followed through with an appeal. Therefore, Academic Affairs evaluated the effectiveness of the academic support policies and structures in place to serve these students and then modified them, introducing a new academic recovery model. The objective of such efforts was to compare the impact of the previous and modified probationary support programs on student success and retention.

A review of the previous academic recovery process, designed for students who completed the fall semester with a cumulative GPA below 1.0, revealed that language used in an academic dismissal letter to these students (see Figure CS1.1) deterred the students from returning. Though students were informed they were academically dismissed and had the right to appeal, most students stopped reading before becoming aware that appealing the decision was an option. A review of the literature underscores the fact that academically at-risk learners at both two- and four-year institutions are less likely to persist before they find themselves on academic probation (Bulger & Watson, 2006). As such, reading language that informs them of their academic dismissal was a possible reason that a high percentage of underrepresented minority students did not appeal. The university replaced the academic dismissal letter and has since shifted its language in the current conditional probation letter (see Figure CS1.2) to invite students back to the institution on conditional academic probation rather than to dismiss and require them to appeal to return.

Academic dismissal letters sent from Academic Affairs prior to the transition to a conditional probation model were curt and direct, with the opening paragraphs stating

> Your grade report from the (Semester/Year) semester warrants this notice of Academic Dismissal from Cabrini College. Please consult your *Undergraduate Catalog* at www. cabrini.edu/catalog for the regulations which govern Academic Probation and Dismissal. If you believe that there were extenuating circumstances that accounted for your poor performance this past semester you may appeal this dismissal. All such appeals must be made in writing by (date).

Figure CS1.1. Excerpt from Academic Dismissal Letter.

Conditional probation letters expressed empathy, eliminating the use of the terms "dismissal" and "appeal" and shifting to the use of terms "conditional probation" and "action plan." The shift in language in this letter resulted in the following:

> A review of your academic transcript in (Semester/Year) shows that you have not met the University's minimum academic grade point average requirements. This warrants notice of **Conditional Probation** at Cabrini University. Please consult your *Undergraduate Catalog* at www.cabrini.edu/catalog for the regulations which govern Academic Warning, Probation and Dismissal. When you applied to Cabrini, your past academic performance showed us you had the potential to be successful in college. We believe that you can be and that you deserve another chance to improve your grades and achieve your goal of earning a college degree. We recognize there may have been circumstances that accounted for your poor academic performance this past semester and that your grades may not demonstrate your abilities or level of commitment to your educational goals. For that reason, we are giving you an opportunity return to Cabrini University next semester.

Figure CS1.2. Excerpt from Conditional Probation Letter.

Language, however, was only one of a multitude of shortcomings hindering student success in the programmatic layout of the academic probation process. An examination of the process indicated that it contained elements that were inconsistent in execution and that accountability was an issue. For example, full-time staff from other areas of the university, rather than trained probationary counselors, were volunteering as probationary counselors. Although some students were being empowered through the process, the student response was dependent on the person assigned to work with the probationary student and the availability of that voluntary, probationary counselor to promote accountability and responsibility.

Kamphoff, Hutson, Amundsen, and Atwood (2007) argued that students on academic probation need ongoing interactions with either faculty or professional staff outside of the classroom to increase their sense of belonging and connection to campus, improve their levels of motivation, and maximize their academic potential. It is true that students must be active participants in their learning environment; however, the learning environment must also actively encourage this participation (Astin, 1984). This encouragement was absent from the academic recovery model that existed at the university prior to 2017, and student success and student retention faltered.

In August 2017, the Department of Academic Advising was established to support retention efforts. This unit brought in two new hires in the roles of director and assistant director/professional advisor. These new staff members worked alongside two additional professional advisors who had many years of experience serving students in academic recovery at the university. The new team worked together to execute the introduction of the conditional probation academic recovery model, which was designed to be holistic and intrusive.

To ensure this intrusive support is embedded in the recovery model, students returning for the spring semester of their first year are required to meet with a probationary counselor during the interim period prior to the start of the spring semester. This initial meeting is designed to establish a mutually agreed-upon action plan, in the form of a conditional probation agreement (see Figure CS1.3), with students facing conditional academic probation status. This action plan includes but is not limited to recurring meetings with the probationary counselor throughout the semester, a series of academic workshops (e.g., study skills, resilience and growth mindset, time management and procrastination, student professionalism) to address the specific needs of the student, and the creation of a manageable course schedule not exceeding 12 academic credits while mandating student attendance.

Academic Conditional Probation Agreement:
Commitment to Action for Improvement Plan

Name_____ Cabrini ID_____ Semester: _____

1. I understand that I have been placed on conditional academic probation because I have not met the University's minimum academic grade point average requirements. I am aware of the following stipulations pursuant to my commitment to return to academic good standing:

    a. In order to be removed from academic probation and return to academic good standing, I will need to earn a **minimum _____cumulative GPA** based on the courses I have selected today. In order to achieve this cumulative GPA, I will need to earn a **minimum _____ term GPA** at the end of this semester.

    b. I understand that if I fail to return to academic good standing, the Academic Review Board will review my progress and   completion of probationary requirements. Based on that review, I will either be dismissed from the University or permitted to return.

    c. I understand that I must remain in good academic standing for the duration of enrollment following this probationary semester at Cabrini and **failure to do so will result in permanent dismissal from the University without the opportunity to appeal**.

    d. I understand that in order to graduate from Cabrini University, I must have a cumulative GPA of 2.0 or higher, and I must meet the minimum major course GPA requirement determined by my academic department.

2. I understand that I am **required to meet with my assigned probationary counselor a minimum of four times** during this semester to review and evaluate my progress, including a midterm grade evaluation meeting. My probationary counselor may contact my faculty at any time during the semester to review grades, attendance, behavior and participation in my classes. My counselor will also review my midterm grade report and warning notices. I also understand that I am **required to meet with my academic advisor before the end of the drop/add period** to discuss my schedule and my commitment to improving my academic performance to successfully graduate with my intended major.

Figure CS1.3 continues on page 141

Figure CS1.3 continued from page 140

3. I understand that I **may not be enrolled in more than 12 academic credits** this semester and that I may not change the academic schedule set during today's meeting without the express permission of the Director of Academic Advising, Assistant Dean for Student Success, or Associate Dean for Retention and Student Success. Additionally, I must **complete all of the classes on my schedule** and will not be permitted to withdraw from any classes, as a withdrawal from any courses will make it more difficult to achieve the required cumulative GPA.

4. I understand that regularly attending and participating in classes will improve my academic performance and that **attendance in all classes is mandatory, including face-to-face, hybrid, and online classes**. I understand that at any time, my probationary counselor can consult with my professors to verify my attendance.

5. I understand that I am **required to attend a minimum of three academic workshops** during the semester as part of this success plan.

6. I have been provided the Making Satisfactory Academic Progress (SAP) handout and understand that this document outlines the necessary criteria to achieve good financial aid standing. I understand that these measures are determined by the Financial Aid Office and are separate from the academic review that will be conducted by the Academic Review Board at the end of this semester to evaluate my progress towards achieving academic good standing. I understand that I am **required to meet with a financial aid counselor before the start of the semester** to review my progress in meeting financial aid satisfactory academic progress criteria that will determine my financial aid eligibility for this semester and following semesters.

7. I have been made aware of the free academic support programs and services that the Center for Student Success (CSS) provides undergraduate students. I understand that using the resources offered by the CSS will reflect my commitment to improving my academic performance and will be positively received by the Academic Review Board during my assessment at the end of the semester.

8. I understand that if I fail to meet any of the mandatory requirements listed above and set forth in today's meeting, I **may be subject to immediate dismissal from the University**. I will be responsible for paying all tuition, fees, room and board charges as noted in the Undergraduate Catalog. I understand that if I am dismissed before the end of the semester, I may lose financial aid, in accordance with Federal, State, and Cabrini regulations regarding aid.

I understand that returning to academic good standing is my goal and that working with my probationary counselor this semester is the University's commitment to helping me achieve my goals. Choosing to make positive changes and demonstrating these changes through action will help improve my GPA and will positively impact the Academic Review Board's assessment of the progress I make this term. This document is evidence of my commitment to take positive steps toward academic improvement.

Signature of Student_____Date_____

CSS Representative_____Date_____

Figure CS1.3 continues on page 142

Figure CS1.3 continued from page 141

> ***Optional:*** I am giving permission for the Center for Student Success (CSS) to contact my parent/guardian to discuss my progress toward achieving academic good standing.
>
> Signature of Student_____Date_____
>
> If you authorize the CSS to contact your parent/guardian, please provide the name and contact information for your parent/guardian in the space below:
>
> _____
>
> _____
>
> _____

Figure CS1.3. Academic Conditional Probation Agreement: Commitment to Action for Improvement Plan

The purpose of the initial conditional probation meeting is strategic in nature, designed to craft a course schedule that will help each student improve their overall GPA while continuing to align with their major goal(s). Often, this schedule requires a student to repeat courses. Additionally, a semester GPA is calculated to give each student a personalized GPA goal they must achieve to get back into good academic standing, referred to as satisfactory academic progress (SAP). The first meeting takes upwards of 60 to 90 minutes to flesh out the conditional probation agreement, make changes to the spring schedule, and review SAP guidelines. The next step is the probationary counselor walking the student to the Office of Financial Aid to make sure all parties understand financial and academic SAP guidelines. Upon completion of the meeting, students walk away with a folder that contains their new schedule, a copy of their probation agreement, and plans for recurring meetings with their probationary counselor during the spring semester.

Once the semester begins, the probationary counselor provides students on conditional academic probation with a weekly attendance tracker for each course. The tracker requires that the instructor sign or initial a form to verify the student's attendance. This procedure assists probationary counselors in evaluating whether or not students are following through on their conditional probation agreement. It's important to note that this attendance tracker is used for purposes that exist beyond academics, particularly to track attendance for student athletes. As a result, requiring students engaging in academic recovery to use a weekly attendance tracker does not reveal to faculty that they are on conditional probation, thus eliminating the potential for faculty bias. In an effort to hold students accountable, the probationary counselor periodically reaches out to the student's faculty throughout the semester to solicit a progress update on the student's academic performance, which includes an additional request for feedback on the student's attendance record.

Although these efforts are each important, the intentionality of the recurring meetings with the probationary counselor (three to four meetings per semester) are most critical. These meetings focus attention on recognizing the student's overt and covert needs and advancing the student forward. Using a strengths-based advising model (Schreiner, 2013), the conditional academic probation program at Cabrini University is structured to motivate rather than discourage students to get back "on track" and to identify, affirm, and apply their strengths to overcome their previous academic struggles.

The first official meeting between student and probationary counselor in the spring is spent reflecting upon the fall semester. The goal is to identify patterns and mistakes that were made and determine what changes each student should consider as they begin a new term. The probationary counselor's purpose is to develop a relationship and rapport with each student and to develop trust so that honest conversations will occur as the semester progresses. Ultimately, the probationary counselor is tasked with making a student aware of behavior discrepancies while encouraging students to change their approach in how they manage time and study and/or how they deal with outside forces that typically affect their best effort. This extensive first meeting sets the foundation for the other mandated meetings that occur within the 15-week term. Anecdotally, it appears that when students are open to change and make a concerted effort to fully engage in their education, improvement in spring courses is notable. It may not be possible to save all students, but this approach to academic probation has led to significant increases in student preparedness and students' transition to improved academic standing.

For situations in which students display a gross lack of compliance with the expectations set forth in the conditional probation agreement, probationary counselors communicate concerns to the dean of academic affairs, who oversees the academic review process. The dean consults with the student's probationary counselor and faculty members to determine the likelihood of the student's academic success and return to good standing by the end of the semester. The dean then meets with the student to reiterate expectations, review the conditional probation agreement, and provide a formal warning that continued failure to meet those expectations may result in dismissal. An additional two-week probationary period is provided for the student to demonstrate positive progress toward achieving their academic goals. Failure to do so generally results in immediate midterm dismissal. While seemingly a harsh penalty, the student receives "withdrawal" grades on their academic transcript for the semester, which is ultimately less damaging to their academic record and GPA than additional failing grades.

Assessment Methods and Design

Academic data were evaluated for all full-time, first-year undergraduate students matriculating between academic years 2014–2015 and 2018–2019. From this population,

188 students met the criteria to be considered for conditional probation, 104 engaged in the previous model prior to the implementation of the modified support initiatives in 2017–2018 and 84 students engaged in the current model. Enrollment, term and cumulative GPA, percentage of credits earned versus attempted, retention to sophomore year, and participation in and completion of probationary support measures were monitored for all 188 students. In the current model, success action plans submitted by students and advising notes from probationary counselors were also reviewed.

Assessment Findings

In a two-year timeframe, the introduction and evolution of the new academic recovery model resulted in a 25.8% increase in retention of conditional probation students, from 14.7% to 40.5%, due in large part to the advising team's commitment to holistic and intrusive support. Although retention is important, it communicates only one part of the story. Evaluating the process of inviting students back to the university on conditional academic probation rather than dismissing them with the right to an appeal revealed that 89% of students eligible for conditional academic probation (two years of aggregate data when evaluating the new recovery process) returned to the University compared to 64% of students who accepted the invitation to appeal their dismissal (three years of aggregate data when evaluating the previous recovery process). This 25% increase of students returning to campus allows the university to live out its mission to provide an "education of the heart" that includes personal coaching as a powerful intervention to encourage students to commit and connect to college (Dalton & Crosby, 2014).

An investigation of the data specific to these two distinct recovery models highlights the value of the mutual relationship, built on trust, between student and probationary counselor (Arcand & Leblanc, 2011; McKeown & Diboll, 2011) in the new conditional probation academic recovery model. One-on-one conversations across the scaffolded professional advising meetings revealed that students who made firm commitments to the holistic academic coaching sessions and academic skills workshops exhibited a greater sense of self-awareness and self-discipline by the conclusion of the semester. Other data confirm a definitive correlation between student engagement with the academic recovery process and improved academic performance and return to good academic standing. Prior to this new recovery model, only 63.6% of students on academic probation improved their GPA from first term to second term. As a result of this new model, 82.6% of students on conditional probation improved their GPA from fall term to spring term. An increase in the number of students transitioning back into good academic standing also increased from 18.7% to 42.5%.

Not only were more students improving their spring GPA in comparison to their fall GPA and achieving good academic standing but they were also increasing the number of credits completed from fall to spring term. Students engaged in the previous recovery model successfully completed only 44% of attempted credits in the spring, whereas the implementation of the conditional probation academic recovery model led to students successfully completing 62.5% of their attempted credits. This change may be attributed to limiting student schedules to 12 credits, ensuring that students have a manageable course load so that they are able to effectively meet the demands of full-time study and apply the techniques presented in the coaching sessions and workshops. Almost 40 years ago, Russell (1981) recommended that a maximum course load for students on academic probation should reflect the minimum for full-time student status because a higher grade-point improvement will occur for a student who earns fewer but higher grades, rather than more average grades. This recommendation is even more pertinent given the current academic landscape in which enrollment shifts have led to more academically underprepared students being admitted to small, private colleges and universities, and the data at Cabrini University accurately reflect this.

At the conclusion of the spring semester, probationary counselors reported that students who adhered to the conditional probation agreement agreed upon at the start of the academic term developed a greater sense of self-esteem and self-confidence in their academic abilities as measured through the dialogue that occurred across monthly meetings. These students observed, first-hand, how a strong work ethic in conjunction with making positive changes to improve study habits correlated with improved academic performance. This confidence increased their self-awareness and led to a newfound motivation that will hopefully carry over to the following semester as students continue to advance their academic progress.

Anecdotal evidence suggests other underlying reasons for the success of the new academic recovery model. For instance, the majority of the students who succeeded in returning to good academic standing seemed to benefit the most from learning how to improve their organizational skills and better manage their time. Kamphoff, Hutson, Amundsen, and Atwood (2007) argued that "students who are able to manage themselves and continuously plan and monitor their behaviors in pursuit of their goals are implementing self-management" (p. 402), and as a result they make better use of their time. As such, this topic was reported as frequently discussed within coaching sessions. When students committed to the process, counselors noted that students developed greater resilience, learning how to address challenges responsibly by adopting a proactive rather than a reactive mindset. In particular, students learned how to make proper use of the support services on campus, such as the Writing Center, Math Resource Center, subject-area peer tutoring, and if eligible, the academic accommodations provided by the Disability Resource Center. They also learned how to interact professionally with faculty, and, most important, how to ask for help when needed. In another example, increased academic outcomes appear to be a result of enhanced levels of maturity. With the guidance of their probationary counselor, students learned to recognize the gaps in their study habits and identify specific areas for improvement. This change required a willingness on the part of the students to display a sense of vulnerability by discussing limitations with their probationary counselors as well as an openness to receive constructive criticism and feedback. The latter is critical in this process, with students reflecting on setbacks as opportunities for personal growth rather than exhibiting a reluctance to accept criticism (Perez, 2015).

At the completion of the Fall 2018 semester, 9.8% of students who did not achieve good academic standing qualified for conditional probation, which reaffirmed the institution's decision to alter its academic recovery model. When reviewing the data that has emerged from the revision of the academic recovery process, it is evident that engagement in the process results in an increase in student GPA, an increase in the number of successfully completed credits, and more students achieving good academic standing by the conclusion of their second semester in comparison to the previous academic recovery model.

Implications for Future Practice

As college enrollment continues to decline (National Student Clearinghouse Research Center, 2019), small private institutions like Cabrini University must recognize that more academically underprepared students will enter our classrooms with high levels of self-doubt. Even before arriving on campus, despite having been admitted to college, these students are likely already feeling impostor syndrome and questioning whether they belong. As a result, many of these students will fail before they succeed. Despite this reality, institutions should prioritize proactive student success initiatives in the first semester and first year that are designed to engage students in curricular and cocurricular settings in an effort to decrease the percentage of students who find themselves on academic probation.

At Cabrini University, students who are evaluated as academically underprepared based on pre-enrollment data are first introduced to professional advisors during the university's summer orientation program. Each incoming student receives a personalized schedule, and academically underprepared students participate in onboarding sessions focused on preparing for the academic expectations and realities of college-level coursework. Once on campus, the foundational piece of the first-year experience is the institution's Learning Community (LC) program. Incoming academically underprepared students are enrolled in LCs comprising 12 to 14 students led by a team of two or three faculty members who intentionally pair and integrate remedial with content-level coursework. These LCs, which specifically enroll academically underprepared students, are built into the fabric and culture of the university, each existing with its own identity. The curricular design of each LC is then supplemented by cocurriculum that extends learning beyond the classroom while building community among the students, their peers, and their LC faculty. However, despite these proactive interventions, some students still struggle academically and land on academic probation. This is why it is of the utmost importance that a strengths-based model (Schreiner, 2013) be established to assist students in overcoming academic failure(s).

To truly engage in the academic recovery process, students must identify personal meaning and passion for engaging in the academic expectations of college. This will serve as the motivation to overcome the hurdles they encounter. Establishing an academic recovery process that embraces a student's return to campus and mandates ongoing dialogue designed not only to identify self-defeating patterns but to unleash student potential is critical. A continuous promotion of optimism can lead to long-term success. As shifts in enrollment occur and more underprepared students are admitted at four-year institutions, colleges and universities have the responsibility and must make it a priority to adapt services to retain these students. This is exactly why a redesign of the academic recovery model was pertinent at Cabrini University to enhance student learning, development, and success.

References

Arcand, I., & Leblanc, R. N. (2011). Academic probation and companioning: Three perspectives on experience and support. *Mevlana International Journal of Education, 1*(2), 1–14.

Astin, A. W. (1984). Student involvement: A developmental theory for higher education. *Journal of College Student Personnel, 25*, 297–308.

Bénabou, R., & Tirole, J. (2000). *Self-confidence and social interactions.* (NBER Working Paper W7585). National Bureau of Economic Research. https://www.nber.org/system/files/working_papers/w7585/w7585.pdf

Bulger, S., & Watson, D. (2006). Broadening the definition of at-risk students. *The Community College Enterprise, 12*(2), 23–32.

Dalton, J. C., & Crosby, P. C. (2014). The power of personal coaching: Helping first-year students to connect and commit in college. *Journal of College and Character, 15*(2), 59–66.

Kamphoff, C., Hutson, B., Amundsen, S., & Atwood, J. (2007). A motivational/empowerment model applied to students on academic probation. *Journal of College Student Retention: Research, Theory & Practice, 8*(4), 397–412.

McKeown, J., & Diboll, M. (2011). Critical friendship in international education reform: Journey to educational cultural convergence. *Mevlana International Journal of Education, 1*(2), 15–26.

Mehaffy, G. (2017, February 3). *Key themes, practices, emerge in re-imagining first year of college.* Strada Education Network. https://www.stradaeducation.org/measuring-the-value-of-education/key-themes-practices-emerge-in-re-imagining-first-year-of-college/

National Student Clearinghouse Research Center. (2019, May 30). *Current term enrollment Spring 2019.* https://nscresearchcenter.org/currenttermenrollmentestimate-spring2019/

Russell, J. E. (1981). Problem areas for the student on probation: The role of the academic advisor. *NACADA Journal, 1*(2), 56–58.

Schreiner, L. A. (2013). Strengths-based advising. In J. K. Drake, P. Jordan, & M. A. Miller (Eds.), *Academic advising approaches: Strategies that teach students to make the most of college* (pp. 105–120). Jossey-Bass and the National Academic Advising Association.

Case Study 2
University of South Carolina:
UNIV 101 Academic Recovery

Mikaela Rea

Institutional Profile

The University of South Carolina is a four-year public institution located in Columbia, South Carolina. As of Fall 2019, the residential campus has approximately 26,700 undergraduate students. Of those undergraduate students, approximately 77% identify as White and 10% identify as African American. Of the remaining undergraduate students, 4% identify as Hispanic, 2.3% identify as Asian, and less than 1% identify as Native American or Pacific Islander. Approximately 3% identify as two or more races, and approximately 1% identify as a nonresident alien. Female students account for 53% of the undergraduate student population, and 44% of undergraduate students come from out of state.

At the University of South Carolina, academic probation is defined as "both an academic standing as well as recovery process for students whose cumulative UofSC GPA is below a 2.00" (University of South Carolina, n.d.) At the end of the Fall 2019 semester, approximately 3% of first-year students received a letter at their permanent address informing them that they were being included in the academic probation process.

Description of Academic Recovery Initiative

All first-year students on academic probation at the University of South Carolina are required to attend at least one appointment with an academic coach at the in the University Advising Center. Each spring, a supplementary Academic Recovery section of the first-year seminar, UNIV 101, is offered to students who were placed on academic probation after their first semester or who wish to retake UNIV 101 for grade forgiveness (available to students receiving a grade lower than C). Like any section of UNIV 101, the Academic Recovery course is co-taught by a teaching team made up of a full-time faculty or staff instructor and a peer or graduate leader. Over 40 years of research supports the idea that peer groups are the primary forces influencing college student development (Astin, 1993; Chickering, 1969; Newton & Ender, 2010). Studies have shown that students who benefit from the work of peer leaders gain increased familiarity with and use of campus resources, development of mature relationships, support in coping through transitions, enhanced academic skills, and greater persistence (Latino & Ashcraft, 2012; Shook & Keup, 2012).

The course maintains the same learning outcomes as other UNIV 101 sections – fostering students' academic success, helping students discover and connect with the University of South Carolina, and promoting students' personal development, well-being, and social responsibility. However, it also emphasizes noncognitive factors such as shame and the cultivation of growth mindsets for students' success (Dweck, 2008). For the teaching team, the Academic Recovery section requires extra creativity and innovative thinking to develop lesson plans and activities that differ from a typical UNIV 101 class since some students may be taking the course for a second time. The Academic Recovery section of UNIV 101 has been offered at the University of South Carolina since Spring 2009.

Student Outreach and Enrollment

Students eligible to take the Academic Recovery section of UNIV 101 receive an email from the Academic Recovery instructor prior to the start of the spring semester. The email uses the structure of a psychologically attuned letter (Waltenbury et al., 2018) to describe academic probation as a learning process rather than a label, acknowledge that many factors can contribute to academic difficulty, communicate that it is not uncommon to face academic difficulty, and offer hope and support. Waltenbury et al. (2018) suggested psychologically attuned letters can reduce the shame, guilt, and stigma students on academic probation may be facing. The email is the first contact with students who may enroll in the Academic Recovery section, so it is important to lay a foundation of care and support. The welcome email also introduces each member of the teaching team and invites students to ask any questions (e.g., How is this different than the UNIV 101 I have already taken? What can I get from taking this course?) before the semester starts. Ultimately, students make the decision to enroll and are accepted into the class on a first-come, first-served basis. It is important to note the possible selection bias at play. Students who decide to enroll in the course may have an intrinsic motivation to be successful.

The Teaching Team

As mentioned previously, the Academic Recovery section of UNIV 101 is co-taught by a teaching team made up of a full-time faculty or staff member and an undergraduate or graduate peer leader. As instructors of the course, the teaching team must work together on each aspect of the course to make it the best possible experience for the students in the class. The instructor will select a peer leader who has already successfully served one semester as a UNIV 101 peer leader. As they would for a regular section of UNIV 101, the peer leader for the Academic Recovery course must be prepared to serve as a mentor, role model, resource, and facilitator for learning.

The teaching team prepares their syllabus together before the start of the spring semester. The peer leader helps by providing insight and creativity, especially important since some of the students enrolled in the course may have already taken UNIV 101. A successful teaching team maintains open, consistent communication; discusses division of responsibilities; and has frequent meetings throughout the spring semester to prepare for class, discuss student issues, and give feedback to one another (Friedman & Hopkins, 2020). The peer leader should be involved in the course delivery each time the class meets. This involvement can range from leading the check-in question at the beginning of the class to taking the lead on the topic for the day. The collaborative effort of the teaching team is woven through course design and implementation. However, peer leaders are intentionally not responsible for grading assignments so that they can maintain peer-to-peer relationships, rather than the peer leader being viewed as another instructor.

Course Design

The Academic Recovery course is intentionally designed to help students by applying theory to practice. Guiding theories include Prochaska and DiClemente's (2018) transtheoretical model of human behavior change, with a specific focus on the four types of precontemplators to support and prepare students in different phases for action and maintenance. Additionally, principles from Dweck's (2008) cultivation of growth mindset are woven throughout the semester. Finally, from the first day of class, there is a focus on diminishing shame and institutional labeling (Brown, 2015; Stearns, 2017). Stearns (2017), in the book Shame: A Brief History, asserted that being labeled by your institution can create feelings of shame. He described shame as an emotional experience that relies on group standard and group enforcement as well as the presence of an audience. There are many potential audiences for this shame, such as family at home when students received the letter informing them they were placed on academic probation, friends at school, and even their peers in the Academic Recovery section. Not only is it important to acknowledge the shame the students feel, but students are encouraged to own it and not be afraid to talk about it. Researcher, storyteller, and psychologist Brené Brown, in her book, Daring Greatly: How the Courage to Be Vulnerable Transforms the Way We Live, Love, Parent, and Lead (Brown, 2012), stated that shame thrives in secrecy and vulnerability and does not equal weakness. Starting on the first day, it is critical to create an environment in which shame won't survive and where the students feel free to be vulnerable with one another and their instructors to make the most of the semester.

On the first day of class, building community and setting expectations for the semester are emphasized. Students begin learning about one another and more about their instructors. The foundation of a community allows safe discussion and creates a sense of belonging. Safe discussion and sense of belonging are critical components for student learning and persistence. Additionally, students who are learning tend to persist, and students who persist will continue learning.

To set expectations for the semester, the instructors ask students to think about the best and worst classes they have had and identify what the teachers and students did in each of those classes. Themes emerge that describe the "best class" as an environment in which the teacher cares about the students, students participate and engage, the teacher grades assignments in a timely manner, and so on. After completing the activity, students and instructors engage in a conversation about how they can work together to make the Academic Recovery class another "best class." Additionally, when students share their stories leading up to the Academic Recovery course, attendance is a recurring theme. This theme is echoed in research by Richie and Hargrove (2005), who found a significant correlation between class attendance and grades. As a way to include students in the design of their course and to provide an accountability mechanism, students create what they believe to be a fair attendance policy for the semester.

A variety of topics are included through the semester, including time management, goal setting, study skills, wellness, values clarification, diversity, and self-identity exploration, to help students better understand themselves, adjust their habits, and begin establishing and working toward their long-term academic and personal goals. For example, one semester, the peer leader created and facilitated a lesson with the goals to get students outside of the classroom, discuss different study strategies, and visit the Student Success Center on campus. At three different study spots on campus, the class discussed a different way to study for exams. The lesson ended at the Student Success Center, allowing students to locate this campus resource as well as to become more familiar with the services they offer.

In class, students are often asked to complete short assignments to give the teaching team an opportunity to coach them individually, as needed. For example, students are given time in class to map out their goals and action steps to accomplish "right-now goals" (i.e., goals for the next couple of weeks), semester goals, one-year goals, and "someday goals" (i.e., goals for the future). Some students had a clear someday goal that made working back to their right-now goals much easier. For example, working backward, if a student's someday goal is to work in the Behavioral Analysis Unit at the FBI, their one-year goal might be to intern at the local police department. Their semester goal might be to interview their criminal justice professor and their right-now goal might be to make an A in their psychology class. Students who struggle to articulate their someday goal find identifying their right-now goals more difficult. For example, if a student does not have a clear picture of where they see themselves in five or seven years, their right-now and semester goals could include making an appointment with a career coach, meeting with a major change advisor, or interviewing a professor for a class that really interests them.

Other important components of the course include midterm reflection essays, group presentations, reflection journals assigned throughout the semester, and a final reflection. The reflection in Spring 2019 was introduced early in the semester because it was incentive-based and two parts. If a student had more than one absence, they were asked to complete a temperature reading to reflect on the semester and their time at the University of South Carolina. The temperature reading is inspired by Satir's (1976) family camp. At family camp, participants started each day with temperature readings that included four components: appreciations, bugs/possible solutions, new information, and hopes and wishes (see Figure CS2.1). We adapted these four components to help the students reflect on the class and their time thus far at the University of South Carolina.

Final Temperature Reading Prompts

Appreciations: What did this experience teach you? What did you learn from this whole year?

Bugs/Possible Solutions: What hurdles do you still need to overcome? How will you do so? Who can help you? What do you need to improve or learn to get there?

New Information: What do you know about yourself now that you didn't know in August? What brought you to these conclusions?

Hopes and Wishes: What's next and how are you going to get there?

(Dial, M., 2019, UNIV 101 *Academic Recovery Section Comprehensive Assignment Packet*)

Figure CS2.1. Final Temperature Reading Prompts.

For the second part of the final reflection in Spring 2019, each student created a personal user manual based on what they had learned and discovered about themselves throughout the semester. The user manual is typically designed to help others understand how to work with the student, but for the Academic Recovery students, it provided an opportunity reflect on and share what they have learned about themselves through the semester. Required components included their name, purpose statement, and self-identified strengths and weaknesses. Students were encouraged to get creative and have fun with the other components to complete the assignment by including information such as warnings like "finds uncertainty frustrating" or by sharing their motivators, values, and personal inventory results as they have learned more about themselves through the semester.

Finally, the class uses a group chat application, GroupMe, and one-on-one meetings as important tools to provide students with continuous support outside the classroom. The GroupMe is created the first day of class, with all students and the teaching team able to connect with one another inside and outside the classroom. GroupMe can be used for a quick check-in at the beginning of class, such as the teaching team asking the students to send a GIF that describes their weekend. It is also a great tool to send reminders and changes about the class as well as for students to connect (e.g., ask who is going to the basketball game that night or if anyone wants to get lunch after class). Through the semester and afterward, the GroupMe chat allows students to easily reach out with questions, connect with one another, and build community.

Additionally, students are required to meet one on one with either the instructor or the peer/graduate leader around the midpoint of the semester. One-on-one meetings are great opportunities for the teaching team to check in with each student, discuss situations specific to the student (e.g., struggling in particular class, having roommate issues), or to follow up on previous information (e.g., How did you statistics test go last week? Did you decide which part-time job you want to apply for?). Both the class GroupMe and one-on-one meetings are great ways to continue to build the community set forth from the first day of class and to continue delivering on the promise of care and support.

Assessment Methods and Design

The first-year seminar course, UNIV 101, has proven to be predictive of student success in other courses taken during the first year in addition to predicting student success beyond the first year. Students who enroll in UNIV 101 typically have higher GPAs and are more likely to graduate. Likewise, students on academic probation who enroll in the Academic Recovery section of UNIV 101 tend to have higher GPAs at the end of the spring semester as compared to those on academic probation who did not enroll in the course. One limitation of the assessment is the intrinsic motivation of students who self-select to enroll in the course.

Each UNIV 101 course administers an End-of-Course Evaluation (EOCE) survey at the end of the semester. The survey is a tool to collect qualitative and quantitative data to assess student satisfaction of the course, perceived learning as a result of the course, and the effectiveness of the instructor and peer leader. On the EOCE survey, the Spring 2018 cohort yielded an 85.7% response rate with $n = 18$. The Spring 2019 cohort yielded an 89.5% response rate with $n = 17$. The Spring 2020 cohort yielded a lower response rate of 61.1% with $n = 11$. Many factors may have contributed to a lower response rate for the Spring 2020 cohort, including factors related to COVID-19 and finishing the semester remotely following spring break.

Assessment Findings

Overall, students who enroll in the Academic Recovery course report that the course was a valuable experience and the content and topics covered were relevant to their needs.

On a scale from 1 (*strongly disagree*) to 5 (*strongly agree*), the means to both statements from the EOCE are consistently over 4.4 out of 5 across several semesters (see Table CS2.1).

In addition to data about the course itself, the students also provide feedback about their instructor and peer or graduate leader. Past data from University 101 Programs has shown the effectiveness of the teaching team in the classroom. In the Academic Recovery section, the teaching team continues to be powerful as a way to promote student learning, growth, and success. Even though a different peer or graduate leader is matched with the Academic Recovery section each year, there has been a consistent instructor since Spring 2018, and the peer and graduate leaders have consistently provided high-quality and high-impact support to the first-year students they serve in the Academic Recovery section. Average responses on the EOCE are consistently over 4.82 on the 5-point scale for items asking if the peer/grad leader was a valuable resource, a valuable part of the overall experience, effective at leading class discussions/activities, and an appropriate role model (see Table CS2.2).

Table CS2.1.
First-Year Student Responses Retrieved from University 101 Programs End-of-Course Evaluations Survey

	Spring 2018	Spring 2019	Spring 2020
Taking University 101 has been a valuable experience.	4.88	4.71	4.64
The content and topics covered in this course were relevant to my needs.	4.71	4.88	4.45

Table CS2.2.
First-Year Student Responses Retrieved from University 101 Programs End-of-Course Evaluations Survey

	Spring 2018	Spring 2019	Spring 2020
My Peer/Graduate Leader was a valuable resource.	-	4.88	4.91
My Peer/Graduate Leader was a valuable part of my University 101 experience.	4.94	4.88	4.82
My Peer/Graduate Leader was effective at leading class discussions/activities.	5.00	4.88	4.82
My Peer/Graduate Leader was an appropriate role model.	5.00	4.88	4.82

Qualitative data is also collected to assess the instructor and peer or graduate leader. Consistently for the past several years, students comment on the teaching team's willingness to be helpful, supportive, approachable, understanding, and relatable. Additionally, on the free response section of the EOCE, students are asked to comment about what they liked most about their University 101 experience. An example comment follows:

> I knew that the class would always be a place where I could be myself. It was also a place where I could ask questions without feeling dumb because my classmates were in similar situations. The atmosphere was always up-beat, but serious when needed to be. The assignments I had were actually beneficial to me and bettering my experience at the University of South Carolina. It also helped me make a lot of friends that I would not have met otherwise.

This comment, along with many others, illustrates the positive impact of building a community within the classroom, creating an environment that diminishes shame and encourages vulnerability. Other comments speak to the importance of intentionally crafting assignments and activities to fit the unique needs of students enrolled in the course: "It taught me how to be better with the exact things that were troubling me most in college and that was extremely helpful."

Beyond the reported satisfaction in the course, on average, students in the Academic Recovery section achieved greater increases in their institutional GPAs than did their peers who did not enroll in the section (see Figure CS2.2). At the end of the Spring 2020 semester, the 16 students enrolled in the Academic Recovery section ($M = 2.51$, $SD = 0.19$) were significantly more likely than the 182 students in the control group ($M = 1.78$, $SD = 0.06$) to end the term in good academic standing, $t(18.39) = 23.62$, $p = .002$ (see Figure CS2.3).

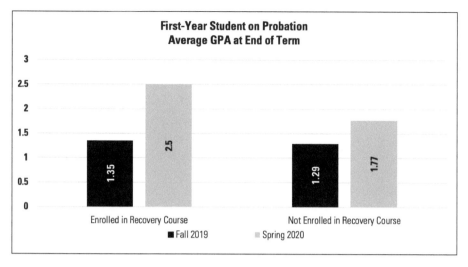

Figure CS2.2. Average GPA at end of term for first-year student on probation. Data retrieved from institutional records at the end of Spring 2020.

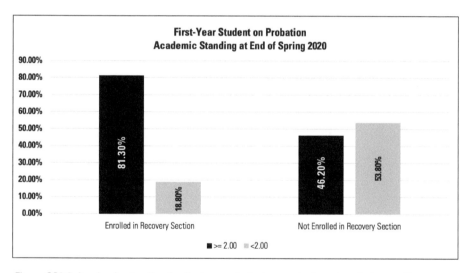

Figure CS2.3. Academic standing for first-year student on probation at end of term. Data retrieved from institutional records at the end of Spring 2020.

Implications for Future Practice

The Academic Recovery section of UNIV 101 has evolved significantly since it began in Spring 2009. Early iterations of this course were instructed by two professional staff members. Now, recognizing the power of peer-to-peer education, the course is co-instructed by a staff member and a peer or graduate leader. Additionally, since Spring 2018, the Academic Recovery section of UNIV 101 has had a consistent instructor. Having a consistent instructor, even though the peer or graduate leader changes from year to year, allows for content and ideas to develop from experience. Although each group of students has unique interests and needs, it is helpful to have a foundation of activities and lessons that work well for this group of students.

Currently, only 19 students can be served each spring semester in the Academic Recovery course since only one section is available. In future years, there may be an opportunity to expand the course offering to allow more than one section. The hope is to give more students the opportunity to reap the benefits of a course that is tailored to fit their needs.

The emphasis on building a community among the students and teaching team is the factor that makes this course so special. As mentioned earlier, the emphasis on community leads to safe discussion and sense of belonging that encourages learning and persistence. Creating a space in which students, especially those who may be feeling particularly isolated or defeated, feel seen and heard largely contributes to students showing up and being active participants in their own learning each week.

In closing, the University of South Carolina is dedicated to providing students with the resources and support to be successful. Many programs, people, and tools are available to help students along their journey. University 101 Programs is a huge part of this student-success initiative, and the Academic Recovery course is another element that allows students to learn, grow, and become the very best versions of themselves and to be successful at the University of South Carolina and beyond.

References

Astin, A. W. (1993). *What matters in college? Four critical years revisited.* Jossey-Bass.

Brown, B. (2012). *Daring greatly: How the courage to be vulnerable transforms the way we live, love, parent, and lead.* Penguin.

Chickering, A. W. (1969). *Education and identity.* Jossey-Bass.

Dial, M. (2019). *UNIV 101 Academic Recovery Section Comprehensive Assignment Packet.* Unpublished.

Dweck, C. S. (2008). *Mindset: The new psychology of success.* Random House Digital, Inc.

Friedman, D., & Hopkins, K. (Eds.). (2020). *University 101 faculty resource manual.* University of South Carolina.

Newton, F. B., & Ender, S. C. (2010). *Students helping students: A guide for peer educators on college campuses.* Jossey-Bass.

Latino, J. A., & Ashcraft, M. L. (2012). *The first-year seminar: Designing, implementing, and assessing courses to support student learning and success: Vol IV. Using peers in the classroom.* University of South Carolina, National Resource Center for the First-Year Experience and Students in Transition.

Prochaska, J. O., & DiClemente, C. C. (1983). Stages and processes of self-change of smoking: toward an integrative model of change. *Journal of Consulting and Clinical Psychology,* 51(3), 390-395.

Richie, S. D., & Hargrove, D. S. (2005). An analysis of the effectiveness of telephone intervention in reducing absences and improving grades of college freshmen. *Journal of College Student Retention: Research, Theory & Practice,* 6(4), 395–412.

Satir, V. (1976). *Making contact.* Celestial arts.

Shook, J. L., & Keup, J. R. (2012). The benefits of peer leader programs: An overview from the literature. *New Directions for Higher Education, 2012*(157), 5–16.

Stearns, P. N. (2017). *Shame: A brief history.* University of Illinois Press.

University of South Carolina (n.d.) *University Academic Probation.* https://sc.edu/about/offices_and_divisions/advising/academic_coaching/probation_and_suspension/academic_probation/index.php#:~:text=Academic%20probation%20is%20both%20an,GPA%20is%20below%20a%202.00.

Waltenbury, M., Brady, S., Gallo, M., Redmond, N., Draper, S., & Fricker, T. (2018). *Academic probation: Evaluating the impact of academic standing notification letters on students.* Higher Education Quality Council of Ontario.

CHAPTER SEVEN

Intentionality and Integration Within Academic Probation Policies and Programs

Richie Gebauer and Michael T. Dial

Although students may have what it takes to be successful, national data indicates that 25% of college students will struggle academically and find themselves on academic probation during their collegiate experience (Greenfield et al., 2013). If students on probation choose to return to their campuses the semester following notification, they find themselves in a transitional period between poor academic performance and either dismissal or recovery (Arcand & Leblanc, 2011). Various scholarly articles have been published and dissertations written about this population of students. However, articles often focus on singular initiatives and individual institutions. On the other hand, dissertations, which can offer a broad treatment of the topic, are often not written for mass consumption, may be difficult to locate, or feature language and analytical concepts that can intimidate campus practitioners. This book seeks to fill this gap in the literature. Throughout it, we've explored the concept of academic probation and examined several potentially high-impact practices for supporting students in academic recovery.

When considering students placed on academic probation, it's easy and common to assume these students were passive, reticent, or underprepared regarding their learning. Students exhibiting a lack of engagement in the classroom or in the context of advising may elicit an assumption that they don't care or are not interested in truly being present. It's in these moments that faculty, staff, and advisors must shift their attention away from teaching and learning toward considering how to redirect students' energy to become engaged (Astin, 1984). The academic recovery process becomes a pathway to influence a change in behavior through establishing a culture of support and a culture of care.

Though it would benefit institutions of higher education if all students were resilient, this isn't the reality. When students encounter academic obstacles, this concept of resiliency comes into focus: "the process of adapting well in the face of adversity, trauma, tragedy, threats, family issues, relational problems, health concerns, or work and financial stress" (American Psychological Association, 2020). For some students, the support structures that typically have been in place in their home environments and through their relationships with teachers and other mentors have prepared them to persevere when encountering failure

(Finn & Rock, 1997). For others, many of whom may find themselves on academic probation, it's possible that the paucity of positive influences in their lives serves as a continuous hindrance in their ability to be successful.

Supporting Academic Recovery Students Through Transition

Students enrolled in institutions of higher education undergo several transitions. Some are common and shared, such as the transition from high school to college and the experience of newfound freedom and responsibility that comes with it. Further progression through the college years may see some students change majors or transfer to new institutions. At some point, most residential students leave on-campus housing for their own homes and apartments, and ultimately many students experience capstones and the transition to post-undergraduate experiences, including enrollment in a graduate degree program or first employment (Schreiner, 2020). Periods of transition can be incredibly precarious experiences for students: "Times of transition can be positive experiences that involve movement toward one's full potential, but they can also be negative experiences that shatter a student's confidence or lead to disengagement from the environment" (Schreiner, 2020, p. 1).

Being placed on academic probation meets all the hallmarks of transition, and this precarious balance between a force for growth and a confidence shattering experience makes institutional choices regarding academic probation so important. Transitions involve change, and change often induces stress reactions. The normal stressors of change compound for students on probation who experience feelings of shock, shame, and inadequacy, as explored in Chapter 1. These students may experience several changes in roles, routines, and relationships as an extension of their probationary status. According to Schreiner (2020), successful transitions are characterized by

> five hallmarks that distinguish them from unsuccessful transitions: (a) students perceive them positively as opportunities for growth; (b) students use healthy coping skills during the transition to approach the transitional activities rather than avoid them; (c) students believe they have the support they need to move through the transition successfully; (d) students access resources during the transition for relevant information, assistance, and support; and (e) students emerge from the transition having grown in personally significant ways. (p. 4)

Institutional leaders and academic support companions (e.g., academic advisors, success coaches, seminar instructors) should aid students in reframing probation as a positive opportunity for personal development, encourage the use of healthy coping mechanisms, push students to utilize resources, and assist students in critical reflection and meaning-making during their time on probation.

Defining Success for Students on Probation

Several traditional models of student success are certainly applicable to the student on academic probation, including retention to subsequent academic terms and persistence to degree. However, the goals and therefore the success measures are likely far more short-term for students in this state of transition. Because so much is at stake for these students (recovery or dismissal), the greatest concern is likely academic recovery itself. This could mean completing a semester with B and/or C grades rather than D grades or worse. In my (Dial's) experience working with students on probation, I have observed several parents dictating a 4.00 semester or loss of parental support for higher education. While understandably frustrated, parents who set these kinds of goals may be setting unrealistically high standards of success for and creating more mental anguish as grades improve but not to the point of perfection. This kind of unrealistic goal may overshadow and undercut more meaningful goals that would aid students in improving their eligibility to return for future semesters. Furthermore, a misplaced focus on academic perfection may inhibit growth in other important measures of success, including "learning gains, talent development, satisfaction and sense of belonging, and student engagement" (Kinzie, 2020, p. xix), each of which may aid the student in academic recovery in immeasurable ways. Additionally, as described earlier, students may struggle in courses and majors in which they lack interest and talent. Aiding recovery students in selecting majors that better align with their strengths, goals, and interests may be an important measure of success and may itself promote a sense of belonging.

Academic Recovery and Student Equity

As indicated earlier in this book in the case study of Cabrini University, academic underpreparedness very often correlates directly with race/ethnicity. More students of color are going to college, with students who identify as a race other than White representing approximately 45% of undergraduate enrollment (Espinosa et al., 2019). As the student body becomes more diverse and institutions continue to enroll more students of color, we may observe an increase in the percentage of students failing to achieve good academic standing, with a disproportionately high percentage of underrepresented, minority students entering academic recovery programs (Hamman, 2018).

A college or university doesn't showcase its commitment to diversity, equity, and inclusion solely by enrolling a more diverse student population. Instead, institutions must commit to being student ready (White, 2016) to serve their underrepresented student populations. Students of color face the challenge of institutional fit, a problem that lies within higher-education institutions that until recent decades were designed specifically for the White, middle- to upper-class, male college student (Barefoot, 2000). As a result, faculty and staff have the responsibility to adapt teaching and learning practices – from the lens of this book, academic recovery initiatives – to enhance student engagement and academic success by meeting students where they actually are, rather than where institutions think they are or expect them to be.

It would be irresponsible to evaluate the academic barriers students of color face in isolation from the negative internal and external forces working against them compared to their White peers: "It is recognized that neither a student's self-view nor school-related behaviors occur independently of the larger social context, that is, family, peers, and the school environment" (Finn & Rock, 1997, p. 222). Negative forces and influences in the K–12 experience of academically at-risk students, many of whom are students of color, alter both the regularity and the quality of the interactions these students have with their peers and teachers (Tyler & Lofstrom, 2009). As a result, it is integral that academic recovery programs identify mentors or advisors and mentoring approaches that are a "right fit" to support students of color. When not done intentionally, "mentoring approaches could disrupt or reproduce race/class/gender inequities" (McCoy et al., 2015, p. 226).

Academic recovery programs should prioritize efforts that promote feelings of belonging, creating a multitude of spaces for students of color to build close relationships with their peers of the same race (Strayhorn, 2017). These relationships create pathways for students to share their experiences to collectively disrupt, combat, and overcome barriers to progress. Academic recovery programs, both consciously and unconsciously, focus on the needs and deficits of students of color rather than using a strengths-based advising approach that not only identifies but magnifies student strengths (Banks & Dohy, 2019). Approaching the academic recovery process from an opportunity lens rather than as a threat to dismissal while surrounding students with their peers (and, if possible, faculty and advisors) of the same race throughout the journey back to good academic standing can increase sense of belonging for and unleash potential in students of color.

In addition to race and ethnicity, it is essential to develop an understanding of all potential variables (e.g., financial struggles pertaining to tuition or purchasing books, family responsibilities that include taking care of children or siblings, balancing school and work to assist with tuition, family related trauma) that may compromise students' time and energy as it relates to academic success. There is not one particular type of student on academic probation. Students engaging in an academic recovery model are not solely underprepared students. In contrast, as mentioned earlier, student athletes, honors students, students from upper-class families, and adult learners all may find themselves in the academic recovery process.

Academic Recovery and Special Student Populations

While likely evident, it's important to note that students in several special populations who either enter the university as high achieving or receive significantly more tailored support than the general student population can and do find themselves in academic distress. Honors students who encounter academic obstacles may experience feelings of depression and begin to identify as unsuccessful (Irwin, 2010) yet mask these feelings with an uplifting and positive attitude despite the academic struggles they're facing (Walsh, 2010). Adult learners attending or reentering college are doing so potentially while juggling a multitude of other life roles in the form of "worker, spouse, or partner, parent, caregiver, and community member" (Ross-Gordon, 2011, p. 26). Though these roles may bring about added maturity, they also bring forth challenges that prevent adult learners from engaging in their academic work and in the campus community in the same ways as traditional undergraduates. Student athletes also have responsibilities that extend well beyond the classroom in terms of practice, strength training, team meetings, and travel and may encounter pressure to prioritize athletic expectations above academic expectations (Jayakumar & Comeaux, 2016). Haslerig (2018) explained that athletes, at times, battle the internal conflict of time investment, assuming investing too much time in one area will detract from the other.

As is evident in respect to the literature, students who are placed on academic probation do not share a set of typical characteristics. Instead, as stated in the introduction to this book, student needs are constantly evolving, and it's the responsibility of educators to continuously assess these needs in an effort to revise and refine the teaching and learning initiatives necessary to meet them. This is done through defining clear student learning outcomes and effective assessment practices designed to evaluate these learning outcomes to yield the student-based evidence needed to strengthen and improve academic recovery functions.

Academic Companioning

Caring professionals have an important role to play in supporting students on academic probation. Arcand and Leblanc (2011) defined the role of academic support professionals using the francophone term "accompagnement scolaire," a process that focuses the supportive relationship as "doing with, rather than doing for" (p. 3). Individual professionals working with academic recovery students provide guidance and context for the university setting. They support students in their development of confidence and self-efficacy while meeting their individual needs.

Several professionals on campus are well suited for this role, but academic advisors often rise to the occasion. According to the National Survey of Student Engagement (NSSE, 2021), students of all racial backgrounds put the most trust in faculty and academic advisors on campus, over other professionals. In fact, "academic advising is perhaps the most important way that first-year students interact with a representative of the institution (Kerr & King, 2005)." Given the powerful role advisors can play in students' lives, it is imperative that academic advisors intentionally engage with their advisees on probation in ways that meet their unique needs (see Chapter 2).

Academic coaches (see Chapter 3) often have smaller caseloads than academic advisors, potentially opening them up to multiple appointments with probationary students. Academic coaching stands out as a comprehensive approach, rather than a series of fragmented services, and as a high-potential program for supporting this unique population of students. Coaches can assist students in making academic plans and developing new academic strategies. These individual connections between advisors/coaches and students are powerful tools to help students successfully navigate transition.

Where Do We Go From Here?

As has been discussed throughout this volume, institutional policies traditionally drive which students find themselves on academic probation, and institutions respond by designing advising and coaching practices and models to support these students with the intent to transition them back into good academic standing. However, when we consider the various populations of students placed on academic probation – student athletes, both academically at-risk and honors students, adult learners, and even upper-class students – it doesn't take long to realize the varying needs of these students and obstacles presented to them. It is critical to assess the various forces that are competing for a student's time and energy. For a curriculum or cocurriculum to achieve its established outcomes, it must appeal to students in a way that evokes the prioritization of their efforts and energy to actively engage with their learning experience (Astin, 1984). As a result, intentionality and integration are critical features of academic recovery models designed not only to increase academic achievement but also to manage the personal bandwidth students need to consciously prioritize academic success.

Intentionality

The one unavoidable challenge facing academic recovery models is that academic recovery is a reactive process, an immediate response to a student's academic struggles. In Chapter 1, Dial discussed the impact and cost effectiveness of designing proactive retention strategies to ensure student persistence. Early intervention and early-alert systems are intentionally established to address initial academic and/or social concerns raised by faculty, staff, or advisors as students engage in the evolving transition that is the first year of college. At times, retention software is used to generate an abundance of pre-enrollment data that then drives curricular and programmatic decisions when considering how campuses will engage their incoming students. Though effective, these efforts to halt student attrition before it occurs are not foolproof, and students encounter obstacles, many times external to the university, that may lead to academic probation. As a result, the academic recovery process is a reactive one.

Despite the notion of reactiveness, institutional leaders engaged in the process of establishing an academic recovery model can be proactive to develop an understanding of where a student's approach went wrong and to intentionally reconstruct that approach for the following semester. Supporting students on academic probation isn't a one-size-fits-all model; it will be unique from institution to institution and potentially from student to student. Therefore, designing an academic recovery model is two-fold. First, advisors of students on probation and in academic recovery should establish an understanding of institutional pre-enrollment data and retention predictors that historically facilitate or hinder student success at their institution. Access to this institutional information in combination with an evaluation of pre-enrollment indicators pertaining to individual academic recovery students is critical information to have prior to mandating one-on-one student advising appointments. This information should influence the design of an intentional action plan that redirects a student's approach to their academics. Second, each institution should reflect on the high-impact and promising practices that successfully engage and retain students, at all levels, on their campus. These often include first-year seminars, learning communities, service learning, capstone experiences, advising, experiential learning, leadership training, student success and support initiatives, and opportunities for engaging pedagogy. Determining the characteristics of the programs that lead to increased student engagement and persistence followed by a consideration of how to embed these same characteristics into an academic recovery program presents an opportunity to move students back into good academic standing. The integration of these two steps, evaluating the potential intersections between each student's individual needs and the defining characteristics of successful first-year programs on campus, means personalizing an academic recovery model to both the institution and the student.

Integration

First-year students are undergoing a significant amount of change as they adapt to a new learning environment that engages them with their peers, university faculty, and staff both in and outside of the classroom. The college experience for upper-class students is constantly evolving as they move deeper into their academic majors, pursue engagement and leadership opportunities on campus while balancing these cocurricular roles with academic success, and consider graduate program and/or job pursuits beyond graduation. Ongoing change and evolution in the lives of students, both within and external to the university, breeds the potential for students to encounter academic struggle. Assisting students to cope and adapt in the face of change is best when the students are able to identify and recognize the value and interconnectedness across their learning experiences.

Ultimately, for students to truly experience integration within an intentional educational practice such as an academic recovery model, probationary advisors on a particular college campus must agree on the meaning of integration and must consider the academic preparedness of the students they're serving (Burg et al., 2009). While the concept of integration may include disciplinary connections, integration of learning has a much broader scope, extending beyond the traditional curriculum and academic disciplines to include various contexts and life experiences and to consider the role of identity in one's life (Barber, 2012). Put differently, the result of integrative learning is connection making (Leonard, 2012), yet students do not necessarily accomplish this on their own. Students must be invited and supported to engage in the process of analyzing their learning experience, which both validates that they are capable of constructing knowledge and results in mutually constructing meaning with others (Baxter Magolda & King, 2004).

It is not enough for an academic recovery model to exist in isolation from other teaching and learning initiatives on campus. Just as research has encouraged the integration of more than one high-impact practice (Schmidt & Graziano, 2016), probationary advisors should consider cultivating an academic recovery model that is integrative in nature, using effective first-year initiatives and high-impact practices to advance academic recovery goals and objectives. Chapter 6 includes an example of this way of thinking: the use of a first-year seminar as a catalyst for effectively supporting students on academic probation. This first-year seminar must be intentional in design rather than replicating the curriculum offered in more broadly focused first-year seminars for general populations of first-year students. Probationary advisors (or faculty) teaching this course may want to evaluate a variety of advising models (e.g., intrusive/proactive, learning-centered, appreciative, strengths-based) and identify a right-fit model that provides a pathway to serve probationary students in the context of a first-year seminar. Ultimately, curriculum is focused on challenging students to reflect on the outcome of the semester that led to academic probation, identifying overt and covert needs that must be addressed to allow for student success, and collaboratively designing an action plan that advances the student forward.

This example of integrating the first-year seminar with academic recovery initiatives is just one approach. However, it is critical that institutions, regardless of approach, strongly consider how best to align program goals and institutional values, thus promoting a collaborative environment. Teaching and learning initiatives rooted in shared learning goals and outcomes are difficult to achieve. However, an environment that promotes effective, cohesive rather than fragmented learning positions students on academic probation with the space to transition back into good academic standing.

Final Thoughts

This book is intended to initiate a conversation about students who find themselves on academic probation. Until now, the scholarship on the impact of academic recovery models on student success and persistence is limited. One might argue that the attention directed toward establishing and strengthening the first-year experience, sophomore programs, and student-success initiatives overall is critical to preventing students from ending up on academic probation. However, a focus on preventative measures without a consideration of academic recovery program design in light of the successes of these programs is futile.

Serving students on academic probation, though important, isn't always a top institutional priority. Yet, this book and the authors who contributed to it have presented a compelling case not only to prioritize academic recovery models but to consider how to establish interconnections among the academic recovery process and other teaching and learning initiatives on campus. It is the responsibility of practitioners to understand who their students are, effectively evaluate their students' needs, and intentionally design an academic recovery model that meets and addresses those needs, shifting a campus to becoming "student ready" rather than expecting students to be "college-ready." The latter represents a shortfall on behalf of the university and promotes privilege over equity. Instead, proactively designing academic recovery initiatives that are intentional and integrative establishes a foundation to reenergize students to engage in their learning, thereby giving it purpose and meaning in unique, individualized ways.

References

American Psychological Association. (2020, September 17). *Building your resilience.* https://www.apa.org/topics/resilience/building-your-resilience

Arcand, I., & Leblanc, R. (2011). Academic probation and companioning: Three perspectives on experience and support. *Mevlana International Journal of Education, 1*(2), 1-14.

Astin, A. W. (1984). Student Involvement: A developmental theory for higher education. *Journal of College Student Personnel, 25,* 297–308.

Banks, T., & Dohy, J. (2019). Mitigating barriers to persistence: A review of efforts to improve retention and graduation rates for students of color in higher education. *Higher Education Studies, 9*(1), 118–131.

Barber, J. P. (2012). Integration of learning: Grounded theory analysis of college students' learning. *American Educational Research Journal, 49*(3), 590–617.

Barefoot, B. O. (1992). *Helping first-year college students climb the academic ladder: Report of a national survey of freshman seminar programming in American higher education* [Unpublished doctoral dissertation]. College of William and Mary, Williamsburg, VA.

Barefoot, B. O. (2000). The first-year experience: Are we making it any better? *About Campus, 4*(6), 12–18.

Baxter Magolda, M.B., & King, P.M. (Eds.). (2004). *Learning partnerships: Theory and models of practice to educate for self-authorship.* Stylus.

Burg, E., Klages, M., & Sokoski, P. (2009). Beyond "parallel play": Creating a realistic model of integrative learning with community college freshmen. *Journal of Learning Communities Research, 3*(3), 63–73.

Espinosa, L. L., Turk, J. M., Taylor, M., & Chessman, H. (2019). *Race and ethnicity in higher education: A status report.* American Council on Education. https://www.equityinhighered.org/resources/report-downloads/

Finn, J. D., & Rock, D. A. (1997). Academic success among students at risk for school failure. *Journal of Applied Psychology, 82*(2), 221–234.

Greenfield, G. M., Keup, J. R., & Gardner, J. N. (2013). *Developing and sustaining successful first-year programs: A guide for practitioners.* John Wiley & Sons.

Hamman, K. J. (2018). Factors that contribute to the likeliness of academic recovery. *Journal of College Student Retention: Research, Theory & Practice, 20*(2), 162-175.

Haslerig, S. J. (2018). Lessons from graduate(d) student-athletes: Supporting academic autonomy and achievement. *New Directions for Student Services, 163,* 93–103.

Irwin, B. D. (2010). Hitting the wall. *Journal of the National Collegiate Honors Council, 11*(2), 43–45.

Jayakumar, U. M., & Comeaux, E. (2016). The cultural cover-up of college athletics: How organizational culture perpetuates an unrealistic and idealized balancing act. *Journal of Higher Education, 87*(4), 488–515.

Kinzie, J. (2020) A new view of student success. In L. A. Schreiner, M. C. Louis, & D. D. Nelson (Eds.), *Thriving in transitions: A research-based approach to college student success.* Stylus Publishing, LLC. xi-xxx

Leonard, J. B. (2012). Integrative learning: A grounded theory. *Issues in Integrative Studies, 30,* 48–74.

McCoy, D. L., Winkle-Wagner, R., & Luedke, C. (2015). Colorblind mentoring? Exploring White faculty mentoring of students of color. *Journal of Diversity in Higher Education, 8,* 225–242.

NSSE. (2021) *The trust gap among college students.* Center for Postsecondary Research, Indiana University School of Education. https://nsse.indiana.edu/research/annual-results/trust/index.html#top

Ross-Gordon, J. M. (2011). Research on adult learners: Supporting the needs of a student population that is no longer nontraditional. *Peer Review, 13,* 26–29.

Schmidt, L. C. & Graziano, J. (2016). *Building synergy for high-impact educational initiatives: First-year seminars and learning communities.* University of South Carolina, National Resource Center for the First-Year Experience and Students in Transition.

Schreiner, L. A., Louis, M. C., & Nelson, D. D. (Eds.). (2020). *Thriving in transitions: A research-based approach to college student success.* The National Resource Center for The First-Year Experience.

Strayhorn, T. L. (2017). Factors that influence the persistence and success of Black men in urban public universities. *Urban Education, 52*(9), 1106–1128. https://doi/org/10.1177/0042085915623347

Tyler, J. H., & Lofstrom, M. (2009). Finishing high school: Alternative pathways and dropout recovery. *The Future of Children, 19,* 77–103.

Walsh, M. (2010). Listening lessons. *Journal of the National Collegiate Honors Council, 11*(2), 33–35.

White, B. P. (2016, March 21). The myth of the college-ready student. *Inside Higher Ed.* https://www.insidehighered.com/views/2016/03/21/instead-focusing-college-ready-students-institutions-should-become-more-student.

ABOUT THE AUTHORS

Kimberly L. Boyd is currently the Dean for Retention and Student Success and an Associate Professor of biology at Cabrini University following a 28-year career in higher education. In addition to her scientific research, Boyd has served as a Teagle Foundation Teaching and Learning Scholar and consultant with the Council for Aid to Education in New York and facilitated workshops nationwide on using performance task-based pedagogies to teach and assess undergraduate students' critical thinking skills. She served as a consultant and exam developer for the Praxis Life Science program for the Educational Testing Service and has received numerous grants from the U.S. Department of Education and National Science Foundation to effect curricular and pedagogical innovation in the science classroom. Boyd holds a PhD from the Department of Molecular Physiology and Biological Physics at the University of Virginia.

Julie Carney-Jones is an Academic Advisor at the University of Delaware (UD) in the College of Health Sciences. Most recently she joined a centralized, team-focused advising office to support first- and second-year students in the health sciences at UD. With 21 years in higher education, Carney-Jones' career has centered on supporting students during their collegiate academic journey through holistic and strengths-based academic advising and recovery. Her advising philosophy is founded on the development of long-lasting relationships with students focused on deepening their self-awareness, sense of self-worth, and belonging; developing grit; and strengthening their academic management skills. Carney-Jones completed a BS in teacher education from Drexel University and an M.Ed from the University of Delaware.

Shana DeRosa is the Director of Academic Advising in the Center for Student Success at Cabrini University. DeRosa has worked with a variety of diverse student populations for the past 16 years, including nontraditional adult learners, traditional-age, transfer, at-promise, first-generation, and undeclared college students, and has worked extensively with students on academic recovery. Her responsibilities have included recruiting students, teaching, and developing curricula for first-year experience courses; serving on crisis response teams; coordinating transfer orientation programs; conducting academic coaching study skills sessions; and collaborating on various retention initiatives. DeRosa regularly provides workshops for faculty and staff on her research passion: proactive, holistic, and developmental advising. She earned an M.Ed in student personnel services and counseling in higher education from Widener University, where she also received a bachelor's in communication studies, broadcasting and journalism.

Michael T. Dial serves as Associate Director of Undergraduate Academic Advising at the University of South Carolina (UofSC). He leads the campus's largest undergraduate advising program, one that supports 14,000 undergraduate students into and through the university. Since 2014, Dial has been involved in first-year and transition initiatives at UofSC including advising, the first-year seminar, early intervention, peer education, and student success programming. In addition to this publication, Dial is a co-editor on NACADA's *Academic Advising Administration: Essential Knowledge and Skills for the 21st Century (2nd Edition)* and serves on the manuscript review board for *Building Bridges for Student Success: A Sourcebook for Colleges and Universities*. Dial previously served on the editorial review board for *E-Source for College Transitions*. He has presented practitioner–scholarship and effective practices for supporting academically at-risk students and those on probation at several national conferences. His other areas of scholarly interest include early alert programs, the first-year experience, and academic advising. Dial earned a BA in recreation administration from Eastern Illinois University and an M.Ed in higher education and student affairs from the University of South Carolina.

Stephanie M. Foote is the Senior Associate Vice President for Teaching, Learning, and Evidence-Based Practices at the John N. Gardner Institute for Excellence in Undergraduate Education and a Lecturer in higher education administration at Stony Brook University. Before joining the Institute staff, Foote was the Founding Director of the Master of Science in First-Year Studies, a Professor of education in the Department of First-Year and Transition Studies, and Faculty Fellow for High-Impact Practices at Kennesaw State University. Foote's research and consultative work span a variety of topics, including the role of first-year seminars and experiential pedagogy on student engagement in the early college experience, transfer students, self-authorship development, engagement and learning in online environments, faculty development, metacognitive teaching and learning approaches, high-impact educational practices, and inclusive teaching practices. Foote earned her PhD in educational administration from the University of South Carolina and received the McGraw-Hill Excellence in Teaching First-Year Seminars Award and the NODA Outstanding Research Award for her dissertation research on the effects of first-year seminar participation on the experience of students in the early college experience.

Dan Friedman is the Executive Director of University 101 Programs at the University of South Carolina (UofSC), where he provides leadership for six academic courses, including the nationally renowned U101 course. Friedman earned his PhD in higher education from the University of Virginia. He is an affiliate faculty member in the Higher Education and Student Affairs program at UofSC. Before coming to UofSC, he served as Director of Freshman Seminar at Appalachian State University and as an Assistant Professor of higher education. Friedman's area of scholarship has centered on the first-year experience, teaching and learning, and assessment.

Richie Gebauer is the Assistant Dean for Retention and Student Success at Cabrini University and serves as Faculty Director of the IMPACT Living and Learning Community. As Founding Director of the university's first-year experience and learning community program, retention and persistence are at the center of Gebauer's work. He is a past president of the National Learning Community Association and has served on the editorial review board for the *Journal of The First-Year Experience & Students in Transition, Learning Communities Research and Practice*, and *E-Source for College Transitions*. His research focuses on the impact of learning communities on the integrative learning practices of students. Gebauer has authored publications advancing the research and practice of learning communities, academic and professional advising, the first-year experience and first-year seminars, and academic recovery programs. Gebauer completed a BA from Franklin and Marshall College, an M.Ed from James Madison University, and an EdD from Cabrini University.

Andrea Harris is the Senior Director of Student Administrative Services for Pepperdine University's Seaver College in Malibu, California. As part of her responsibilities, she supervises both the frontline student services department and the staff academic advisors. She also has a dotted line to the Office of the Dean to ensure that all policies and practices are consistent with the expectations of the college. Harris is the academic representative to the Student Care Team, which meets weekly to ensure that all students in need receive comprehensive care, and she manages the college's probation/dismissal and reinstatement policies. Harris enjoys heavy metal music and lives in Los Angeles with her husband, son, and dogs.

Paige McKeown serves as the Assistant Director for Undergraduate Advising and Academic Intervention at the University of South Carolina (UofSC). She has worked in the advising field at UofSC for six years and transitioned to a career in higher education from K-12 school counseling. She earned a bachelor's in social studies education from Wake Forest University and a master's in counseling from the University of Pennsylvania. McKeown, a nationally certified counselor (NCC) and career development facilitator (GCDF), is working toward completing her PhD in educational psychology and research at UofSC. Her specific research interests include students' self-regulation skills, mental health, social supports, and academic success strategies in the high school-to-college transition. McKeown has been published in *Academic Advising Today* and has presented regionally and nationally on advising and intervention best practices.

Caleb Morris (he/they) is an Academic Advising Educator at the University of South Carolina (UofSC) in the centralized University Advising Center. In triplicate roles as an Exploratory Advisor, Academic Coach, and Undergraduate Studies Advisor, Morris has supported over 2,000 students transitioning between major and academic standing, including students on academic probation. In 2022, NACADA recognized Morris with the Outstanding Advisor Award in the New Advisor category. A champion of access and inclusion, Morris has received institutional awards for leading diversity, equity, and inclusion efforts in academic advising and has presented on the topic at conferences. In addition to advising, Morris teaches the first-year seminar and senior capstone experience courses at UofSC. Morris earned a Bachelor of Arts in history and a Master of Education in higher education and student affairs, both from UofSC.

Catherine Nutter is Senior Director of University Advising at Texas Tech University. Nutter's career in education has spanned several decades and levels, from K-12 teaching and administration, to adjunct faculty at the community college level, to administration and instruction at the university. Her work at Texas Tech includes leadership in academic advising for undeclared/undecided students, students on a health careers path, and students in academic recovery, as well as chairing the Committee on Advising, Retention, and Student Success. Nutter has published several articles and presentations with the Consortium for Student Retention Data Exchange and the National Symposium on Student Retention, including "Undecided: A Good Decision for Retention" and "A Little Advice: Making Data Matter in Academic Advising." Nutter holds bachelor's and master's degrees in English and a PhD in higher education research.

Mikaela Rea serves as an Undergraduate Academic Advisor at the University of South Carolina (UofSC), where she also enjoys teaching. She has taught many sections of the first-year seminar and a leadership development seminar for juniors and seniors. Rea has given multiple presentations related to peer leadership based on work in her previous role in University 101 Programs at UofSC. Rea holds a BA in psychology and an M.Ed in higher education and student affairs, both from UofSC.

Dottie Weigel is an Associate Professor of higher education and Director of the Graduate Program in Higher Education at Messiah University. Her research interests include transition in the first college year, with a focus on the experiences of third-culture and international students. Before her faculty appointment at Messiah University, Weigel served in various administrative roles within first-year programs. She also co-edited and published *Transitions*, a textbook for first-year students at the University of South Carolina. Weigel is an active member of professional student affairs organizations such as NASPA and ACPA and served as the Bottom Line editor with *About Campus*. She also served as a review board member for the *Journal of The First-Year Experience & Students in Transition*. In May 2019, Weigel was honored with the Preis Outstanding Graduate Teaching Award at Messiah University. An advocate for graduate students, she is committed to helping students stay abreast of trends and issues in higher education.

Dallin George Young is an Assistant Professor in the College Student Affairs Administration and Student Affairs Leadership graduate programs at the University of Georgia. His research focuses on a line of inquiry that investigates how novices are trained, socialized, and educated as they move from the periphery to full participation in academic communities of practice. His research and practice includes: theoretical perspectives to interrogate student transitions into the academy; how graduate and professional students learn the rules, knowledge, and culture of their fields; the transformative potential for students engaged in peer leadership; and the (differential) impacts of educational structures on the success of students in transition.

INDEX

NOTE: Page references followed by *f* indicate figures; those followed by *t* indicate tables.

A

ability, disaggregating outcome measures by, 125

abstract conceptualization, 113

academic advisors. *See* advisors and advising

academic and curricular gateways, 121
  lenses for assessing, 128–9t

academic capital, 10

academic coaching
  academic recovery and, 4, 80–1, 166
  at Cabrini University, 135
  curricular knowledge and, 71–2
  division/unit/department housing, 69t
  engagement planning and campus involvement, 77, 78f
  as individualized personal interactions, 63
  navigating campus resources, 79–80
  organizational contexts and, 68–71
  probation experience navigation and, 4
  reasons to establish, 64–6, 65t
  review of, 10–11
  self-assessments and strengths identification, 75–6
  terminology, 64
  training considerations, 70

Academic Coaching and Career Enhancement for Student Success (ACCESS), at Florida Atlantic University, 69

academic community role, academic probation and, 4

academic companioning, 165–6

academic culture shock, 63

academic deans, reinstatement responsibility and, 26

academic difficulties as not uncommon, 20. *See also* academic probation; roadblocks, common

academic intervention. *See also* early-alert programs; intrusive advising or interventions; mandatory interventions
  beyond faculty referrals, 93–5
  group, 17–18, 30, 32
  individual, 18–19
  intermediate, 16, 16f
  passive, 16, 16f, 95
  policies, 15
  proactive, 71t, 88
  reactive, 88
  with undergraduate students, 97–9, 98f
  value and effectiveness of, 99
  voluntary, 16, 16f, 17

academic major, reinstated student success and change in, 26

academic plans
  reinstatement and, 26
  University of South Carolina, 72, 73–5f

academic probation. See also academic recovery; institutional policies
  academic companioning and, 165–6
  affirmation and validation in first-year seminars and, 111–2
  aligning first-year seminar goals with, 108–9, 110–111f

student success
grit as predictor of, 43
psychologically attuned probation notifications and, 22
reinstated students, variables in, 26
and support initiatives, 167
Student Success in College: Creating Conditions that Matter (Kuh, Kinzie, Schuh, Whitt, and Associates), 108–9
student-affairs staff, 90–1, 91f
students. *See also* holistic student needs
agency in education and, 132–3
assessment process involvement of, 131
campus ready, shifting campus to student ready from, 168
evaluation of transition by, 3–4
fiscal implications of incomplete college experience for, 10
impacts of academically losing, 8–10
intrusive interventions and, 85
reinstatement responsibility and, 26
students of color. *See also* race and racial minorities
institutional fit issues for, 163–4
study-skills courses or workshops, 17, 30
success measures, 163
success team members, 46
Suchan, J. J., 25, 27, 29
Sun-Selışık, Z. E., 76
Sunstein, C. R., 15
support
in 4S system, 4
in academic recovery program continuum, 16, 16f
level of, reinstatement and, 26
of students during academic probation, 162
surprise or shock, academic probation and, 7

Suskie, L., 125, 126, 127, 132
suspension
duration, academic success of reinstated students and, 26
institutional policies on, 23–5, 23f
Swail, W., 9
Swecker, H. K., 38
Swing, R. L., 104

T
taking charge, probation and, 3
Tampke, D. R., 83
teaching teams, 150–1, 155
technology, early-alert programs and, 84, 89–90, 96
temperature readings, UofSC prompts for, 153, 153f
Texas Tech University, Academic Success Workbook, 59–62
text messages, 90
Thaler, R. H., 15
three-part journals, reflection using, 114
Tinto, V., 16, 38, 63
Tirole, J., 2
top-down early-alert programs, 88–9
Tovar, E., 6
traditional-age students, 6
training, for academic coaches, 70
transfer students, 16
transitions
academic probation as, 2–4, 3f
mandatory interventions and, 33
successful, characteristics of, 162
transtheoretical model (TTM) of human behavior change, 85–7, 86f
precontemplator types in, 97–9, 98f, 151
trauma, family-related, 164
Trombley, C. M., 29–30
Trowler, P., 15